METAPHORS OF MINISTRY

11/9/15

— Submitter Credits
   2 wks — should I
— Next overseer remind
              Dr Woods?

METAPHORS OF MINISTRY

Biblical Images for Leaders and Followers

David W. Bennett

Wipf & Stock
PUBLISHERS
Eugene, Oregon

Wipf and Stock Publishers
199 West 8th Avenue, Suite 3
Eugene, Oregon 97401

Metaphors of Ministry
Biblical Images for Leaders and Followers
By Bennett, David W.
Copyright©1993 by Bennett, David W.
ISBN: 1-59244-504-7
Publication date 1/28/2004
Previously published by Baker Book House/Paternoster Press, 1993

Contents

Part Three: Following the master in church leadership today

List of tables

1

Introduction

During his three years of public ministry, Jesus focused much of his time and attention on the development of the twelve people who would become the leadership core of the earliest Christian community. He selected them for an intensive program of personal spiritual development and practical ministry experience, in preparation for the day when he would return to heaven and commission them to make disciples from every nation. Jesus trained the Twelve to be leaders in his church.

Down through the centuries church leaders have continued to study the Gospels to discover patterns of leadership development that can be applied to their own historical and cultural context. Yet the words 'leader' and 'leadership' do not appear in the Gospels. In fact, Jesus says surprisingly little to his disciples about their future role as leaders, at least in any explicit way. Why is this? Could it be that leadership has more to do with learning to follow than learning to command, supervise, or manage? Could it be that effective leadership depends more on right attitudes than on mastery of certain skills? Could it be that it is more important for the leader to understand what he or she has in common with other followers of the Lord than to focus on what sets the leader apart from the rest?

Leadership has been defined by many theorists as a process of influence. To understand how Jesus prepared the disciples to be leaders, we can begin by studying what he said about how they would influence others. Thus, even if we cannot find paragraphs in which Jesus delineates detailed job descriptions for the future leadership of the disciples in the Jerusalem church, we can find passages that describe the impact that he expected them to have on the lives of other people. Many of the insights we need are embedded in the images which Jesus used to describe his followers. Terms like 'witness', 'servant', 'salt' and 'harvester' are full of implications for the role of the spiritual leader.

We must approach the issue of leadership on Jesus' terms, not ours. The concepts and values that he shared with his disciples may not be the familiar categories of our contemporary management textbooks or our manuals of church administration. The metaphors he chooses may not imply the same patterns of leadership behavior that are familiar in our own churches.

My starting point for this research is the confession of the Lordship of Jesus Christ. I hold the teaching and example of Jesus and his apostles to be the authoritative norm for ministry in the church, for all cultures and for all times. Although the principles will be applied differently in various contexts, Jesus' standards are the plumbline by which I intend to measure all other leadership patterns.

I also start with the premise that the Bible is the inspired, authoritative, and infallible Word of God, a reliable source of historical data as well as divine truth. Therefore, although I recognize difficulties in the precise chronological reconciliation of the Gospel accounts, I accept them as trustworthy historical records. I therefore assume that events and teachings actually occurred in the contexts described, and that a general harmonization of the four accounts is both possible and desirable. I also hold to conservative views on the authorship of the New Testament letters, considering them to be the work of the individuals to whom they are traditionally attributed, and therefore to be reliable samples of the teaching of these early leaders themselves, rather than later creations of the church.

My goal in this study is to discover the basic patterns of the style of leadership for which Jesus was preparing his disciples, patterns which would become the foundation for leadership in the early church. I will endeavor to define some of the basic concepts, values, and behaviors which were to guide the disciples in their leadership roles after Jesus ascended to heaven.

The method I have chosen begins with an examination of the terms which Jesus used to describe his disciples. In reading carefully through all four Gospels as well as the early parts of Acts, I have identified over thirty terms in parables, teaching, direct address, exhortations, and so forth. Relying primarily on inductive study of the English and Greek texts, I have examined each of these terms in context. I have attempted to get a feel for the meaning of each word-picture by seeing how it functions in each particular passage, and by comparing Jesus' uses of the same term in different contexts.

I have noted which words appear most frequently. There may be some surprises, because the images we stress most often in our own churches are not necessarily the ones used most frequently by Jesus. There are also terms which are missing from the vocabulary of Jesus, and I will offer some explanations of why this may be.

I have also looked for patterns in how, where and when Jesus introduced each of these images of leadership. I will suggest some reasons for why he used certain metaphors early in his encounters with the disciples, why he left others toward the end of his ministry with them, and why other images become increasingly prominent as he approaches the cross.

I have limited the first part of this study to terms actually found on the lips of Jesus, as recorded by the Gospel writers. Of course I am assuming that the terms used are indeed Jesus' terms, and not simply a reflection of later theological reflection by the early church.

In chapter three I will a propose a taxonomy for the various terms, and will identify some of the main dimensions of contrast. A comparison of the terms in the light of this analysis will suggest some overall themes that characterize Jesus' teachings about patterns of leadership.

In the second part of this study we will explore the use and development of these terms by the writers of the New Testament. We will also study the new images that are introduced by Paul, Peter, and others, noting how these compare to the pictures drawn by Jesus. In that part of the study we will incorporate observations from studies of first-century culture and language that help us to understand the ideas associated with these terms. Just as we did in the Gospels, we will look for common themes that underlie the images found in the New Testament, and see how these correspond to the themes identified in the teaching of Jesus. At the end of Part Two, an expanded taxonomy of terms will be presented, incorporating the observations from the entire study, but continuing to highlight the terms used by Jesus in his instruction of his disciples.

Before launching into the biblical study, we need to consider a few observations about the importance of images in a study of church leadership. Lakoff and Johnson insist that: ' ... metaphor is pervasive in everyday life, not just in language but in thought and action. Our ordinary conceptual system, in terms of which we both think and act, is fundamentally metaphorical in nature' (1980:3). A metaphor helps us to understand a thing in terms of something with which we are already familiar. With a creative leap of the imagination, we are able to perceive a previously undiscerned similarity, and to open up new avenues of insight. Metaphors sharpen our observations, and help us to see patterns and relationships; they awaken feelings and attitudes, and can alter the way we behave (Barbour 1976:12–14). 'Good metaphors shock,' says Sallie McFague, 'they bring unlikes together, they upset conventions, they involve tension, and they are implicitly revolutionary' (1982:17).

'Metaphor is one of our most important tools for trying to

comprehend partially what cannot be comprehended totally: our feelings, aesthetic experiences, moral practices, and spiritual awareness' (Lakoff and Johnson 1980:193).

Imagery becomes especially important, therefore, in our attempts to fathom a God whom we cannot see, and to live in the context of realities that transcend space and time. We need images to help us to comprehend the spiritual community of which we are a part, and to understand the place of leadership in that community, which, as Jesus taught, often functions quite differently from society as a whole. For this reason also, a study of images of leadership cannot be separated from an examination of images of the church.

For example, Gibbs (1987:53–80) illustrates how six contemporary images of the church are correlated with differing expectations of the leader. In the Venerable Institution, the leaders give ceremonial headship and patronage. In the Business Organization, people expect a 'go-getter' leader and a centralized executive structure. Where the church is seen as a Happy Family, people want the leader to be an empathetic encourager. In the Supercharged Community, they desire inspirational, visionary prophets. When the church is a Celebrity's Fan Club, the leaders must be gifted performers. The sixth image, the church as Complex Organism, is a composite of the first five.

Messer (1989) also comments on the diversity of contemporary images for the ministry. After citing some traditional biblical and historical images, he lists a number of recent ones: counselor/therapist, administrator, professional, player/coach, enabler, facilitator, midwife, clown, mana person, storyteller, wagonmaster, and pastoral director. Then he suggests a number of fresh images of his own for the church and its ministry today: Wounded Healers in a Community of the Compassionate; Servant Leaders in a Servant Church; Political Mystics in a Prophetic Community; Enslaved Liberators of the Rainbow Church; Practical Theologians in a Post-Denominational Church; and a Public Ministry in a Global Village.

Minear (1960) has identified ninety-six biblical analogies describing the church,[1] as well as sixteen images that refer to the functioning of leaders within the church.[2] He says:

> In every generation the use and re-use of the Biblical images
> has been one path by which the church has tried to learn
> what the church truly is, so that it could become what it is
> not. For evoking this kind of self-knowledge, images may be
> more effective than formal dogmatic assertions (1960:25).

14

There is no single 'master image' which fully embraces the totality of church life and leadership. Dulles cautions us that we must be prepared to 'work simultaneously with different models' if we are to 'do justice to the various aspects of the Church as a complex reality' (1987:14). As Minear says: '. . . no one figure can be selected as the dominating base line of all thought about the church. The writers start their thinking not from one image, building upon its foundation a complex set of figurative constructions, but they seem to start from a reality that lies beneath and behind all the images. No writer makes any single image serve in a passage of any length as the only or the sufficient analogy of the community of faith' (1960:222). Each picture allows us to view the whole from a somewhat different perspective. It is only as the different perspectives are combined and compared that we will begin to develop an understanding of the wholeness that they describe. Dillistone warns that 'there is always a danger either of concentrating on a single analogy or of coming to infer that an analogy is to be accorded a literal or a univocal interpretation' (1986:83).[3]

Sometimes we are not fully aware of the metaphors, expressed or implied, that shape our values and responses. For example, Tillapaugh (1982) argues that the church in America today has turned too much inward, taking a defensive stance toward the world, viewing itself as a 'fortress' rather than unleashing people for ministry in the world. McFague (1982) is concerned about the use of predominantly patriarchal imagery that causes many women to feel specifically excluded from the life of the church. Küng warns that 'all too easily the church can become a prisoner of the image it has made for itself at one particular period of history' (1967:22); the same warning could be applied to the church leader.

There are many debates in the church today about the most appropriate images to capture the imagination of present-day Christians, and to direct and inspire the work of church leaders. The place to begin, however, is with a thorough understanding of the terms that Jesus introduced to his disciples.

Since most of the terms Jesus used are metaphors, rather than literal descriptions of his followers, we will sometimes speak collectively of 'images of discipleship.' However, we recognize that some of the terms are not 'metaphors' in the strict sense, but rather words describing roles which the followers are to assume, such as the term 'disciple', or words that have literal meanings but which carry associations that go beyond those meanings, such as 'the Twelve.'

15

Jesus as well as his apostles had many choices, in the terms they selected and in the roles with which they decided to identify. We can learn much from the words they chose to use as well as the words they avoided. Jesus was calling a new community into being. We cannot conclude that simply because Jesus used a term that was familiar to his hearers, that therefore he applied it in exactly the same way as it had been used in the rest of society. Nor can we assume that, when Jesus suggested a metaphor, the point of comparison was necessarily the first one that would have occurred to his hearers, or to us. That is why we must begin with careful inductive study of the terms in the contexts where they are used, employing caution in the use of sociologically oriented exegetical studies,[4] and even greater caution in the use of etymologically based word studies.[5]

Notes

1   He groups them into four 'master' images—people of God, new creation, fellowship of faith, and body of Christ—as well as a cluster of minor images. Küng (1967) employs a similar grouping, discussing the church as People of God, Creation of the Spirit, and Body of Christ. Dulles (1987), drawing on a blend of biblical as well as historical images, describes five models of the church—as institution, mystical communion, sacrament, herald, and servant—then proposes a sixth model which he finds more satisfactory: 'community of disciples.'

2   Purkiser (1969) finds seventeen New Testament metaphors for ministers, as well as eleven more generic terms.

3   For example, Stevens (1987:178; note 8) observes that Larry Richards errs in seeing the church only in relational terms, rather than also in terms of mission, because of his exclusive focus on the 'Body' image.

4   An exegete who has done sociological and cultural investigation of the ancient world may be tempted to see only the similarities between the biblical situation and the larger context, rather than paying sufficient attention to the differences. R.R. Wilson (1984) warns that since sociology is interested in general patterns, it can therefore 'tend to neglect unique phenomena' (p. 13), and that therefore one needs 'to balance social theory with a thorough examination of the textual evidence' (p. 26).

5   For this reason I have chosen to cite word studies from the three-volume work, *The New International Dictionary of New Testament Theology*, edited by Colin Brown (Grand Rapids: Zondervan, 1975), from here on abbreviated as DNTT. Unlike earlier standards like Kittel's *Theological Dictionary of the New Testament*, this reference work explicitly acknowledges the pitfalls of failure to give sufficient attention to context, and tries to avoid the dangers of over-reliance on etymologies (1:10).

2

Description of terms

In this chapter I will describe how the terms function in the passages where Jesus uses them. Thus each image will be allowed to stand on its own, with little reference to parallel terms, or to the usage of the word elsewhere in the Bible. But in chapter three I will propose a hierarchy of relationships between the terms, based on the data presented in this chapter, and in Part Two I will comment on the usage of the various images elsewhere in scripture. For ease of reference, the description of these terms has been organized alphabetically, according to their English transliteration.

adelphos, adelphe (brother, sister)

In terms of the sheer number of occurrences, one of the terms used most frequently by Jesus is 'brother' (*adelphos*). It appears several times in the Sermon on the Mount, in the sections on anger and reconciliation ('if anyone is angry with his brother ... your brother has something against you ... be reconciled to your brother' Matthew 5:21–24), love for enemies ('if you greet only your brothers' Matthew 5:43–48), and judging others ('...the speck of dust in your brother's eye ... How can you say to your brother ... remove the speck from your brother's eye' Matthew 7:1–5; cf. Luke 6:41–42). Then in Matthew 18:15–35, Jesus teaches his disciples about how to respond to the 'brother' who sins against them, and who needs to be forgiven again and again.

In each case Jesus introduces the term in the context of inter-personal tension. The explosion of anger, the long bitter grudge, the perception of a defect in the other, the suffering of a personal injury each tempt us to maintain distance between ourselves and the other person. Yet in these very situations, Jesus reminds his disciples that they are connected to one another; they are members of a family, they are brothers. They cannot separate themselves from one another any more than they can cancel the bonds that tie them to their own families. It is true that those who are closest to them can hurt them most deeply, and will probably hurt them most often. But Jesus reminds his disciples that they remain brothers, and must seek reconciliation.

17

The word 'brother' is primarily a reciprocal word, a description of an egalitarian relationship. Brothers are fundamentally peers. Yet the brother relationship among the disciples does not remove the possibility for discipline or the exercise of authority within their community. In Matthew 18 Jesus insists that the brother who sins must be disciplined strongly if he refuses to listen to admonition; if he persists, he will be excommunicated, treated like an outsider, expelled from the fellowship. Yet, Jesus says in a similar passage in Luke 17:3, if there is repentance, the brother must be forgiven. There is a fundamental bond that remains and must be restored.

The egalitarian implications of the word 'brother' are highlighted in Matthew 23, in the passage where Jesus is rebuking the hypocrisy of the status-seeking Pharisees, with their love for prominent positions and distinctive titles. Jesus specifically warns his disciples: 'You are not to be called "Rabbi," for you have only one Master and you are all brothers (*pantes de hymeis adelphoi este*)' (23:8). In the preceding verses Jesus criticizes the Pharisees for doing everything for show. They do not practice what they preach; they burden others, but give no help in lifting those burdens; they do everything for people to see; they love places of honor at the banquets and the most important seats in the synagogues; they yearn to be recognized in public places and to have people address them with honorific titles. All of these practices feed their pride, their sense of being separate from and above the people. They do not want to be seen as 'among', but 'over'.

But the disciples of Jesus must not imitate these errors. They are, Jesus reminds them, brothers first of all. They are not 'over' but 'among.' And they are also 'under.' They have one one Master/teacher (*didaskalos*), one Father in heaven (*ho pater ho ouranios*), one teacher/leader (*kathegetes*) (23:8–10). The image of 'brother' is introduced to emphasize that the disciples are all on the same level ground, all equally responsible to God as Father.

The use of the word 'brother' implies the recognition of a bond. In the parable of the sheep and the goats, the King rewards the righteous because 'whatever you did for one of the least of these brothers of mine, you did for me' (Matthew 25:40). Whoever is called the King's brother is identified with the King in the closest possible way.

Even when Jesus predicts Peter's denial, he encourages Peter by telling him: 'When you have turned back, strengthen your brothers' (Luke 22:32). Jesus knows that after such a tragic failure, Peter will not feel very much like a part of the community; yet he remains a brother among brothers. Similarly, after his resurrection appearance to the women, Jesus says, 'Go and tell my brothers (tois adelphois mou) to go to Galilee' (Matthew 28:10; cf. John 20:17). These are warm words, spoken in a context where the disciples might have felt ashamed and distant from Jesus, because they had all deserted him at the time of his arrest. But Jesus moves to close the gap by the use of the term 'brother.' In so doing, he reminds the disciples that they are not only brothers of one another, but also brothers to him.

When his own natural family wanted to see him, Jesus replied that 'whoever does the will of my Father in heaven is my brother (adelphos) and sister (adelphe) and mother (meter)' (Matthew 12:48–50; cf. Mark 3:33–35 and Luke 8:19–21). That is, those who obey and trust God are included in a new spiritual family, with bonds that are even more fundamental and enduring than those that tie individuals together in biological families. The word 'brother' implies personal relationship to Jesus and to the community of faith. Jesus' lack of deference to his natural family members is more understandable in the light of the information provided in Mark 3:21, where we learn that Jesus' family had gone to take charge of him, because they were convinced that he was out of his mind. Yet in a kinship-oriented society like Israel, still it must have been startling for people to hear of a bond that was even deeper than that of the natural family.

Notice that though the relationship between Jesus and the disciple is initiated by Jesus, it is cemented and confirmed by the willing response of the follower; only the ones who do the will of the Father (Matthew 12:50; Mark 3:35), who hear God's word and put it into practice (Luke 8:21), are included in the circle of Jesus' brothers and sisters.

apostolos (apostle)

The verb apostello (to send) appears frequently in the Gospels, in reference to the sending of Jesus by the Father (e.g. Matthew 15:24; John 5:36), and the sending of the disciples by Jesus (e.g. Matthew 10:5; John 17:18). Jesus also uses the word often in his parables to describe servants sent on assignments by their masters (e.g. Matthew 20:2; Mark 12:1–6).

But the noun apostolos, referring to the messenger who is sent, and transliterated by the English word 'apostle' occurs only a handful of times in the Gospels, most often in Luke, usually as a designation for the twelve disciples. On two occasions, however, Jesus uses the word *apostolos* in reference to his followers.

The first instance is the appointment of the Twelve, recorded in Mark 3:13–19 and Luke 6:12–16. The importance of this occasion is emphasized by Luke's observation that Jesus spent the entire preceding night in prayer. When morning came, Luke tells us, 'he called his disciples to him and chose twelve of them, whom he also designated apostles' (6:13). Then, in both Mark and Luke, comes the listing of the twelve names.

The initiative of Jesus in this whole process is evident. The apostles were not volunteers. Jesus chose the time. Jesus chose the place. Not all of the followers of Jesus were embraced in the choice. No, Mark includes the explicit statement that Jesus 'called to him those he wanted, and they came to him'(3:13). Luke also implies Jesus' initiative through his statement that Jesus called (*prospho-nesen*) his disciples and chose (*eklexamenos*) twelve.

The enlistment of the disciples in the process of leadership development began with the action of Jesus. There was an open invitation to follow Jesus, and to listen to his teachings, but not a corresponding invitation for all to be part of the inner circle who would be 'with him' and who would be sent out 'to preach and to have authority to drive out demons' (Mark 3:13, 14). It was only these twelve, selected and gathered by Jesus' deliberate choice, who would enter into the more intensive course of leadership develop-ment, and whom Jesus would designate (*onomasen*) as apostles (Luke 6:13; the phrase in Mark 3:14 is essentially the same, but based on a less certain text; the word order in Luke places the emphasis on the word *apostolous*).

To emphasize this act of narrowing and selecting, Luke notes that Jesus chose 'from them' (*ap' auton*), that is from the larger group of disciples. Thus not every disciple is described by the term 'apostle.' There are some roles in the community of Jesus which are 'by invitation only.' The selection appears to have taken place in full view of the other disciples, not in some secret ceremony of initiation. Thus the special leadership role of these twelve would have been clearly demarcated in the eyes of the entire group of Jesus' followers.

The authority of Jesus over these twelve is also implied in the act of naming: Simon he nicknamed 'Peter', the rock, and James and John he designated as the 'sons of thunder.'

The 'sent ones' would have two basic responsibilities. First, they were called together to be with Jesus, that is, to share a common life, to enter into a personal relationship with him and with one another. In the second place, they were called to share in a task, to announce a message (*keryssein*) and to exercise authority (*exein exousian*) over the powers of darkness. Thus they would share in the divine authority. Their influence would be more than mere moral persuasion; rather they were authorized to speak and to take action as representatives of the Messiah himself.

The one other occasion in the Gospels where Jesus uses the word *apostolos* is in John 13:14–16, just after he has washed the disciples' feet. He tells them:

> Now that I, your Lord and Teacher, have washed your feet, you also should wash one another's feet. I have set you an example, that you should do as I have done for you. I tell you the truth, no servant is greater than his master, nor is a messenger (*apostolos*) greater than the one who sent him (*tou pempsantos auton*).

Jesus has clearly stated his own position of leadership. He is the Lord (*kyrios*), the one who holds the authority, and he is the teacher (*didaskalos*), the one who has the knowledge. But he has set an example of service of the lowliest kind. What is demonstrated by the greater can certainly be expected from the lesser. Therefore the disciples are obligated to do for one another what Jesus has done for them.

Jesus supports his point by arguing that the servant is 'not greater' than his master—in other words, the servant is commonly acknowledged to be less than his master. For a servant to say that certain work is beneath his dignity would be to imply that he has greater status than his master. Similarly, says Jesus, the messenger, or apostle (Jesus is speaking in generic terms of one who is sent by another, not specifically of the Twelve), is not greater than the one who sent him.

When Jesus first designated the Twelve as apostles, there was an emphasis on the special privileges of intimacy with Jesus and participation in his mission that they would enjoy. They would share in his authority as proclaimers of the divine word and conquerors of demons. But here Jesus reminds them that no matter how much authority the 'apostle' may have, he remains one who has been sent by another. His authority is not autonomous, but derived.

It would have been very easy for the apostles to focus on those whom they were greater than, rather than to remember that they themselves were under authority, and were not independent agents. The sentence structure of verse 16 clearly puts *apostolos* parallel with *doulos*, and the sender with the master, thus emphasizing that to be an apostle is first to be a servant.

Yet in the very next verses of John 13 Jesus returns to the theme of the high status and privilege of the one who is sent. In verse 18 he reminds the disciples that he has chosen (*exelexamen*) them, that they are in this circle by his initiative, not their own. But in verse 20 he says: 'I tell you the truth, whoever accepts anyone I send (*pempso*) accepts me; and whoever accepts me accepts the one who sent me.' Jesus' reference to the Father's sending recalls the phrase at the beginning of the passage (13:3) where John states that Jesus knew that 'he had come from God' (*apo theou exelthen*). So then Jesus himself has been sent by God, a position of high authority and privilege, yet he stoops to wash feet. Similarly the disciples are privileged to be sent into the world as messengers, apostles, of Jesus. The one who welcomes them welcomes the Son of God. Yet the apostles, like the one who sent them, are called to serve in humility.

diakonos (servant)

The two words used most frequently by Jesus to express the idea of servanthood are *diakonos* and *doulos*. They frequently occur together in the same passages; many of those verses will be discussed in the section on *doulos*. How shall the two words be distinguished? One pattern that emerges is that when the emphasis is on the task, the responsibility, on obeying orders and being under authority, the word used is *doulos*. But when the emphasis is on the rendering of personal service, or when the stress is on the attitudes of humility and love which should inspire the service, then the word more likely to be used is *diakonos*.

The word *diakonos* means literally 'to wait at table,' to render service during a meal. This sense is found in Jesus' parable in Luke 17:8 where the servant is commanded by his master to prepare the supper and to serve it, and in the surprising description in Luke 12:37 of the master who turns the tables and thanks the faithful servants by waiting on them himself!

The image of the *diakonos* is often connected with Jesus' teachings on humility. For example, Mark refers to an argument between the disciples on the road to Capernaum about who was the greatest (a topic that came up frequently among the Twelve). The disciples were embarrassed to tell Jesus what they had been discussing. So he called them together, and sat down, as a symbol of his own authority. Then he said: 'If anyone wants to be first, he must be the very last, and the servant of all (*panton diakonos*)' (Mark 9:35). The servant of all would make no distinctions concerning whom he would serve and whom he would not. Such servanthood is an unqualified act of surrender to be available to anyone to whom the master sends us.

Then Jesus used a child as an illustration of the kind of humble attitude God was looking for. The parallel account in Matthew records Jesus' statement: 'Whoever humbles himself like this child is the greatest in the kingdom of heaven' (Matthew 18:4). Luke's account includes the statement: 'He who is least among you all—he is the greatest' (Luke 9:48).

4.1

A similar dispute broke out when James and John requested positions of honor at the right and left hand of Jesus (Matthew 20:20–28 and Mark 10:35–45). Jesus replied by pointing out the contrast between the harsh and arrogant rule of the Gentile authorities, and the humble servanthood to which he was calling his disciples. He said, 'Whoever wants to become great among you must be your servant (*hymon diakonos*)' (Matthew 20:26), then concluded with the citation of his own example: 'For even the Son of Man did not come to be served (*diakonethenai*), but to serve (*diakonesai*), and to give his life as a ransom for many' (Mark 10:45).

Luke 22 records yet a third argument on the same topic, following the Last Supper. As in Matthew 20, Jesus contrasts the practices of Gentile rulers with the standards expected of his followers. He says:

> The kings of the Gentiles lord it over them (*kurieuousin auton*); and those who exercise authority over them (*hoi exousiazontes auton*) call themselves Benefactors (*euergetai*). But you are not to be like that. Instead, the greatest (*ho meizon*) among you should be like the youngest, and the one who rules (*ho hegoumenos*) like the one who serves (*ho diakonon*). For who is greater, the one who is at the table or the one who serves (*ho diakonon*)? But I am among you (*en mesoi hymon*) as one who serves (*ho diakonon*) (Matthew 20:25–27).

In that Jesus had just finished washing the disciples' feet, the illustration of his service to them was fresh in their minds. Jesus was not rebuking the desire to be great, or denying that there could be authority or rule within his community. Rather he was teaching that the attitude underlying every action was to be that of the humble servant.

Matthew records yet another example of the association between the word *diakonos* and the attitude of humility. In the midst of a scathing denunciation of the Pharisees for their hypocrisy, their preoccupation with outward appearance, and their clamoring for recognition, Jesus says: 'The greatest among you will be your servant (*hymon diakonos*). For whoever exalts himself will be humbled, and whoever humbles himself will be exalted' (23:11–12).

The greatest act of humility and self-emptying servanthood by far is seen in Jesus' giving of his life 'as a ransom for many' (Matthew 20:28; Mark 10:45). The word *diakonos* is used once more by Jesus in John 12, in association with his imminent death. He tells a short parable about the kernel of wheat which must fall into the ground and die in order to become fruitful (12:24). He reminds the disciples that, 'The man who loves his life will lose it, while the man who hates his life in this world will keep it for eternal life' (12:25). And then he says: 'Whoever serves (*diakonei*) me must follow me; and where I am, my servant (*ho diakonos ho emos*) also will be. My Father will honor the one who serves (*diakonei*) me' (12:26).

Thus to serve Jesus is to follow him, to stay with him no matter where the path may lead, even to suffering and death.

dodeka (twelve)

All four Gospel writers refer to the disciples on a number of occasions as 'the Twelve' (e.g. Matthew 26:14; Mark 4:10; Luke 18:31; John 20:24). But only once is it recorded that Jesus referred to them by this term. In John 6:70, when many were turning back and no longer following him, Jesus said, 'Have I not chosen you, the Twelve (*hymas tous dodeka exelexamen*)? Yet one of you is a devil!'

The emphasis on Jesus' choice of them, and the correspondence to the twelve tribes of God's chosen people Israel, suggest that a deeper symbolic significance is implied in the number. Jesus did not just happen to choose twelve, rather than eight, or fifteen. In

Matthew 19:28, on the road to Jerusalem, and again during the Last Supper, in Luke 22:30, Jesus promises his disciples that in the coming kingdom they will sit on twelve thrones, judging the twelve tribes of Israel. This promise suggests that the disciples represent the new Israel, the new people of God drawn together by their allegiance to the Messiah. But it also implies that they will have leadership roles in the believing community, both in this age and in the age to come.

doulos (servant)

When Jesus speaks to his disciples of servanthood, he has two aspects in mind. First is the service rendered to God as the supreme authority to whom they owe their allegiance, and the second is the service which they render to people as an expression of humility and love.

In the Sermon on the Mount, Jesus warns his disciples: 'No one can serve (douleuein) two masters (kyriois). Either he will hate the one and love the other, or he will be devoted to the one and despise the other. You cannot serve (douleuein) God and money' (Matthew 6:24; cf. Luke 16:13). The relationship of service involves obedience, but it is more than that; it is also a matter of allegiance. The conflict that Jesus describes is not a conflict in chains of command, but rather a matter of divided affections. The key words are love and devotion, in contrast to hating and despising. Thus, says Jesus, the service that God requires springs from an exclusive allegiance.

Many times in his parables Jesus compares his followers to servants (douloi), whether of a king, or head of a household, or landowner. For example, in the parable of the unforgiving servant (Matthew 18:23–35), a servant who has been forgiven a huge debt by the king refuses to release his fellow-servant (syndoulon) from a much smaller obligation. In the parable of the prodigal son, the older son complains about all the years he has served his father without special recognition (Luke 15:29).

In the parable of the talents (Matthew 25:14–30), a man entrusts various large sums of money to his servants, expecting them to invest the resources wisely during his absence. The huge amounts of money involved illustrate the significant level of responsibility that the Lord entrusts to his servants. The strong reaction of the master to the servant who fails to exercise stewardship shows the

25

great importance Jesus places on the disciples' diligence in using effectively the resources they have been given for the task of ministry.

In a similar story, the parable of the ten minas (Luke 19:12–27), the amounts of money are much smaller, and the emphasis is on the long delay that will precede the coming of the kingdom. The story stresses the importance of making the most of opportunities in the meantime. The faithful servants are rewarded by being given authority over several cities. They are not released from their continuing obligation to serve, but they gain the privilege of broadened responsibility. Both parables teach that servanthood involves responsibility and accountability, and that faithful service will be rewarded.

The association of servanthood with responsibility is also found in Jesus' comments in Matthew 24:45–51 (cf. Luke 12:42–46) about the 'faithful and wise servant (*ho pistos doulos kai phronimos*)' whom the master puts in charge of his other servants (*oiketeias*) to give them their food at the proper time. This servant has other servants under him. And he is rewarded by being placed in charge of all his master's possessions (24:47). In contrast, the wicked servant is described as mistreating his fellow-servants (*tous syndoulous*). Thus even though he has responsibility over others, he still remains a servant not just 'over,' but also 'among.' Luke follows his telling of this story with Jesus' warning to the servant who has been entrusted with much, but who does not obey (Luke 12:47–48).

Similarly, in Mark 13:34, during the Olivet discourse, Jesus speaks about a person who leaves his house and places his servants (*tois doulois autou*) in charge, each with his own task (*ekastoi to ergon autou*). Each servant is given authority (*exousia*) over a particular area.

In Luke 12:35–38, Jesus paints a beautiful portrait of the high regard which the master has for his faithful servants. He pictures a man returning from a wedding banquet to find his servants waiting for him. Jesus says, 'I tell you the truth, he will dress himself to serve, will have them recline at table and will come and wait on them.' What a startling and unexpected expression of the master's approval!

The standard of service that God expects is revealed vividly in Luke 17. Jesus has just told the disciples that they must be prepared to forgive again and again the brother who sins against them repeatedly. Apparently overwhelmed by these high standards, the

26

disciples cry out, 'Increase our faith!' (17:5). Jesus speaks of the power of faith as small as a mustard seed, but then goes on to raise the standard even higher. He describes a servant (doulos) who has been plowing or looking after the sheep. After the servant finishes his work in the fields he is expected to prepare supper for the master and to wait on his needs. Only then can he prepare his own meal. And in all of these tasks he is not to expect any special thanks from the master, because he is merely performing his duty. Thus Jesus concludes: 'So you also, when you have done everything you were told to do, should say, "We are unworthy servants; we have only done our duty"' (17:10). When the disciples keep the commands of Jesus, they are not to congratulate themselves on their extraordinary accomplishment, or to expect special recognition; they are only doing their duty; the same would be expected of any servant. The truly valuable servant will find ways to serve that go beyond the mere commands of the master; he will delight to identify needs of the master, and to fulfill them before he is even asked to do so. The true servant has his master's welfare on his heart at all times.

To be Jesus' servant is to be identified closely with him in all respects, including his suffering. In Matthew 10, Jesus warns the disciples about the persecution which they are going to suffer because of their association with him, telling them that they must not expect any better treatment than he himself has received. He says: 'A student is not above his teacher, nor a servant (doulos) above his master (ton kyrion autou). It is enough for a student to be like his teacher, and the servant (ho doulos) like his master (hos ho kyrios autou)' (10:24–25). Jesus makes a similar statement ('a servant is not greater than his master') in a similar context (a warning about persecution) in John 15:20. Then again, in John 13:16 we find the same quotation, when Jesus exhorts the disciples to wash one another's feet, and not to consider beneath their dignity the sort of humble work that their Master was willing to do.

Although Jesus used the metaphor of the servant frequently in reference to his disciples, he saw its limitations. Although the 'servant' image conveyed the ideas of accomplishing a task, fulfilling a responsibility, and being under authority, it could not express the quality of intimate relationship that Jesus enjoyed with his disciples. Thus he said to his disciples in John 15:15: 'I no longer call you servants (doulous), because a servant does not know his master's business (ti poiei autou ho kyrios). Instead, I have called you friends (philous), for everything that I learned from my Father I have

27

made known to you' (cf. comments under *philos*). When Jesus said 'no longer', he reminded them of what a dominant metaphor 'servant' had been in his teaching so far.

Yet to be a servant implies not only allegiance to the Lord. It also involves an attitude of humility toward others. In Matthew 20:20–28 (cf. Mark 10:35–45) we find James and John making the request, through their mother, to be given the two positions of greatest prominence in the kingdom, sitting at Jesus' right and left. Jesus has just told the disciples that he is going up to Jerusalem to suffer and to die (Matthew 20:17–19), but they do not grasp the implications. Anger erupts from the ten toward the presumption of the two, probably out of jealousy that the others did not think to make the request first!

Jesus corrects their attitudes by drawing a contrast between leadership in pagan society and leadership in his community: 'You know that the rulers of the Gentiles (*hoi archontes ton ethnon*) lord it over them (*katakyrieuousin auton*), and their high officials (*hoi megaloi*) exercise authority over them (*katexousiazousin*)' (20:25). The *kata-* compounds express looking down, subjugation, oppression, abuse of power and authority. But that is not to be the case with the Twelve. Jesus says, 'Whoever wants to be great among you must be your servant (*hymon diakonos*), and whoever wants to be first must be your slave (*hymon doulos*)' (20:26–27). Then Jesus cites his own example of service, in contrast to the typical patterns of the world: '. . . just as the Son of Man did not come to be served, but to serve, and to give his life as a ransom for many' (20:28).

Notice that here Jesus does not call the disciples to be servants in a general sense. No, he exhorts them specifically to be servants of one another. That is much more difficult. To serve their master is expected. But to serve their competitors is far more challenging. They are to be so busy lifting one another up that they forget about their own ambitions, and instead become caught up in the joy of seeing one another succeed. Instead of focusing on being over, they are to place themselves willingly under; and in so doing, they will become great. Thus the image of 'servant' expresses humility, and the willing withdrawal from the competition for status and power.

28

eklektos (chosen)

Although many of the terms Jesus uses for his disciples convey very vivid pictures, this one is less concrete. Because of the long history of the reference to Israel as God's chosen people (Deuteronomy 10:15; Isaiah 41:8), Jesus' reference to his followers as chosen ones, or the 'elect', evokes images of them as the new Israel, the true remnant. It is a term which emphasizes the privileges which they enjoy as objects of God's gracious choice.

Jesus uses the related verb, *eklegomai* (to choose), several times in the Gospel of John in reference to his disciples: 'Have I not chosen you, the Twelve?' (6:70); 'I know those I have chosen' (13:18); 'You did not choose me but I chose you' (15:16); 'I have chosen you out of the world' (15:19). Elsewhere he uses the noun, *eklektos*, on two occasions.

The first instance is Luke 18, in the parable of the persistent widow. Having described how the reluctant judge finally gives in to the widow's pleas, Jesus draws the application: 'Will not God bring about justice for his chosen ones (*ton eklekton auton*) who cry out to him day and night?' (18:7). Jesus' use of the term 'chosen' expresses a guarantee of protection and preservation for those who must endure hardship and persecution. Those whom God has selected and embraced in his love will never be abandoned to their enemies.

The same theme of protection in the midst of adversity is expressed through Jesus' use of the term *eklektos* during his discourse on the Mount of Olives, recorded in Matthew 24 and Mark 13. In response to the disciples' questions about the end of the age, Jesus describes a time of increasing stress and persecution. But then he adds the word of hope: 'If those days had not been cut short, no one would survive, but for the sake of the elect (*tous eklektous*) those days will be shortened' (Matthew 24:22). Mark records the same statement, with an additional modifying phrase: '. . .the elect, whom he has chosen' (Mark 13:20).

Jesus warns that false prophets and false Messiahs will appear so convincing that even the elect would be deceived, 'if it were possible' (Matthew 24:24; Mark 13:22). That qualifying phrase, recorded by both evangelists, implies a promise that those whom God has chosen will nevertheless be preserved from final deception. Then comes another promise the sending of God's angels to 'gather his elect (*tous eklektous autou*) from the four winds, from the ends of the earth to the ends of the heavens' (Mark 13:27; cf. Matthew

24:31). The inclusion of the personal pronoun 'his', in reference to the elect, emphasizes the bond between God and his people.

Once again, as in Luke 18, we see this metaphor introduced as part of a comforting promise, that God will come to the rescue of his people before the time of suffering overwhelms them completely. He has committed himself to protect and preserve those who are his, those whom he has chosen.

ergates (worker)

In Matthew 9:37–38, when he saw the helplessness and spiritual needs of the crowds who constantly pursued him, Jesus addressed his disciples: 'The harvest (*ho therismos*) is plentiful but the workers (*hoi ergatai*) are few. Ask the Lord of the harvest (*tou kyriou tou therismou*) to send out (*ekbale*) workers (*ergatas*) into his harvest (*eis ton therismon autou*).'

Here is a metaphor that stresses the task, as well as the link of accountability between the workers and the Lord of the harvest. As we see in Matthew 10, the disciples became the answer to their own prayer. They became the workers thrust out into the field. They did not volunteer, but were sent out. The word *ekbale* may imply a forceful act, in view of the possible reluctance of the one sent.

In Luke 10:2, when Jesus sends out the seventy-two, the same call to prayer for workers (*ergatas*) is issued. Both Matthew 10 and Luke 10 record Jesus' saying, 'The laborer (*ho ergates*) is worthy of his hire,' as justification for the disciples to receive food and lodging from those to whom they preach.

Jesus refers to the work of the disciples as a kind of harvesting in John 4 as well. After speaking with the woman by the well in Samaria, he prepares the disciples for the great spiritual response which they are about to encounter among the townspeople, saying, 'Open your eyes and look at the fields! They are ripe for harvest (*leukai eisin pros therismon*) ... I sent you to reap (*therizein*) what you have not worked for' (4:35, 38).

In Matthew 20 the term *ergates* appears once again when Jesus tells the parable of the workers in the vineyard. The owner of the vineyard is called *oikodespotes* in verses 1 and 11, and *ho kurios tou ampelonos* in verse 8. Both terms emphasize that he is the one in authority. The owner goes out to hire (*misthosasthai*) workers (*ergatas*). Different ones are enlisted to work at various hours of the day, but all receive the same wages at the end. The parable as a whole teaches that the Lord has the sole right to determine how his servants are rewarded. Any complaints are evidence of ingratitude and lack of submission.

Thus the image of 'worker' is associated with a task to be done, with submission and accountability to the Lord's authority, and with the prospect of ultimate reward.

ge (soil)

All three synoptic Gospels record the parable of the soils, in which Jesus describes four different ways in which people respond to the message of the kingdom of God (Matthew 13:1–23; Mark 4:1–20; Luke 8:4–15). Three of the soils are unfruitful. Only one, the good soil (ten kalen gen), produces a crop.

The first soil, described as the path, never allows the seed to grow at all. The rocky soil produces growth only temporarily, and the thorny soil prevents the plants from maturing or bearing fruit. But the good soil, as Jesus describes it in Matthew, represents the one who hears the word (akouon), who understands it (synieis), and who bears fruit (karpophorei) (13:23). Mark's account adds that the good soil represents those who welcome (paradechontai) the word, and Luke notes that these are people with good and noble hearts who retain (katechousin) the word and persevere in it. But in all three passages, the emphasis is on the fruitfulness of the good soil (karpophorei in Matthew; karpophorousin in Mark and Luke), in contrast to the unfruitfulness of the thorny soil (akarpos ginetai in Matthew and Mark; ou telesphorousin in Luke). Matthew's and Mark's accounts also draw attention to the size of the crop produced by the good soil—thirty, sixty, or even one hundred times what was sown.

What does fruit represent? In agricultural terms, the fruit is the part that is eaten, or sold for income, or exchanged for other goods, or saved to plant for the next year's crop. The fruit is something useful. It points to the fulfillment of the purpose for which the crop was planted in the first place. No farmer would be satisfied with sowing if no fruit resulted. Thus this image of discipleship implies that there is a task to be accomplished, a purpose to be fulfilled. To be a follower of Jesus is not merely to enter into a personal relationship, but also to embark on a mission in which effectiveness can be evaluated, and in which failure is possible.

In each case the constant is the sower and the seed. The variable is the soil. This image, therefore, draws attention to the response of the disciple. The true follower of Jesus is not one who merely hears his word, but who also responds in obedience. Discipleship is not a passive state, but an active engagement.

halas (salt)

One of the best-known metaphors used by Jesus to describe his disciples occurs in the Sermon on the Mount, where he says, 'You are the salt of the earth (*to halas tes ges*)' (Matthew 5:13). Many have offered explanations of the significance of salt in the society of that time, but the two aspects of salt that appear most prominently are enhancement of flavor and preservation from decay. Thus, through this illustration, Jesus is highlighting the distinctive identity of his disciples as those who display God's character before the world and who help to rescue people from the judgment to come.

The image of salt implies that the disciples are going to influence their society. It summons them to the task of penetration and renewal. The followers of Jesus will have an observable impact on their world, not so much through their actions as through their very character as salt.

Yet, Jesus warns, it is possible for salt to lose its saltiness, and hence to become ineffective and useless, good for nothing except to be thrown out and trampled. The danger of salt losing its distinctive character is also mentioned by Jesus in Luke 14:34: 'Salt is good, but if it loses its saltiness, how can it be made salty again? It is fit neither for the soil nor for the manure pile; it is thrown out' (cf. Mark 9:50).

halieus (fisherman)

The very first metaphor which Jesus applies to his followers occurs in the familiar invitation: 'Come, follow me and I will make you fishers of men (*halieis anthropon*)' (Matthew 4:19; Mark 1:17). Although this has become one of the most familiar illustrations for discipleship, it is not used again by Jesus, nor is it taken up by any of the New Testament writers. Perhaps the reason why it is so prominent in our thinking is that it is the first image that Jesus uses to describe the life into which he is inviting his disciples.

Jesus issues his initial call to discipleship in terms of a task to be done, a mission to be accomplished. The mission focuses on the transformation of people. But the promise of effective influence in the lives of others is preceded by the command: 'Come, follow me,' or 'Come after me' (*deute opiso mou*). These are the words of a leader to a potential follower, as our English word 'leader' carries the image of one who goes ahead. Thus the invitation to the disciples as future leaders begins with the necessity of learning to be followers.

The ministry of leadership begins with the invitation of Jesus, with his call and initiative, not with volunteer enlistment. And the process of leadership development is also under his direction. Jesus says, 'I will make you (*poieso hymas*) fishers of men.' That is, what the disciples become will be what Jesus makes them.

In chapter five of his Gospel, Luke records the call of the first disciples, including many details that are not mentioned by either Mark or Matthew. He tells how Jesus got into the boat belonging to Simon Peter, and from there taught the crowds that lined the shore. Then he describes Jesus' command to Peter to let down the nets one more time, in spite of Peter's protest that an entire night of fishing had produced nothing. After the miraculous catch of fish, which nearly sank two boats, Jesus said to Peter: 'Don't be afraid; from now on you will catch men (*anthropous esei zogron*)' (5:10). The noun *halieus* (fisher) does not appear in the words of Jesus in this account (although Luke uses it to introduce the scene in 5:2); but the equivalent image is conveyed by the vivid participial phrase. The words 'from now on (*apo tou nun*)' emphasize the radical discontinuity with their former life. They are crossing a threshold. They are embarking on a life of apprenticeship, in preparation for a new vocation.

hetairos (friend)

Jesus' use of this term for friend differs considerably from his use of the other term, *philos*, also translated friend. Whereas *philos* conveys an attitude of warmth and welcome, *hetairos* connotes a certain coolness and reserve. *Philos* draws the other close. *Hetairos* maintains the distance.

In the parable of the workers in the vineyard, recorded in Matthew 20:1–16, the landowner says to the hired servant who is complaining about his wages: 'Friend (*hetaire*), I am not being unfair to you' (20:13). Although the hired servants in the parable all represent followers of Jesus, the ungrateful worker, addressed as 'friend', is one with whom the master is not at all pleased.

In a similar spirit, in the Garden of Gethsemane, Jesus acknowledges the kiss of Judas by saying, 'Friend (*hetaire*), do what you came for' (Matthew 26:50). Jesus is greeting a betrayer, not a loyal companion who has remained with him in the Upper Room.

In other contexts, too, the word *hetairos* seems to convey this note of reserve. For example, in Matthew 11:16, Jesus compares his generation to children who complain to their companions (*tois heterois*) who will not sing their tunes or dance to their instruments. Again, in the parable of the wedding banquet (Matthew 22:1–14) the king addresses the man who failed to wear wedding clothes as 'friend (*hetaire*)' (22:12), just before throwing him outside into the darkness.

Thus it seems that each time the word *hetairos* is used, it connotes some displeasure or annoyance, perhaps the way we employ the word 'buddy' today, where the term can be used with warmth, but is often used as a euphemism to soften the anger that smolders under the surface.

hyios (son/child)

Jesus' first usage of this metaphor to describe his disciples occurs in the Beatitudes, where he promises, 'Blessed are the peacemakers, for they will be called sons of God (*hyioi theou*)' (Matthew 5:9). The children of God are those who share his character, in whom can be seen the family resemblance. Later in the Sermon on the Mount Jesus exhorts his disciples to love their enemies and to pray for their persecutors so that 'you may be sons of your Father in heaven (*hyioi tou patros hymon tou en ouranois*)' (Matthew 5:45). The remainder of that paragraph builds to the climax in verse 48: 'Be perfect (*teleios*), therefore, as your heavenly Father is perfect.' Once again, then, to be a child of the Father is to imitate the Father's character. In a similar passage in Luke 6:35–36, Jesus summons his disciples to be 'sons of the Most High (*hyioi hypsistou*)' by being merciful as their Father is merciful.

In reply to the question about the woman with multiple husbands, Jesus refers to those who will enter the age to come as 'children of God (*hyioi theou*)' and 'children of the resurrection (*hyioi tes anastaseos*)' (Luke 20:36). Then in Matthew 13:38, in the explanation of the parable of the weeds, Jesus says that the good seed are the 'sons of the kingdom (*hyioi tes basileias*).' The children of the King are the children of God.

These are direct references to the disciples as children of God.

34

But there are also numerous passages in which Jesus, speaking to his disciples, implies the same relationship by referring to God as 'your Father' (Matthew 5:16, 45, 48; 6:1, 4, 6, 8, 14, 15, 18, 26, 32; 7:11; 10:20, 29; 13:43; 18:14; 23:9; Mark 11:25; Luke 6:36; 11:13; 12:30, 32; John 20:17). Notice that the great majority of these references are found in Matthew, and in particular, in the Sermon on the Mount. Furthermore, in teaching the disciples to pray, Jesus encourages them to address God as 'Our Father' (Matthew 6:9; Luke 11:2). Of course, there are also numerous verses in which Jesus refers to God as 'the Father' (e.g. Matthew 28:19; Mark 13:32; John 4:23) or as 'my Father' (e.g. Matthew 26:39; Luke 22:29; John 10:29), especially in the Gospel of John. But here we are focusing on the passages which reveal Jesus' emphasis on the specific, personal relationship between the disciples and their heavenly Father.

These passages repeatedly associate two things with the image of the disciples as children of the Father: first, the family resemblance, the similarity in character between the Father and the children; and second, the tender care that the Father shows toward his children, listening to their prayers, providing for their needs, and rewarding them for their faithful service.

hyios tou nymphonos (guest of the bridegroom)

Jesus introduces this metaphor in answering a question about why his disciples, unlike the disciples of John the Baptist and the Pharisees, do not fast. He replies: 'How can the guests of the bridegroom (hoi hyioi tou nymphonos) mourn while he is with them? The time will come when the bridegroom (ho nymphios) will be taken from them; then they will fast' (Matthew 9:15; cf. Mark 2:19; Luke 5:34). Although the three Gospel writers employ slightly different wording, all use the phrase hyioi tou nymphonos.

This is an image of joy, of celebration in the midst of companions. But the focal point is the bridegroom, who represents Jesus. The guests are derivative and subordinate. They have no role apart from the bridegroom. Their function is to keep the celebration focused on him and to share in his joy.

The wedding imagery is found in a two other parables recorded by Matthew. In Matthew 22:1–14 (cf. Luke 14:16–24), the parable of the wedding banquet, the king's invited guests refuse to come, and even mistreat the messengers. So the king sends out his servants into the streets in order to fill the wedding hall with guests. Those who are invited include both good and bad. They are distinguished only by their willingness to respond to the invitation. They have no other qualifications. Jesus uses this illustration to picture his followers as those who have been included in the community of celebration solely by the gracious act of God, not through any merit of their own.

In Matthew 25:1–13, the image of the wedding banquet appears once again in the parable of the ten virgins. Those who are allowed to enter are the ones who took along extra oil, and therefore were able to keep their lamps burning when the arrival of the bridegroom was later than expected. Here again the disciples are compared to participants in a wedding celebration.

hyperetes (servant)

The word *hyperetes* (servant) is used by Jesus of his disciples in just one passage. In his examination before Pilate, Jesus is asked, 'Are you the king of the Jews?' (John 18:33). And after a brief interchange Jesus says, 'My kingdom is not of this world. If it were, my servants (*hoi hyperetai hoi emou*) would fight in order to prevent my arrest from the Jews' (18:36). In the Gospels, the word *hyperetes* is generally used to describe the officers who aid those in positions of leadership such as judges and chief priests. For example, in Matthew 5:25 Jesus urges his disciples to settle disputes quickly with their adversaries, so that they are not handed over to the judge, who may in turn hand them over to the officer (*toi hyperete*) who will throw them in prison. Throughout John the word is used to describe the officers sent by the chief priests and Pharisees to place Jesus under arrest (7:32; 18:3, 12, 18, 22; 19:6).[1]

In these contexts the *hyperetes* had as his main function the carrying out of the orders of another. He is one who helps, who assists in the task. His role is defined with reference to the one he serves. In using this metaphor of his disciples, Jesus was indicating that their function was to assist him in his ministry, and to carry out his commands.

klema (branch)

In John 15 Jesus says, 'I am the true vine (*he ampelos he alethine*),' comparing his disciples to branches. This is the only occurrence of this metaphor in the Gospels, or indeed, anywhere in the New

Testament. Yet its placement in the Upper Room discourse, and the number of verses given to the development of the illustration, testify to its importance.

Two kinds of branches are contrasted here—those that bear fruit and those that do not. The unfruitful branches are cut off (*airei*); after they are thrown away they wither and are burned. In contrast, the fruitful branches are cut only partially, in order to prune them (*kathairei*), so that they will bear even more fruit. In both cases parts are removed; yet in the first instance the branch is removed, whereas in the second instance it is improved.

The branch derives its life only through remaining in the vine. That is its sole source of productivity. It has no vitality in itself. In the same way, says Jesus, the disciple's growth and influence depend entirely on his union with Christ. The product of his life, whether in development of godly character or in impact on the lives of others, derives solely from his vital relationship with the Master. The proof of genuine discipleship is found in the production of abundant fruit, the result of consistent dependence on Jesus the true vine.

mathetes (disciple)

Numerous times the Gospel writers speak of the followers of Jesus as his 'disciples.' In fact, this is the term most commonly used to refer to those who responded to Jesus' call. But Jesus himself also employed this term often in application to his followers. For example, in Matthew 10:42, he says, 'If anyone gives even a cup of cold water to one of these little ones because he is my disciple (*eis onoma mathetou*), I tell you the truth, he will certainly not lose his reward.'

The word 'disciple' (*mathetes*) is often paired with 'teacher' (*didaskalos*). For example, when Jesus sends his disciples ahead to arrange for the Passover meal, he instructs them to say to a certain man, 'The Teacher (*ho didaskalos*) says: My appointed time is near. I am going to celebrate the Passover with my disciples (*ton matheton mou*) at your house' (Matthew 26:18; cf. Mark 14:14; Luke 22:11). Or again, in Matthew 10:24 and Luke 6:40 Jesus says, 'A student (*mathetes*) is not above his teacher (*hyper ton didaskalon*).' In the Matthew passage, the application is that the disciple can be expected to experience the same sort of persecution suffered by his teacher; in Luke, the saying is set in the context of warnings against hypocrisy, and is used to make the point that the goal of the disciple's training is ultimately to be like his teacher. Jesus says, 'Everyone who is fully trained (*katertismenos*) will be like his teacher (*hos ho didaskalos autou*)' (Luke 6:40). Thus to be a disciple is not to be a mere listener in a classroom; rather it is to learn a pattern of life, to adopt the lifestyle of the teacher. Although the disciple is under the authority of the teacher, it is a relationship which the student enters voluntarily, born out of his desire to become like the teacher.

In four passages Jesus defines the qualifications for those who want to be known as his disciples. In Luke 14, we read that large crowds were following Jesus. Apparently many were getting caught up with his popularity, swept along in the adventure without reflecting deeply on what they were doing. So Jesus speaks to them about the cost of discipleship. In verse 26 he lists virtually every primary relationship of kinship: father, mother, wife, children, brothers, and sisters. And he says that the one who comes to him (*erchetai pros me*) must hate (*misei*) all these, and even his own life. Apart from this radical commitment, expressed through the hyperbolic reference to hatred, one cannot be Jesus' disciple (*ou dunatai einai mou mathetes*). Thus it is not enough simply to come to Jesus; one must also surrender unconditionally to him.

In verse 27 Jesus says further that one cannot be his disciple unless he carries his own cross and comes after Jesus (*erchetai opiso mou*). There is a difference between coming to Jesus and coming after Jesus. The first is merely encounter; the second is active obedience.

Discipleship, says Jesus, involves not only surrender of family ties, and giving up the right to self-preservation, but also the willingness to part with every material possession. He warns, 'Any of you who does not give up everything he has cannot be my disciple' (14:33). Discipleship therefore is a radical commitment, a bond which looses all other bonds, a direction which gives life one and only one central point of reference. To be a disciple is to turn from, and to turn to. It is to sever the old loyalties and to follow after Jesus, not distracted by ties to possessions or family or even by instincts of self-protection.

Three more definitions of discipleship are given by Jesus in the Gospel of John. In John chapter 8, Jesus addressed 'the Jews who had believed him (*tous pepisteukotas autoi*)' (8:31); but as the subsequent conversation demonstrated, their belief was quite superficial. So Jesus raised the issue of true discipleship. Were these people indeed the devoted followers that they seemed to be? He said, 'If you hold to my teaching (*meinete en toi logoi toi emoi*), you are truly my disciples (*alethos mathetai mou este*)' (8:31). Thus Jesus implied that there are those who followed, who associated with Jesus, but who were not really learning from him as their teacher; they were not reorienting their worldview or adjusting their behavior in light of his revealed truth.

In verse 32, Jesus states one of the benefits enjoyed by the person who holds to his teaching: 'Then you will know the truth, and the truth will set you free.' In verses 34 through 36 Jesus explains the sort of freedom he has in mind—freedom from the compulsion to commit sin. So then, the teaching of Jesus changes life at the behavioral and ethical level. To be a disciple means not only to receive an infusion of knowledge but also to undergo a transformation of character.

Jesus' next statement about discipleship is found in his introduction of the 'new commandment' in John 13. After urging the disciples to love one another just as he has loved them, he says, 'By this all men will know that you are my disciples (*emoi mathetai*) if you love one another' (13:35). The command to love is not new in itself (cf. Leviticus 19:18) but the measure of that love is new. The standard is now the self-sacrificing love that led Jesus to wash the feet of the disciples, and which would soon lead him to death on the cross for their redemption. The disciples are to display this love so consistently and openly that even people outside the community of faith will recognize that such love can only be explained by its source in the disciple's relationship to Jesus.

Jesus' final statement on the evidence for true discipleship is found in John 15:8. He has been teaching about the vine and the branches, and the focus has been on the goal of fruit-bearing (cf. comments on *klema*). Branches that bear fruit are pruned so that they will produce even more (15:2). Only those branches that remain in the vine are capable of bearing fruit (15:4–5). God is glorified when much fruit is borne (15:8). But more than that, abundant fruitfulness is the mark of true discipleship: 'This is to my Father's glory, that you bear much fruit, showing yourselves to be my disciples (*genesthe emoi mathetai*).' It is the visible products of the life, the good deeds that glorify the Father (cf. comments on *halas* and *phos*) and the beneficial impact upon others, enlisting them as followers of Jesus, that prove the genuineness of discipleship.

So then, when in Matthew 28:18–20 Jesus sent the disciples out with the command, 'Go and make disciples (*matheteusate*) of all nations (*panta ta ethne*),' there was a context which the disciples would have understood. In the first place, Jesus had enlisted them as his disciples. Now he was exhorting them to go and do the same, to lead others into the same process of deepening relationship and ministry development into which he had conducted them. In the second place, Jesus had defined the characteristics of a true disciple in terms of unqualified commitment, faithfulness to his word, love for fellow-disciples, and abundant fruit-bearing. The mission of the disciples was now to go out into the world to enlist and to develop that sort of person—to 'make disciples'!

The mission had two aspects. First, they were to baptize the disciples in the name of the Father and of the Son and of the Holy Spirit, that is, to call them to repentance and to public identification with the community of the Messiah. Second, they were to teach them to observe (*terein*) all things that Jesus had commanded (*panta hosa eneteilamen hymin*). Note that the emphasis was not on teaching them all things, but on teaching them to obey. Again we see that the emphasis in discipleship is not merely on the cognitive but also on the behavioral.

Jesus assures the disciples of an ongoing relationship with them: 'Surely I am with you always, to the very end of the age.' The disciples will remain disciples of the Master. They will never 'graduate' from the school of discipleship, or cease to be disciples. But they have the task of inviting others to join them as disciples of the one Master (cf. Matthew 23:8–10). They are not called to enlist disciples of themselves, but rather disciples of Jesus.

martys (witness)

After explaining to the disciples how all the events of his suffering, death, and resurrection were fulfillments of scripture, Jesus said to them: 'You are witnesses of these things (*hymeis martyres touton*)' (Luke 24:48). The role of the witness was to attest to the reality of certain events in a public setting. Thus the witness had a twofold role: first to verify the evidence, that is, to heighten the credibility of the statements made; and secondly, to proclaim the truth to others, making the facts known publicly. The witness was someone who had had an experience, who could testify to what he had seen or heard personally (cf. 1 John 1:1–3).

Martys

40

Similarly, in Acts 1:8, Jesus' final words to his disciples are recorded by the author, Luke: 'You will be my witnesses (*esesthe mou martyres*) in Jerusalem, and in all Judea and Samaria, and to the ends of the earth.' Here the emphasis shifts from witness to events to witness on behalf of a person.

In both passages there is an emphasis on the nations. Luke 24:47 says that 'repentance and forgiveness of sins will be preached in his name to all nations (*eis panta ta ethne*), beginning at Jerusalem.'

Other variations of the same metaphor occur several times in Jesus' conversations with his disciples. In sending out the Twelve, Jesus says, 'On my account you will be brought before governors and kings as witnesses to them and to the Gentiles (*eis martyrion autois kai tois ethnesin*)' (Matthew 10:18). The *martys* is the one who gives the word of testimony, while the *martyrion* refers to the testimony given. Notice again the reference to the nations. In his account of the Olivet discourse, Mark includes the same phrase, *eis martyrion autois*, and follows it with another explicit reference to the nations: 'And the gospel must first be preached to all nations (*eis panta ta ethne*)' (Mark 13:9; cf. Luke 21:13, where there is reference to the *martyrion* but not to the nations).

One more example is found in John 15:27, where Jesus uses the related verb, after warning the disciples of the persecutions they will suffer because of their identification with him: 'You also must testify (*martyreite*), for you have been with me from the beginning.'

In summary, then, the image of the 'witness' is associated by Jesus with firsthand experience, public proclamation, worldwide ministry, and the suffering of persecution.

misthios (hired servant)

In three of his parables, Jesus refers to hired servants. In the story of the prodigal son, the repentant young man longs to be taken back as one of his father's hired servants (*misthioi*, Luke 15;17, 19). And in John 10, Jesus contrasts the good shepherd's genuine concern for the sheep with the careless attitude and lack of commitment of the hired servant (*misthotos*), who runs away when the wolf attacks (John 10:12–13). But in neither of these cases does Jesus use the hired servant as an illustration of his follower.

In the third story, however, the hired servant is an image for the disciple. In Matthew 20:1–16, Jesus describes a landowner who hires (*misthosasthai*, 20:1) workers at different hours of the day to

41

go to work in his vineyard. Later in the story Jesus refers to these laborers as 'workers' (*ergatas*, 20:8). They work under the supervision of a foreman (*toi epitropoi*, 20:8). Although the noun *misthios* is not used in the story, this role for the workers is implied. In using this image, Jesus makes the point that each worker will be rewarded for his labors, but that the amount of the reward is entirely under the discretion of the landowner (*oikodespotei*, 20:1; *ho kurios tou ampelonos*, 20:8), who represents the Lord.

nepios (child)

In Luke 10:21–23, following the return of the seventy-two from their mission, Jesus praises God because he has 'hidden these things from the wise (*sophon*) and learned (*syneton*), and revealed them to little children (*nepiois*)' (10:21; parallel to Matthew 11:25–27). Jesus says that the only ones who really know the Father are the Son and those to whom the Son reveals the Father. God has hidden these things (*ekrypsas*) from some and revealed them (*apekalypsas*) to others. Here Jesus' use of the image of the child to describe his disciples underscores their ignorance apart from divine revelation. Whatever they understand is by the gracious action of God.

oiketes (servant)

Following the parable of the shrewd manager, Jesus says to his disciples: 'No servant (*oiketes*) can serve (*douleuein*) two masters (*kyriois*). Either he will hate the one and love the other, or he will be devoted to the one and despise the other. You cannot serve both God and money' (Luke 16:13). The *oiketes* is a kind of servant named for his sphere of service; that is, within the household (*oikos*), in contrast to servants who work in the fields, or who manage business interests, or who assist the chief priests. Like other kinds of servants, he is under the authority of a master (*kyrios*), and shares the function of serving expressed by the verb *douleuein*.

In the use of this metaphor, Jesus reminds the disciples that they can have only one ultimate authority for their lives, but also that they are members of God's household.

42

oikiakos (member of the household)

The only occurrences of this word in the New Testament are in Matthew 10, where Jesus gives instructions to the Twelve before sending them out. He speaks of the persecutions that the disciples will encounter as they go into the world as his witnesses, and warns them that they can expect no better treatment than he has received himself. He then cites three role pairs, each expressing inequality of status and authority: student with teacher, servant with master, and members of the household (*tous oikiakous autou*) with the head of the house (*ton oikodespoten*). Jesus compares himself to the head of the household, who has been called Beelzebub, the prince of demons. The disciples, as 'members of the household', can therefore expect even worse treatment (Matthew 10:24–25).

This metaphor expresses both connection and inequality. On the one hand, the disciples are members of the household, with all the associated rights and privileges. On the other hand, their role is defined in relation to the head of the house. They are under his authority, and responsible to him for their tasks. They are not his peers, even though they share a common life.

oikonomos (manager)

Only once does Jesus use this metaphor to describe his followers. However, in the parable of the shrewd manager, recorded in Luke 16:1–12, Jesus provides a vivid description of the function of the *oikonomos*. In that parable a rich man has a manager who is in charge of his possessions. The manager is accountable to the rich man, and his effectiveness is measured by how well he invests the resources in ways that benefit the rich man; if the manager is found guilty of wasting the owner's resources, he will be put out of his job. The manager has considerable freedom to negotiate with the various people who owe money to the rich man. In this parable, the manager is commended for his shrewdness in using material resources to accomplish his goals, not for his dishonesty in the process. Jesus uses the shrewd manager to illustrate the importance of good stewardship in handling material possessions, and in managing that which belongs to another. But in this story, the shrewd manager himself is not used as an image for the disciple.

Yet in Luke 12 Jesus does use an *oikonomos* as an illustration of a disciple. There Jesus is speaking of the importance of being ready for his return, and of making good use of resources in the light of the coming judgment. He introduces a short parable: 'Who then is the faithful and wise manager (*ho pistos oikonomos ho phronimos*), whom the master puts in charge of his servants to give them their food allowance at the proper time?' (12:42). The manager who does what he is supposed to will be rewarded by being placed in charge of all the master's possessions (12:44). But the one who abuses the menservants and maidservants, and who indulges himself in gluttony and drunkenness, will be punished.

Thus the *oikonomos* is one who holds a position of responsibility. He can be in charge of people as well as possessions. But notice that in verses 43, 45, and 46 the oikonomos is referred to as 'servant' (*ho doulos*). That is, he occupies a position of authority, but he also remains under authority. The 'manager' (*oikonomos*) fulfills a particular function within the larger category of 'servant' (*doulos*).

paidion (child)

On several occasions Jesus uses a child as an illustration of the sort of qualities that should characterize his followers. For example, in Matthew 18:1, his disciples ask him, 'Who is the greatest in the kingdom of heaven?' The parallel passages in Mark 9:33–37 and Luke 9:46–48 show that the question arose out of an argument among the disciples about which of them in particular was the greatest. Jesus replies by calling over a little child, and saying, 'Whoever humbles himself like this child (*hos to paidion touto*) is the greatest in the kingdom of heaven' (Matthew 18:4). Using the strongest possible negative expression, Jesus says, 'Unless you change and become like little children, you will never enter the kingdom of heaven' (18:3). He goes on to speak of the importance of welcoming even a child (18:5), and of the seriousness of causing one of the little ones (*ton mikron*) who believe in him to sin (18:6). He warns against the temptation to look down on these little ones (18:10), reminding the disciples of the guardian angels who are watching (18:11). He affirms that the heavenly Father does not want one of them to be lost (18:14). When Jesus speaks of 'little ones' in these verses, he is probably continuing the reference to the child, who is standing there in the midst.

Jesus was issuing a warning, a rebuke of the attitude that led to the question about greatness in the first place. The disciples were inclined to shoo the children away (cf. Matthew 19:13–15, with parallels to Mark 10:13–16 and Luke 18:15–17). But the person who did not consider a child to be very important, said Jesus, showed a fundamental lack of humility, and therefore was unfit to enter the kingdom of heaven. These warnings were issued not to unbelievers, or to the undecided, but to those who were already following Jesus. The humility of a child, illustrated in a welcoming attitude toward the child, was an essential mark of true discipleship.

Jesus also uses the child as an illustration of the sincere and simple faith which is required of the disciple. In Luke 18:17, when parents bring babies to Jesus to have him touch them, Jesus states bluntly, 'Anyone who will not receive the kingdom of God like a little child (hos paidion) will never enter it.'

On one occasion, Jesus addresses the disciples affectionately as 'children.' In John 21, after the resurrection, when he sees six of the disciples fishing on the Sea of Galilee early in the morning, Jesus calls out to them, 'Friends (paidia), haven't you any fish?' (John 21:5). Here it seems to be a term of endearing address, somewhat as one might use the term 'boys' to talk to male comrades in English.

pais (manservant) and paidiske (maidservant)

The word pais[2] appears a number of times in the Gospels, sometimes to designate a child, but more often in the sense of 'servant' (including the reference to Jesus as the Servant of the Lord in the quotation from Isaiah 42 found in Matthew 12:18). The word paidiske is used of the maidservant who recognized Peter outside the house of the high priest (Matthew 26:69; Mark 14:66, 69; Luke 22:56; John 18:17).

Jesus brings both terms together in Luke 12:42–46 in his story about the manager (oikonomos) whom the master (ho kyrios) puts in charge of his servants (tes therapeias autou). When the master's return is delayed, the irresponsible manager begins to beat the menservants (tous paidas) and the maidservants (tas paidiskas).

Thus the terms pais and paidiske seem to be used of the servants of lowest status, either in age or responsibility, not of those who were given responsibility over others, like the oikonomos. In this parable, the more direct comparison with the disciple is the oikonomos/doulos, but there may also be a comparison implied between the pais/paidiska and the believer who is under the authority of another in the community of faith. Even though that one may be low in status, or weak in position, the master will not

45

allow abuse of that one to go unpunished. Every servant, no matter how lowly, is under the protection and care of the master, who represents the Lord.

philos (friend)

On two occasions Jesus refers to the disciples as his 'friends'. The first is in Luke 12, while Jesus is making his way to Jerusalem. In a discourse warning his disciples about the hypocrisy of the Pharisees and the prospect of deadly persecution, he says: 'I tell you, my friends (*tois philois mou*), do not be afraid of those who kill the body and after that can do no more' (12:4). Jesus does not use this form of address to the crowds, but only to those who are intimately associated with him in his sufferings. It is a term of affection, of love, derived from the verb *phileo* (to love). It is a word that denotes companionship, closeness, camaraderie.

Jesus uses the verb *phileo* to describe the love of the Father for the Son (John 5:20), the Father for the disciples (John 16:27), and the disciples for Jesus (John 16:27). But he also uses *phileo* in reference to the love of family members for one another (Matthew 10:37) and the love of the Pharisees for positions of prominence (Matthew 23:6). Jesus employs the noun in several of his parables (e.g. Luke 11:5–9; 15:3–10) and refers to Lazarus as 'our friend' (John 11:11).

Thus the word 'friend' was part of Jesus' vocabulary long before the Last Supper, including references to his followers. But not until John 15 does Jesus draw out the full meaning of the word, applying it to his relationship to the disciples. Here, after repeating the great new commandment, 'Love each other as I have loved you' (15:12; cf. 13:34–35), Jesus affirms that the greatest demonstration of love (*agape*) is that one lay down his life for his friends (15:13). So then the discussion of friendship is set in the context of the highest expression of love (*agape*).

Jesus says to his disciples: 'You are my friends if you do what I command. I no longer call you servants, because a servant does not know his master's business. Instead, I have called you friends, for everything that I learned from my Father I have made known to you' (15:14–15). Here Jesus expresses what may seem to be a surprising dimension of friendship, at least in those cultures where friendship is seen as a peer relationship, a reciprocal term that carries no hint of hierarchy or inequality. Jesus announces that the test of true friendship is the disciples' willingness to obey his commands, specifically, the command to love one another. Similarly, in verse 10, Jesus says that just as he demonstrates his love for the Father by obedience to the Father's commands, so the disciples must demonstrate their love for Jesus by obeying Jesus' commands.

Thus the essence of friendship lies not in the abolition of authority, or in the removal of role distinctions, but rather in the appropriate expression of love. And when one is under the authority of another, the most appropriate expression of love, and hence friendship, is obedience.

The servant and the friend of Jesus are alike in that both have the obligation to obey. However, they are different in that the servant (*doulos*) does not know his master's business. The master owes the servant no reasons or justifications. But Jesus made known to the disciples everything that he had heard from the Father—all the context, the reasons, the purposes for acting as he did.

When Jesus says, 'I no longer call you servants (*ouketi lego hymas doulous*),' he is not saying that the relationship of servanthood has ceased, that the disciples should not call themselves Jesus' servants, or that he will no longer refer to himself as Master (cf. John 13:13).[3] Rather he is saying that 'servant' is no longer an adequate metaphor to convey all the dimensions of intimacy that the disciples have come to enjoy with Jesus. Nothing less than the word 'friend' will do to express the richness of communication and love that have come to characterize the relationship.

phos (light)

In the well-known passage from the Sermon on the Mount, Jesus addresses his disciples: 'You are the light of the world (*to phos tou kosmou*)' (Matthew 5:14). The purpose of the light is to be seen, so that people will be drawn to praise their Father in heaven. The disciples are to be like a city on the top of a hill, and like a lamp put on its stand, not hidden under a bowl (5:14–16).

Each aspect of this metaphor speaks of widely dispersed influence. The disciples are to be a light for the world (*tou kosmou*). They are intended to radiate to everyone in the house (*pasin tois en tei oikiai*). Their light is meant to shine before men (*emprosthen ton anthropon*). The disciples, in other words, are supposed to have an impact on others, drawing them to glorify and praise the Lord. That is their fundamental ministry task.

The light, says Jesus, consists of their good deeds (*hymon ta kala erga*). Thus their primary influence is that of setting an outstanding example.

Jesus identifies his followers with light in a couple of other passages as well. In Luke 16:8, in the parable of the shrewd manager, Jesus alludes to the 'people of the light (*tous hyious tou photos*)', and in John 12:36 he urges the crowd in Jerusalem: 'Put your trust in the light while you have it, so that you may become sons of light (*hyioi photos*).'

poimen (shepherd)

Generally in the Gospels the shepherd metaphor is applied to Jesus, not to the disciples (cf. Matthew 26:31; Luke 15:3–7; John 10:11). The disciples are most often described as sheep, not as shepherds (cf. comments on *probaton*). Yet on one occasion, after the resurrection, Jesus instructs a disciple explicitly to do the work of a shepherd. Yet even here the noun *poimen* (shepherd) is not used, but rather two related verbs.

The passage is John 21. Following the miraculous catch of fish, and breakfast together on the shore, Jesus asks Peter the first of three penetrating questions that correspond to Peter's threefold denial. 'Simon son of John, do you truly love me more than these?' When Peter answers, 'Yes, Lord, you know that I love you,' Jesus replies, 'Feed (*boske*) my lambs (*ta arnia mou*)' (21:15). A second time Jesus poses the question, Peter affirms his love, and Jesus responds with a command: 'Take care of (*poimaine*) my sheep (*ta probata mou*)' (21:16). Then comes Jesus' third question, Peter's repeated protest of love, and Jesus' third admonition: 'Feed (*boske*) my sheep (*ta probata mou*)' (21:17).

Three times Jesus tells Peter to do the work of a shepherd. Jesus includes the more general word for tending a flock (*poimaine*) in between uses of the more specific word for feeding and pasturing (*boske*). He begins by pointing to those who are the younger, more tender sheep, those most in need of care, the lambs; but he exhorts Peter to care for the whole flock as well. Peter's obedience in taking up the task of shepherding will be the evidence of his genuine love for Jesus.

Notice that Jesus refers all three times to 'my lambs', 'my sheep.' The sheep belong to Jesus, not to Peter. The disciple, even as shepherd, remains a servant, caring for the property of another.

The emphasis is not on the authority of the shepherd, or the leadership of the shepherd, but on the loving care rendered by the shepherd, and on the accountability of the shepherd to the owner of the sheep. As used by Jesus in this context, the shepherd is a very tender, personal, care-oriented image, though in other passages the verb *poimaino* can convey a strong sense of authority and rule (cf. Revelation 2:27; 12:5; 19:15).

Although these verses in John are the only ones where a follower of Jesus is described explicitly in shepherding imagery, the shepherding role of the disciples is hinted at in one other place. In Matthew 10:6, Jesus sends the Twelve to 'the lost sheep of Israel.' Thus he implies that the disciples will participate in the shepherd's work of gathering the flock.

probaton (sheep)

One of the metaphors that Jesus uses frequently to describe his followers is that of 'sheep' (*probaton*), as well the related words translated 'flock' (*poimne* and *poimnion*). In Matthew 10, when Jesus sends out the Twelve, he warns them: 'I am sending (*apostello*) you out like sheep (*hos probata*) among wolves' (Matthew 10:16). This is a picture of helplessness, of vulnerability. The disciples must rely on God, for as sheep, they have no natural defenses.

In Matthew 26:31, as well as the parallel in Mark 14:27, once again it is the vulnerability of the sheep that is in focus. Following the Last Supper, Jesus leads his disciples out onto the Mount of Olives. There he sadly predicts that all of them will fall away and desert him. He quotes from the prophet Zechariah these words: 'I will strike the shepherd (*ton poimena*) and the sheep of the flock (*ta probata tes poimnes*) will be scattered.' Here the emphasis is on the dispersion of the sheep that happens so quickly when the shepherd is removed. Sheep do not naturally stay together without a shepherd.

In Luke 12 Jesus tells his disciples not to worry about the physical necessities of life, such as food or clothing, because God knows their needs, and will provide for those who seek first his kingdom. He reassures them, 'Do not be afraid, little flock (*to mikron poimnion*), for your Father has been pleased to give you the kingdom' (12:32). The image again is one of helplessness. But the Father has committed himself to see that the needs of the sheep are provided. The Shepherd guarantees the sheep's security.

In the familiar parable of the sheep and the goats (Matthew 25:31–46), the sheep (*ta probata*) are placed to the king's right and the goats (*ta eriphia*) to his left. The sheep are identified as those blessed by the Father (25:34), the 'righteous' (25:37, 46) who have shown kindness to the brothers of the King. The focus of the parable, however, is on the separation which the King performs, like a shepherd (*hosper ho poimen*, 25:32), not on the characteristics of sheep.

In John 10 Jesus introduces an extended description of himself as the Good Shepherd. Although the emphasis of the passage is on the self-sacrificing love of the shepherd, there are also many comments about the sheep. The sheep are called by name (10:3) and know the shepherd's voice (10:4, 27); that is, they have a personal relationship with the shepherd; the disciples are not anonymous faces among the crowd. The sheep know the shepherd just as the shepherd knows the sheep (10:14–15, 27). The sheep are led out (*exagei*) by the shepherd (10:3); they follow (*akolouthei*) him (10:4, 27); they are dependent on the shepherd for guidance; thus disciples do not take their own initiative or choose their own paths. The sheep owe their very lives to the shepherd and to his willingness to lay down his life for theirs (John 10:11); they are fully secure in his care (10:28–29).

Thus in John 10 the metaphor of the sheep conveys ideas of intimacy, dependence, obedience, and security. But there is another dimension suggested in verse 16, where Jesus says that there remain some sheep who are yet to be gathered into the flock. Here there are hints of evangelism and outreach, leading to the growth of the flock. This is the activity of the shepherd, not the sheep, it is true, but Jesus' statement implants an expectation among the sheep that they must be prepared to welcome others into their circle.

sitos (wheat) and *sperma* (seed)

After presenting the parable of the wheat and the weeds (Matthew 13:24–30, 36–43), Jesus explains to his disciples that 'the good seed (*to kalon sperma*) stands for the sons of the kingdom' (13:38). The Son of Man sows these seeds in the field, which represents the world, where the good seed grows alongside the weeds sown by the devil. Not until the end of the age can the two be separated. At that time, says Jesus, the wheat (*ton siton*, grown from the good seed) will be harvested and gathered into the barn, while the weeds will be tied in bundles and burned. In verse 43 the image changes, and Jesus says: 'Then the righteous will shine like the sun in the kingdom of their Father' (cf. comments under *phos*).

The point of the parable is that the weeds and the wheat cannot be separated until the end of the age. In attempting to uproot the one, you would destroy the other. Thus the disciples are called to live alongside unbelievers in the world. They are not to attempt to withdraw into isolated communities, but are to live among the people of the world, trusting that at last they will be vindicated and revealed as the objects of God's special protection and choice.

The metaphor of the seed occurs again in John 12:24, where Jesus speaks of the imminent approach of his time of suffering. He compares the disciple to the kernel of wheat (*ho kokkos tou sitou*) which must fall to the ground and die before it can produce many other seeds (*polyn karpon pherei*). As in the images of the soil and the vine (cf. comments on *ge* and *klema*), the emphasis is on fruitfulness. The goal, the purpose of the seed is to produce more seeds. The disciple who refuses to pay the cost necessary for fruitfulness proves himself to be no true servant of Jesus. Here the image of the seed implies sacrifice, and participation in the sufferings of Christ, in order to accomplish the mission.

teknion (little child) and *teknon* (child)

After the departure of Judas from the Upper Room, Jesus addresses the disciples with this endearing term: 'My children (*teknia*), I will be with you only a little longer' (John 13:33). Jesus uses this tender expression in telling the disciples that he must soon leave them. He knows that this revelation will arouse some fear and uncertainty among them, so he addresses them gently, like a parent with young children.

In Matthew 9:2 (and in the parallel passage in Mark 2:5), Jesus speaks to the paralyzed man who has been let down through the roof by his friends: 'Take heart, son (*teknon*), your sins are forgiven.' Jesus uses this term at the very outset of the encounter, communicating warmth and acceptance to a person who may have been feeling quite conspicuous, uncertain, and ill at ease under the circumstances.

Mark 10:24 records one other incident where Jesus addresses his disciples as *tekna*. After the disciples react with amazement to Jesus' statement about the difficulty of a rich man being saved, Jesus says, 'Children (*tekna*), how hard it is to enter the kingdom of God!' Again, the use of this term communicates love and reassurance in a situation of uncertainty.

therapeia (servant)

In Luke 12:42, Jesus asks, 'Who is the faithful and wise manager (*oikonomos*), whom the master (*ho kyrios*) puts in charge of his servants (*tes therapeias autou*) to give them their food allowance at the proper time?' A few verses later these servants are referred to as menservants (*paidas*) and maidservants (*paidiskas*) (12:45). In the parallel passage found in Matthew 24:45, the noun *oiketeias* is substituted for *therapeias*.

From other usages of the noun *therapeia* and the related verb *therapeuo*, it appears that the emphasis of the word group is on personal care. Thus the *therapeia* as servant is one who waits upon the master, who renders personal assistance.

Notes

1   The word is also used in Luke 4:20 of the synagogue attendant. Stambaugh and Balch note that this person 'took care of the building, kept order during the service, made announcements, led the prayers if necessary, and administered corporal punishment in accordance with the Law' (1986:49).

2   Braumann (DNTT, I:280–281) notes that a distinction is made between *paidion*, the baby or little child, and *pais*, the child between seven and fourteen years old. He says that the term *pais* 'also suggests the child's lowly position in society and his ancient function as slave. It can therefore also mean servant or slave.' However, these distinctions are not rigidly observed in the LXX.

3   Moltmann (1977:114–121) has a section entitled 'Friendship with Jesus', in which he claims that in this statement, 'The relationship of servants to God, the Lord, comes to an end' (p. 118). Along a similar line, in developing the idea of God as a friend, Sallie McFague (1982:177–192) says, 'The model of friend for God... moves away from hierarchism and toward egalitarianism. It also has strong immanental tendencies; we are no longer under but with and in God' (p. 181). However, as I have argued in the preceding paragraphs, Jesus is not abolishing the concept of servanthood, nor of authority and submission, but rather is adding a new and unexpected dimension to the discipleship relationship.

Table 1

Taxonomy of terms used by Jesus for his followers

1.0 People

    1.1 Emphasis on Relationships

        1.11 Relationship by birth
            1.111 Member of household (*oikiakos*)
                1.1111 Sibling
                    1.11111 Brother (*adelphos*)
                    1.11112 Sister (*adelphe*)
                1.1112 Child
                    1.11121 Child/son (*hyios*)
                    1.11122 Child (*teknion*)
                    1.11123 Child (*teknon*)
                    1.11124 Child (*nepios*)
                    1.11125 Child (*paidion*)

        1.12 Relationship by appointment
            1.121 Chosen (*eklektos*)
            1.122 Twelve (*dodeka*)

        1.13 Relationship by voluntary association
            1.131 Friend
                1.1311 Friend (*philos*)
                1.1312 Friend (*hetairos*)
            1.132 Wedding participant
                1.1321 Friend of bridegroom (*hyios tou nymphonos*)
                1.1322 Virgin with lamp
                1.1323 Guest at wedding banquet
            1.133 Disciple (*mathetes*)

    1.2 Emphasis on Tasks

        1.21 Task executed under the authority of another
            1.211 Servant (*doulos*)
                1.2111 Relationship words
                    1.21111 Hired servant (*misthios*)
                    1.21112 Low status servant
                        1.211121 Manservant (*pais*)
                        1.211122 Maidservant (*paidiske*)
                    1.21113 Member of household (*oiketes*)

              1.2112 Function words
                  1.21121 Personal helper (*therapeia*)
                  1.21122 Assistant for tasks (*hyperetes*)
                  1.21123 Server for meals (*diakonos*)
                  1.21124 Manager (*oikonomos*)
            1.212 Shepherd (*poimen*)
            1.213 Worker (*ergates*)
            1.214 Apostle (*apostolos*)

        1.22 Task executed independently
          1.221 Witness (*martys*)
          1.222 Fisherman (*alieus*)

2.0 Things

    2.1 Emphasis on Relationships

      2.11 Sheep (*probaton*)

    2.2 Emphasis on Tasks

      2.21 Images related to growth
        2.211 Soil (*ge*)
          2.2111 Productive soil
          2.2112 Unproductive soil
             2.21121 Pathway
             2.21122 Rocky soil
             2.21123 Thorny soil
        2.212 Branch of vine (*klema*)
          2.2121 Fruitful
          2.2122 Unfruitful
        2.213 Wheat (*sitos*)
          2.2131 Seed (*sperma*)

      2.22 Images related to dispersion/influence
        2.221 Salt (*halas*)
          2.2211 Savory
          2.2212 Lost savor
        2.222 Light (*phos*)
          2.2221 On lampstand
          2.2222 Under a bowl

3

Relationships between the terms

In the previous chapter, thirty-five terms used by Jesus to describe his disciples were listed. How are these terms related to one another in their usage? In Table 1 I have proposed a taxonomy for these images. The statements made in the following paragraphs are conclusions drawn from the data supplied in the previous chapter; the reader should refer to the appropriate sections for specific examples and verse references.

The first major division is between comparisons to people (1.0) and comparisons to things (2.0). Both of those larger categories are further subdivided into images that emphasize the personal relationships of Jesus' followers (whether to Jesus or to one another) and images that focus on the tasks which Jesus' followers are expected to perform.

Comparisons to people— emphasis on relationships (1.1)

The relationships pictured in this category have been further divided according to how they were formed—whether by birth, by appointment, or by voluntary association. Members of the same household (1.111), included in the generic word *oikiakos*, would most often be included from birth, including children who had been born to the servants; and there would also be people who had come into the household through marriage. However, the images selected by Jesus are those who are related biologically, as siblings (both brothers and sisters), and as children.

Five different words are used in the comparisons of the disciples to children—*hyios*, *teknion*, *teknos*, *nepios*, and *paidion*. When the word *hyios* is used, it is generally associated with reference to God as Father; the emphasis of the comparison is placed on the resemblances between the child and the Father, and on the tender care which the Father has for the child. *Teknon*, along with the diminutive form *teknion*, is used by Jesus only in direct address; but it too is a term that conveys an attitude of love and assurance. When *paidion* is used in direct address, it also carries the same feeling.

Hyios and *teknon* can be used of adults as well as children, in that they refer primarily to biological origin when used in a literal sense; but *nepios* and *paidion* picture little children. *Paidion* is the term generally used in the Gospels for children who are brought by their parents to Jesus, or whom Jesus heals; it is used of Jesus when he was only eight days old (Luke 2:21), and also for a girl who was twelve years old (Mark 5:39–41). When Jesus uses the term *nepios* for his disciples, he is referring to their ignorance, and their dependence on divine revelation. He uses the figure of the *paidion* to teach the qualities of humility and simple faith.

Two of the terms used by Jesus have to do with relationships that come about through appointment (1.12)—not through birth, but through an act of selection. As we saw in the last chapter, the term 'chosen', *eklektos*, suggests the comparison of the disciples to God's new Israel, his new chosen people. It is often used to convey the reassurance that God will protect his people in spite of difficulties and persecution. The reference to the disciples as the Twelve, *dodeka*, implies their leadership role in this community of chosen people, corresponding to the twelve patriarchs of Israel; although the patriarchs received their positions through birth, the Twelve are appointed by Jesus.

Then come the terms that are drawn from various forms of voluntary association (1.13). Two words are used for 'friend'. The first one, *philos*, implies a relationship of love and intimacy. The second, *hetairos*, conveys a tone of coolness and displeasure. Jesus uses *hetairos* in his parables, and in addressing Judas, but with his faithful followers he uses *philos*.

Several of the parables picture Jesus' followers as participants in a wedding (1.132). Two of the images, friends of the bridegroom and virgins with lamps, refer to people who would already be close associates of the bride and groom. But in the parable of the wedding banquet, Jesus compares his disciples to people who have been gathered in from the streets to share as guests in the celebration. The friends of the bridegroom are used to picture the joy of the disciples in fellowship with their Lord; the virgins are used to teach the necessity of watchfulness; and the hastily assembled guests are used to emphasize the unmerited grace of God's call.

The third type of voluntary association is the disciple (*mathetes*) with his teacher (1.133). Some might argue that this word should be classified under 'tasks' (1.2) rather than 'relationships' (1.1), since the disciple certainly has duties assigned to him. But as Jesus uses

56

the term, the emphasis is on close association with and devotion to the teacher, becoming like him in pattern of life, and even sharing in his sufferings. Therefore, it should be seen as a term primarily descriptive of an intimate, as well as purposeful, relationship.

Comparisons to people—emphasis on tasks (1.2)

The second set of images drawn from people is those that emphasize the execution of a task. The disciple is not only one who is invited into a personal relationship with Jesus and with the other disciples, but also one who has work to do. This work may be done independently, or may be assigned by someone else. Most of the metaphors used by Jesus in this category involve a task that is assigned by a superior, who represents the Lord.

The most common image by far is that of the servant. Nine different words are used for servants in Jesus' illustrations. The most general term seems to be *doulos* (1.211). The main emphasis of this word is the bond of allegiance and submission to authority that ties the *doulos* to his master (*kyrios*). References to the *doulos* figure prominently in Jesus' teachings about diligence, responsibility, accountability, and stewardship. The image of the *doulos* is also important when Jesus speaks of identification with his sufferings, and of following his example of humility, willingly functioning 'under' rather than 'over.'

Within the general category of 'servant', there are a number of words that highlight particular aspects of the relationship between the servant and the master, or between the servant and the other servants (1.2111). For example, some servants are hired on a temporary basis (*misthios*), whereas others are permanent members of the household (*oiketes*). Jesus uses the *misthios* in one instance to illustrate his teaching on rewards, but in another to contrast the hired shepherd who has no personal commitment to the flock with the good shepherd who genuinely loves the sheep and is willing to die for them. The words *pais* and *paidiske* seem to imply a relationship of low status within the household; these servants are the youngest, or those with least responsibility; yet Jesus shows that they too come under the protection of the master.

Several other words for servant focus on the particular functions which they perform (1.2112). The *therapeia* seems to be a personal helper, performing services that directly benefit the master, whereas the *hyperetes* focuses more on carrying out assignments under the orders of the master. Thus the *therapeia* is a better image for ministries of compassion and personal care, whereas the *hyperetes* image is better suited for the execution of tasks, especially where struggle or conflict is involved. The *diakonos* is one who helps to serve the meal. Jesus uses this image repeatedly to express lessons in humility, especially in the context of arguments among the disciples over who is the greatest; *diakonos* is also used in reference to Jesus' voluntary sacrifice of his own life. Finally, the *oikonomos* is the servant who carries broad responsibilities; he is the manager of the master's possessions, and sometimes of other servants. Jesus employs this image to teach about stewardship of opportunities as well as resources.

Three other images complete the list of those who execute their tasks under the direction of another. The shepherd (*poimen*), as used by Jesus, is an illustration of the one who cares for sheep that belong to Jesus, the Master; it is used not as an image of authority, but as one of personal, loving care. The worker (*ergates*) appears in Jesus' teaching in the context of spiritual harvest; the follower of Jesus is one who helps to gather in those who are ready to come to faith. This image is also used in Jesus' teaching about future rewards. Then comes the apostle (*apostolos*), who is a messenger sent by a superior. Although we might tend to think of the apostle primarily in terms of his authoritative role within the church, Jesus uses the term to emphasize that the apostle is under the authority of the one who sends him.

The two other task-related terms employed by Jesus do not emphasize the connection to the authority of another (1.22). One is witness (*martys*), describing the one who gives public testimony to personal experiences and observations. Jesus often associates this term with the worldwide mission of the disciples, and with the persecution which they will suffer because of their open expression of allegiance to him. The other term is fisherman (*alieus*). Jesus employs this image to describe the disciples' new vocation of calling others to repentance.

Yet neither of these roles is entirely independent either. The witness is a witness to Jesus, by the command of Jesus, and is persecuted for his identification with Jesus. The fisher of men is 'made' so by Jesus, and enters that profession by following after Jesus. Therefore, although these illustrations do not convey as strong a picture of being under authority as the previous set (1.21), neither do they imply tasks performed autonomously.

Comparisons to things— emphasis on relationships (2.1)

Although most of the images Jesus uses for his followers are comparisons to people, several are comparisons to things. But only one of these metaphors is used to illustrate lessons about the disciple's relationship to the Lord or to other believers.

Frequently Jesus refers to the disciple as a sheep (*probaton*), and to the disciples collectively as a flock. Yet they are always his flock, not the flock of any other disciple. The image of the sheep emphasizes the personal bond between Jesus and his followers; it conveys ideas of protection and loving care. The metaphor also suggests the weakness and vulnerability of the disciples, who must depend on the shepherd for direction, for food, and for defence.

Comparisons to things—emphasis on tasks (2.2)

Within the illustrations that are drawn from things, and which focus on the task, a further division can be made, between images that are related to growth and those that are related to dispersion and influence. The images of growth (2.21) are drawn from the world of agriculture.

First, Jesus compares his listeners to soil (*ge*). Only one kind of soil produces a crop. The other three soils—the pathway, the rocky soil, and the thorny soil—are unproductive. The good, productive soil represents the follower who not only hears Jesus' words, but also welcomes and obeys them.

A similar comparison between the productive and the unproductive can be seen in the illustration of the branches of the vine (*klema*). Those who remain steadfastly united to Jesus and to his word are the good branches, that yield abundant fruit. But the unfruitful branches are thrown away.

A third agricultural metaphor is the wheat (*sitos*) whose growth springs from a seed (*sperma*). Jesus employs this image on one occasion to explain why the believers and the unbelievers will continue to live alongside one another, and will not be separated in the present age. In another instance he uses the seed as a parable of the life laid down in order to produce more life.

The two remaining images focus on the influence which the disciples will have as they disperse into the world (2.22). Both images speak of a contrast between effectiveness and ineffectiveness. The useful salt (*halas*) is contrasted with salt that has lost its savor, and is therefore good for nothing anymore. The light (*phos*) that is set on the lampstand and illumines the whole house is set over against the light that is hidden under a bowl. Both metaphors are used to emphasize the widespread influence that the disciples are expected to have—salt that seasons the whole earth, and light that illumines the entire world.

4

Major themes

Again and again in the images used by Jesus to describe his disciples, certain themes emerge. These form the basic structure of the style of life for which Jesus was preparing his followers. These were the patterns that would shape the early Christian community, and which would become the standards for its leaders. In this chapter I will suggest seven fundamental themes.

1. Function

The disciple is called to participation in a community as well as to a task.

In the metaphors drawn from people as well as from things, we find some that highlight the bond of commitment and love that tie the followers of Jesus to one another and to their Lord, and others that emphasize the mission for which the disciples have been enlisted. The words that speak of the relationship between Jesus and his followers include child (*hyios, teknion, teknos, nepios, paidion*), friend (especially *philos*), disciple (*mathetes*), and sheep (*probaton*); the words brother (*adelphos*) and sister (*adelphe*) point to the connection between the followers. On the other hand, the whole cluster of servant words (including *doulos* and *diakonos*), as well as several other images like apostle (*apostolos*), fisherman (*alieus*), shepherd (*poimen*), salt (*halas*), and light (*phos*), focus on the disciple's life of active service and influence in the world, carrying out the task of ministry in Jesus' name.

It is very easy for the spiritual leader to lose this balance between task and relationship. Some become so intent on nurturing the community of faith as a loving family that they become ingrown, neglecting the tasks of evangelism and service to the world. Others become so goal-oriented and determined to mobilize every believer for action that they do not pay sufficient attention to the needs of the people for personal nurture, encouragement, and reconciliation. Jesus' disciples are to remember that they are both brothers/sisters and servants.

2. Authority

The disciple is under authority.

Over half of the metaphors chosen by Jesus describe someone who is under the authority of another. Often the word selected is one member of a familiar role pair, such as child (of a father, *pater*), servant (of a master, *kyrios*), or disciple (of a teacher, *didaskalos*). Other images of those under authority include the shepherd (*poimen*) who tends a flock that belongs to another, the worker (*ergates*) hired by the landowner (*oikodespotes*), the apostle (*apostolos*) commissioned by his superior, and the sheep (*probaton*) obeying the voice of the shepherd.

It is interesting to note that even though the disciples are being prepared for spiritual leadership in the church, Jesus places far more emphasis on their responsibility to God's authority, than on the authority which they themselves will exercise. There is far more instruction about the role of following than about the role of leading.

3. Responsibility

The disciple exercises authority.

Even though the emphasis of Jesus' instruction is on obedience to authority rather than on the exercise of authority, nevertheless Jesus does employ images that describe the follower as one who is given responsibility for others. On two occasions, Jesus promises the Twelve that in his coming kingdom they will sit on thrones judging the twelve tribes of Israel (Matthew 19:28; Luke 22:30); this is a strong and unmistakable image of authority.

In his parable about the manager (*oikonomos*) in Luke 12, Jesus pictures the disciple as one who is placed in charge of other people as well as possessions. Similarly, in the parable of the ten minas (Luke 19:12–27), the faithful servants are rewarded by being given responsibility over entire cities. Jesus' instructions to Peter in John 21 about performing the work of a shepherd also imply a role of leading and guiding within the Christian community. Jesus' references to the apostles contain clear statements of the authority which they will exercise over demons. As ones sent by God, the apostles proclaim the message about the coming kingdom with the very authority of God; in fact, says Jesus, the one who receives them is receiving the One who sent them.

Therefore, there is no contradiction in Jesus' mind between being under authority, and being responsible to exercise authority. Frequently in the Gospel of John, Jesus speaks of his own obedience as the Son to the Father, yet in John 13 he affirms that the disciples are correct to call him their master and teacher.

4. Derivation

The disciple is one who has responded to the call of Jesus.

Yet no matter how much authority the disciple may exercise, his role and his responsibilities are always derived from his prior call. The disciple is fundamentally a responder, not an initiator. As Jesus reminds the disciples in John 15:16, 'You did not choose me, but I chose you.' The disciple is a branch of the vine, not the vine itself; apart from the vine the branch can produce nothing. The disciple has no philosophy of his own to expound; he is only an *apostolos*, a messenger commissioned by another. He is a servant assigned to a master, a child born to a father, a guest invited to a wedding, soil receiving the implanted seed. Yes, there are images of growth and influence—but the source of life lies elsewhere, not in the disciple himself.

This theme is closely related to the theme of authority. But it goes even deeper. Jesus reminds the disciple through these images that everything comes from God. As Jesus expresses it in John 15:5, 'Apart from me you can do nothing.' To use a fresh metaphor, the spiritual leader is not a creative musician, composing his own tunes; rather he is an arranger of the song sung by the Master. Nor is the leader an inventor and entrepreneur, dreaming up a product and then marketing it; no, he is the distributor for a precious commodity supplied to him. The ministry is always derivative, never *sui generis*. The disciple is not autonomous; he lives in relationship to a fixed reference point—the life, the word, and the example of his Master.

5. Status

Disciples are on the same level in relationship to God, even though they may have different areas and amounts of responsibility.

In Matthew 23 Jesus reminded the disciples in very strong terms that they were all brothers, all children of one father, all students at the feet of the same teacher. Among the followers of Jesus there were to be none of the status-seeking games and political maneuvers that characterized the life of the Pharisees. On other occasions as well, Jesus contrasted the life of servanthood with the grasping for power and the abuse of authority that was so typical of pagan rulers. The disciples were not to strive for the right to be 'over,' but rather were to focus on their role 'among,' as brothers, and on opportunities to place themselves 'under,' as servants.

On the other hand, Jesus was not establishing a kind of radical egalitarianism where any sort of internal authority structure in the community was seen as a denial of brotherhood, or where any difference in level of responsibility was seen as an attack on the principle of spiritual equality. No, his illustrations, such as the parable of the minas and the talents, described believers who were given differing degrees of responsibility. And as has been noted already, Jesus' references to the apostle, the shepherd, and the manager are images that imply the existence of authority roles within the community.

Jesus' focus is not on particular structures of leadership in the community, but rather on the attitudes that should characterize the leaders. He tells his disciples that even the teachers of the law and the Pharisees should be obeyed in their role as teachers of the Mosaic law (Matthew 23:2), but that their hypocritical practices must be rejected. Jesus himself never surrendered his authority role within the Twelve, yet he called the disciples his brothers and his friends.

6. Identification

To be a disciple is to identify with Jesus, both in his pattern of life and in his suffering.

As Jesus says in Luke 6:40: 'Everyone who is fully trained will be like his teacher.' To be a disciple, Jesus emphasizes, is not merely to comprehend a body of truth, or even to perform an assigned task, but rather to adopt a pattern of life. Jesus defines 'disciple' in terms of unqualified commitment, and firm adherence to Jesus' words and patterns of love. He uses the image of the child to emphasize that the child should resemble the Heavenly Father. The disciple is described as salt and light. Thus true disciples are not to be identified simply on the basis of their knowledge, or their accomplishments, but on the basis of their character, their attitud commitments—in short, their likeness to Christ.

One of the sternest tests of identification with Jesus is the willingness to participate in his sufferings. As we have seen, the images of the servant (*doulos* and especially *diakonos*) as well as the witness (*martys*) are closely associated with the experience of hardship and persecution. In John 12 Jesus also uses the image of the kernel of wheat which must fall into the ground and die in order to be fruitful.

Spiritual leadership is not a position of privilege which exempts one from suffering. Rather, the leader, like Jesus, must be willing to be the first to set the example of laying his life down, and of obeying at the cost of death. The leader must not be like the hired hand who runs away and deserts the sheep when he sees the wolf coming. Rather, the leader must be prepared to share in his Master's suffering. As Jesus said, 'Whoever serves me must follow me; and where I am, my servant also will be' (John 12:26).

7. Accountability

The disciple will be evaluated by the Lord, in terms of his character as well as his service.

Many of Jesus' illustrations draw a contrast between effectiveness and ineffectiveness in service, between those who fulfill their intended purpose and those who do not. The good salt is contrasted with the salt that has lost its savor. The lamp is intended to be placed on the lampstand, not to be hidden under a bowl. Some branches remain in the vine, and therefore become fruitful; others do not, so are cut off. The good soil produces crops of thirty, sixty, or one hundred times what was planted; but neither the pathway, the rocky soil, nor the thorny soil yield anything of value.

The good shepherd, who cares for the sheep, is contrasted with the hired hand who has no personal commitment to their welfare. Some virgins provide extra oil for their lamps; others fail to do so. The unprofitable servant does only his duty; the irresponsible manager fails to provide for the other household servants.

Repeatedly Jesus' parables make reference to rewards—the master's words of 'Well done,' the assignment of responsibility over cities, the promise of ruling on thrones. But equally often there are references to disciplines and punishments—a guest without a wedding garment thrown outside into the darkness, an unfruitful branch cut off, a lazy and unproductive servant stripped of his responsibility.

Through images like these Jesus teaches that discipleship is serious business. It is more than participation in the life of a warm and loving family. The disciple is held responsible for growth in character development, and for productive investment of resources and opportunities. A time of judgment is coming, when the disciple's life and work will be evaluated; and there will be losses as well as rewards. The spiritual leader is not exempt from this evaluation, any more than any other disciple.

5

The choice of metaphors

On what basis did Jesus select his metaphors for the description of his disciples? In this chapter we will show how Jesus chose terms suited to his listeners, and avoided terms whose associations did not reinforce the lessons he was trying to teach.

Appropriate metaphors

Jesus chose images that were appropriate to the culture, appropriate to the disciples' stage in the process of leadership development, and appropriate to the particular circumstances in which he taught them.

APPROPRIATE TO THE CULTURE

Jesus drew his illustrations from the common materials of life that would have been familiar to his hearers. He spoke of relationships in the family, of children with their father, and brothers with sisters. He described scenes from the household, in which some servants assisted in the preparation of the meals, while others worked in the fields.

Some illustrations came from everyday work—shepherds and fishermen, land owners and managers, court officers and personal assistants. Other metaphors were drawn from common social relationships and community celebrations—friends and associates, members of the wedding party and guests at a banquet. Everyday objects and sights were used to teach lessons in discipleship—salt, lamps, vines, flocks of sheep and goats, ripe fields of wheat, beaten-down pathways, thorns and rocks.

Some of Jesus' illustrations echoed the images used by prophets of Israel from centuries before: the chosen people, the servant, the vine, the brother, the friend of God, the messenger.

Jesus was speaking mainly to the common people, whose lives were intertwined with their fields and their flocks, or their boats and their nets. And therefore most of his illustrations were drawn from these spheres. His metaphors needed no explanations. They carried familiar associations of smell and feel and sound. They evoked feelings and memories. People had watched virgins with their lamps at weddings, and had listened to the testimony of witnesses

.ey used salt to preserve their food, and had heard
.o one another in the marketplace.

of a metaphor is that it awakens associations, stirs
embodies values. It focuses our attention, highlight-
.tails, and encourages creative new insights. But the
.etaphor depends largely on the familiarity of the image
that ser v. .s the basis for the comparison. An illustration that must
first be explained in order to be appreciated loses much of its
impact. Jesus chose metaphors that were close to his listeners.

APPROPRIATE TO THE STAGE IN LEADERSHIP DEVELOPMENT

Jesus did not introduce all the metaphors at once in his encounters
with his disciples. Certain patterns can be discerned in the arrange-
ment of, and emphasis on, certain illustrations at different points in
the disciples' pilgrimage.

To begin with, all four Gospel writers cite as the earliest
metaphors used by Jesus those that focus on the task. Matthew and
Mark record the statement, 'Follow me, and I will make you fishers
of men' (Matthew 4:19; Mark 1:17). In the parallel account in Luke,
Jesus says to Peter the fisherman, 'From now on you will catch men'
(Luke 5:10). John does not record the call of the fishermen, but does
report another incident from early in Jesus' ministry, the encounter
by the well in Samaria; there Jesus invites the disciples to join him in
the work of spiritual harvest (John 4:35–38). Thus Jesus' initial call
to the disciples was to join him in a task, proclaiming the good news
of the kingdom of God, inviting lost men and women to repent and
believe, and to join the community of the Messiah.

His last words to the disciples contained a similar emphasis on
the task. He reminded them that they were to be his 'witnesses', and
commissioned them to go and 'make disciples' of all the nations. But
in between the initial call and the final commission, there was a
consistent emphasis on images that spoke of the close relationships
into which Jesus' followers were being called.

The focus on relationships began very early in Jesus'
instructions to his disciples. Numerous times in the Sermon on
the Mount (Matthew 5–7) Jesus spoke of the disciples as children
of the heavenly Father and as brothers of one another. In Mark 2
Jesus compared his disciples to friends of the bridegroom who
were so caught up in the joy of the celebration that they could not
think of somber activities like fasting. The next chapter records the
occasion on which Jesus said that those who did the will of God

were his brother and sister and mother (Mark 3:31–35).

The themes of brotherhood and relationship to God as his children remain prominent throughout Jesus' ministry to his disciples. But the most intimate description of Jesus' love for the disciples, and theirs for him, does not come until the night of the Last Supper, in John 15. There Jesus says, 'I no longer call you servants... Instead, I have called you friends' (John 15:15). The 'task' word, 'servant', although an accurate description of the relationship in many respects, is no longer adequate; it cannot express the intimate love, or the free communication, that exists between Jesus and his followers. The word 'friend' must be summoned into service. Jesus could not have made such a statement early in his ministry, before the bonds of deeper trust and commitment had been forged with the disciples through months of travel and ministry together. Some metaphors were appropriate from the very outset; others needed more time.

The whole cluster of 'servant' images becomes much more prominent in Jesus' teaching toward the end of his ministry, as he and the disciples make their way to Jerusalem for the last time. The disciples are finally understanding that Jesus is the Messiah, the Son of God. Following Peter's clear profession of faith at Caesarea Philippi, Jesus begins to speak more frequently of his impending sufferings. But the disciples are filled with visions of the coming glories of the kingdom; they are thrilled with the prospect of sitting on their thrones judging the twelve tribes of Israel. Soon the seeds of ambition begin to erupt in open competition and arguments. So Jesus begins to speak more often of the role of the servant, who places himself humbly at the disposal of the other, and who willingly follows his master along the path of suffering. Thus almost all of the servant teachings of Jesus are found in the later chapters of the Gospels, in Matthew 18–25, Mark 9–13, Luke 12–22, and John 12–15. The longer a person has been involved in the process of leadership development, the more likely it is that he may start to struggle with ambitious pride, and may need to be reminded that his purpose is to serve, not to rule.

I believe that it is also significant that Jesus did not refer to any of the disciples as 'shepherd' until after the resurrection, when he spoke to Peter in John 21. Until that time, the emphasis is on their role as sheep. The crucial lesson for each disciple to learn early was how to be a follower. Only after he had learned to follow well could he be trusted to lead.

APPROPRIATE TO THE PARTICULAR CIRCUMSTANCES

Jesus chose his illustrations wisely in view of the particular circumstances of the people he was addressing. For example, when he extended the initial call to fishermen by the lake shore, he promised to make them 'fishers of men.' But as far as the Gospel writers record, he did not use this metaphor again, because the others he called were from different vocations.

When speaking of the interpersonal tensions that were bound to arise in a closely knit community, Jesus reminded the disciples that they were brothers (see comments in Chapter Two on *adelphos*). He knew that they would be tempted, when injured, to put distance between themselves; but he insisted that they recognize the bonds that joined them as members of the same spiritual family.

When arguments arose among the Twelve concerning who was to be the greatest, Jesus responded by setting a child in the midst of them as an illustration, or by describing the characteristics of a servant. When his followers began to assume that the kingdom was going to be established in the very near future, Jesus told parables that pictured servants whose masters went away for long periods of time, servants who were responsible to make wise investments in the meantime.

Jesus' metaphors are deliberately chosen with great care to be appropriate to the culture, appropriate to the stage in the disciples' leadership development, and appropriate to the life circumstances.

Missing metaphors

As we have already seen, Jesus drew his illustrations from numerous objects, activities and roles of everyday life. We have detailed thirty-five images that he uses to describe his followers. Yet there are some significant omissions. There are a number of words that Jesus does not use for his followers, even though these social roles would have been very familiar to Jesus' listeners.

In the first place, Jesus does not use any of the numerous words compounded from the root *arch-* , which have to do with rule, and which carry a strong tone of authority. At least sixteen of these words occur in the New Testament (*archegos, archiereus, archipoimen, archisynagogos, architekton, architelonos, architriklinos, archon, hekatontarches, hekatontarchos, patriarches, politarches, stratopedarches, tetrarches, chiliarchos, Asiarches*), but none of them are ever applied to the disciple of Jesus, with the exception of Paul's description of himself in 1 Corinthians 3:10 as an 'expert builder' who laid the foundation for others to build upon.

Although Jesus tells numerous stories involving masters and servants, and often uses the word *kyrios* (master), he never compares his disciple to the master—only to the servant. Even the illustrations of those who have responsibility over others picture those who are themselves servants; the *oikonomos* who manages his master's household and possessions, or the *poimen* who tends the flock of another.

Jesus describes his followers as a family, but he never refers to any of the disciples as a 'father.' On the contrary, in Matthew 23:9 he warns, 'Do not call anyone on earth 'father,' for you have one Father, and he is in heaven.' Even in the passages where he speaks so clearly of his followers as a spiritual family, he refers to 'brother and sister and mother', but not to 'father' (Matthew 12:50; Mark 3:35; Luke 8:21). We have also seen Jesus' reserve in speaking of the disciples as shepherds, until late in his ministry with them—and even then, the focus is on the tender care of the shepherd for the sheep, not on the authority with which he leads them.

Yet the references to following are very numerous—the disciple (*mathetes*) with the teacher, the servant with the master, the sheep with the shepherd. Jesus places far more emphasis in the development of his disciples on their following than on their leading. He avoids altogether the terms that evoke images of strong authority, or that encourage comparison with political rulers. He uses far more images that encourage the disciples to think of themselves as 'among' or 'under' than those that imply 'over.'

Another set of images notable by their absence are those drawn from the temple and its worship. Although the apostles Paul, Peter, and John each take up the metaphor of 'priest' in the description of the believer, Jesus never does. Perhaps because of the corruption of so much of the temple worship in Jesus' day, as well as the opposition from so many of the priests, and the involvement of the chief priests in political maneuvers with the Roman government, Jesus chose not to draw illustrations from this sphere. With his emphasis on the disciples as brothers to one another, Jesus may also have wanted to avoid any hints of élitism that may have been implied in the use of priestly language.

6

Family members and citizens

In the next several chapters we will explore how the New Testament writers develop and add to the terms used by Jesus for his followers. We will follow the order of the taxonomy shown in Table 1.

Rural and urban images

As the gospel spread outward from Judea and Galilee, Christian communities began to take root in the major cities of the Mediterranean world. The action in the book of Acts takes place not along the seashore, or on the mountainside, but in the crowded marketplace, the tentmaker's shop, the theater, and even the city jail. The context is no longer primarily rural, but urban. The languages spoken are usually not Hebrew or Aramaic but Greek and possibly Latin. The focus shifts from the temple at Jerusalem to the temple of Diana in Ephesus and the altar to the unknown god in Athens. Accompanying this shift in context comes a shift in images. Wayne Meeks observes:

> Paul was a city person. The city breathes through his language. Jesus' parables of sowers and seeds, sharecroppers and mud-roofed cottages, call forth smells of manure and earth, and the Aramaic of the Palestinian villages often echoes in the Greek. When Paul contructs a metaphor of olive trees or gardens, on the other hand, the Greek is fluent and evokes schoolroom more than farm; he seems more at home with the clichés of Greek rhetoric, drawn from gymnasium, stadium, or workshop. Moreover, Paul was among those who depended on the city for their livelihood (1983:9).

Yet most of the basic images used by Jesus to describe his followers are repeated and elaborated by the teachers and writers of the early church. The shift from rural to urban brings some new vocabulary, with distinctive accents, but not a totally new language of discipleship. The same terms and themes employed by Jesus emerge again and again.

Household images

As we have seen, Jesus used many images to describe the relationships among those he had called together as his followers; one of the most common of these metaphors was the family. Jesus encouraged his disciples to address God in prayer as 'Father', and to see one another as brothers and sisters. The whole cluster of images related to the family becomes one of the most important metaphors in the New Testament.

Although the noun *oikiakos* (member of a household, Matthew 10:25), occurs only once in the Gospels, the synonymous term *oikeios*, as well as the root term *oikos* (house, household), are very prominent in the remainder of the New Testament. The *oikos* was the most important and fundamental structure of the Hellenistic world. Neither Hebrew nor Greek have a word for the nuclear family as we know it today, with parents and children living together as an isolated unit (Goetzemann, DNTT II:247). Rather, the basic form of social organization was the household, which consisted of not only the immediate family, but also various combinations of slaves, freedmen, friends, clients, laborers, business associates and tenants, as well as other relatives, all under the authority of the 'head of the household', the senior male member of the most prominent family (Tidball 1984:79–81; Malherbe 1983:69; Meeks 1983:31). John Hall Elliott summarizes it like this:

> *Oikos* ... is my house and home with all its personnel and property, my family and lineage, my 'given identity', the place where I 'belong' and exercise my personal and communal rights and responsibilities, my moral obligations (1981:24).

In order to understand the associations of this image for first-century Christians, it is important to appreciate the strong bonds of solidarity and loyalty that tied members of a household together. Participation in the common history of the head of a family was even more important than biological descent in bonding society together (Minear 1960:166). Members of a household would embrace whichever religion had been chosen by the head of the house (Tidball 1984:81; cf. Cornelius, Acts 11:14; Lydia, 16:15; Philippian jailer, 16:31; Crispus, 18:8). Abraham Malherbe emphasizes the intimacy of these connections:

The household members' loyalty to the interests of the household was so strong that it could rival loyalty to the republic. The closeness of the household unit offered the security and sense of belonging not provided by the larger political and social structures (1983:69).

In his letter to the Galatians, Paul[1] reminds them of the special obligations and loyalty they owe to one another as members of the 'family of believers (*tous oikeious tes pisteos*)' (Galatians 6:10). He uses the same word in Ephesians to tell Jews and Gentiles that Christ has overcome the estrangement and hostility that formerly kept them apart: 'You are fellow-citizens with God's people and members of God's household (*oikeioi tou theou*)' (Ephesians 2:19). To be a member of God's household is to belong, to be related, to be intimately interconnected.

In giving instructions to Timothy about the qualifications of church leaders, Paul says that a person's leadership in the home demonstrates fitness for leadership in the church. With this parallel fresh in mind, Paul explains that that he has written about these matters so that 'you will know how people ought to conduct themselves in God's household (*en oikoi theou*), which is the church of the living God' (1 Timothy 3:15).

Other New Testament writers also refer to the community of believers as God's household. Twice the author of Hebrews describes Jesus as presiding over God's *oikos*—first, as Son (Hebrews 3:6), and then as high priest (Hebrews 10:21). In his first letter, Peter warns Christians that, 'It is time for judgment to begin with the family of God (*apo tou oikou tou theou*)' (1 Peter 4:17).[2]

Although the first-century household was broader than the nuclear family as we know it today, the terms most commonly used in the New Testament to describe the relationships between believers were drawn from the innermost circle of relationships— brother, sister, father, mother, son and daughter.

BROTHERS AND SISTERS

Twice in his first letter Peter refers to the community of believers as 'the brotherhood (*adelphotes*)' (1 Peter 2:17; 5:9). Some form of the word *adelphos* (brother) is found in every New Testament book except Titus and Jude. From Acts through Revelation, fellow-Christians are called 'brother (*adelphos*)' over 200 times and 'sister (*adelphe*)' several times as well. Sometimes the reference is to individuals (e.g. 'our sister Phoebe', Romans 16:1; 'Tychicus the dear brother', Ephesians 6:21). Timothy is called 'brother' five times, four times by Paul (2 Corinthians 1:1; Colossians 1:1; 1 Thessalonians 3:2; Philemon 1) and once by the author of Hebrews (13:23).

Even the leading apostles are called 'brother', such as Paul (by Ananias in Acts 9:17 and 22:13; by the Jerusalem elders in Acts 21:20, and by Peter, in 2 Peter 3:15); and John (referring to himself, in Revelation 1:9).[3] In Acts 15, two verses underscore that the leader is also a brother: Judas and Silas are called 'leaders among the brothers (*andras hegoumenous en tois adelphois*)' (15:22), and the letter to the Gentile Christians is addressed from 'the apostles and elders, your brothers (*hoi apostoloi kai hoi presbyteroi adelphoi*)' (15:23). Thus a community of brothers and sisters can still have leaders, and those who are leaders nevertheless remain brethren. The equality of status implied in the term 'brother' does not disallow differentiation in leadership roles.

Sometimes the term 'brother' or 'sister' is used in a general sense to denote 'fellow-Christian' ('Suppose a brother or sister is without clothes', James 2:15; cf. Romans 14:10; 1 Corinthians 7:12; 1 Thessalonians 4:6; 1 John 2:9). Other times it refers to the whole group of Christians in a given locality: 'Peter stood up among the brothers' (Acts 1:15); 'All the brothers greet you' (1 Corinthians 16:20).[4] The plural 'brothers' is also used in commands or statements concerning Christians in general (Hebrews 2:11–12, 17; 1 John 3:14; Revelation 12:10).

Most often, however, the term 'brothers' is used in direct address, by a speaker to his listeners, or an author to his readers. Thus Peter refers to the disciples in the Upper Room (Acts 1:16), to the crowds on the day of Pentecost (Acts 2:29), to the Jerusalem council (Acts 15:7), and to the churches to whom he wrote (2 Peter 1:10). The Twelve address their fellow-believers as 'brothers' in Acts 6:3; Stephen uses the same term with the Sanhedrin in Acts 7:2, as also does Paul in Acts 23:1, 5–6. Paul addresses his readers as 'brothers' numerous times in his letters to the Romans, Corinthians, Galatians, Ephesians, and Thessalonians; so also do James and the author of Hebrews.

It is interesting to note that whenever 'brother' or 'brothers' is used in direct address, it is to a fellow-Jew (whether believing or non-believing) or to a fellow-Christian.[5] Among Jews, of course, the term is appropriate because of their shared physical descent through Abraham, Isaac, and Jacob. Among Christians, however, whether Jew or Gentile, the word 'brother' attests to the new spiritual family connection formed through common faith in Jesus Christ.

The use of the term 'brother' among members of a religious community was not unique to the Christian church. This terminology had been used for generations in Judaism, as well as in other religions (W. Günther, DNTT, I:254–257). Best describes the term 'brother' as a sign of social equality[6] as well as communal solidarity:

> When Paul terms his converts his brothers this indicates that he and they stand on the same level for by its very nature 'brother' is a reciprocal relation. The first Christians derived the term from Judaism, but it was also one which Paul's Gentile converts could appreciate since it was in use in so many contemporary cults. It serves to distinguish those within a community from those outside by creating a bond between those within (1988:132).

Malina (1981:94–121), in a very useful discussion of kinship and marriage in the New Testament world, notes the special closeness of the brother/sister relationship. This point should be kept in mind when reading exhortations such as Paul's command to Timothy to treat 'younger women as sisters, in all purity' (1 Timothy 5:2), or the instruction to greet one another with a holy kiss (Romans 16:16; 1 Corinthians 16:20; 2 Corinthians 13:12; 1 Thessalonians 5:26; 1 Peter 5:14).

CHILDREN

The closeness of family relationship is also conveyed in the numerous terms denoting parent/child relationships. Each of the terms for 'child' that Jesus used for his disciples—*hyios, teknion, teknos, nepios,* and *paidion*—are taken up by other New Testament writers as well.

Just as Jesus used the image of 'child of God (*hyios tou theou*)' to teach that his followers should imitate the character of their heavenly Father, so Paul invokes the metaphor in teaching the Corinthians about their need to live a life of separation from the world (2 Corinthians 6:18)[7]. Jesus also used the 'son (*hyios*)' image to teach about the tender care of God for his children; in this same spirit the author of Hebrews assures his readers that God's disciplinary actions are proof that 'God is treating you as sons (hos hyiois)' (12:7), an expression of his love.

Paul uses the hyios terminology in Romans and Galatians to describe the Christian's deliverance from bondage and fear (Romans 8:14, 19; Galatians 3:7, 26; 4:7). The Christian is no longer a slave, or a prisoner, or under the supervision of a tutor. Sonship is an image of maturity and freedom,[8] of privilege and elevation of status. In the same way the author of Hebrews celebrates Christ's action in 'bringing many sons to glory' (2:10), and John records God's announcement in the vision of the new heavens and new earth: 'He who overcomes will inherit all this, and I will be his God and he will be my son' (Revelation 21:7).

In each of these references to hyios, every Christian is seen as a child of God. However, hyios can also be used in a narrower sense, by a senior leader referring to a younger believer. Peter conveys greetings from 'my son Mark' (1 Peter 5:13), expressing a depth of respect and love for this younger man.

The word teknon[9] is similarly used in two senses to describe believers as God's children, but also to refer to younger or newer members of the fellowship as spiritual children in relation to their leaders. Only senior members of the community use the term in this second sense.

In Romans 8, Paul uses teknon interchangeably with hyios to speak of the privileges of freedom and rights of inheritance that accompany sonship (verses 16–17, 21); similar themes accompany his use of this word in Galatians 4:28, 31. The apostle John likewise expresses amazement at the privilege that is ours in being called God's children (1 John 3:1–2). In several other passages, believers are reminded that they are God's children, responsible to display the family resemblance as part of the call to holy living (Ephesians 5:1–2; Philippians 2:15; 1 Peter 1:14–17; 1 John 3:10; 5:2).

On several occasions Paul appeals to those whom he has nurtured or led to the Lord, calling them his tekna, his children:

> I am not writing this to shame you, but to warn you, as my dear children (1 Corinthians 4:14);

> I am sending you Timothy, my son, whom I love (1 Corinthians 4:17);

> I speak as to my children—open wide your hearts also (2 Corinthians 6:13);

> My dear children, for whom I am again in the pains of

childbirth until Christ is formed in you (Galatians 4:19);

. . . to Titus, my true son in our common faith (Titus 1:4);

I appeal to you for my son Onesimus (Philemon 10).

In each of these passages we can hear the strong tone of Paul's affection and intense concern, combined with a sense of responsibility for the welfare of his spiritual children.

Several times in his first letter, the apostle John refers to his readers as 'dear children (teknia)', a nursery term, closely related to teknon, that denotes a little child rather than offspring in general. It is not surprising that the 'apostle of love', probably well along in years at the time of writing, would use such a tender expression for his spiritual family.

Nepios is the word for infant or young child; it 'carries the overtones of helplessness, inexperience, and simplicity' (Braumann, DNTT, I:281). As we have seen, Jesus uses the term in Luke 10:21–23 to contrast the 'wise' of this world, who remain ignorant of God's truth, with the 'little children' to whom the things of the Spirit have been revealed. In each of the three places where this metaphor is taken up by the New Testament authors, it is used to describe believers as they are, but not as they should be. Paul scolds the Corinthians for being 'mere infants in Christ' (1 Corinthians 3:1), still needing milk and not ready for solid food, because of their jealous rivalries and fixation on human personalities. In Ephesians 4:14–16 he looks forward to the day when, after the equipping gifts have produced unity and maturity, 'we will no longer be infants', troubled by doctrinal instability. Similarly the author of Hebrews contrasts the infant, still living on milk, with the mature person who has learned to distinguish good from evil (Hebrews 5:13). In each of these instances the metaphor is used with a tone of rebuke. Everybody starts as an infant, but nobody needs to remain as an infant.

The remaining word for 'child' used by Jesus in reference to his followers is paidion. The author of Hebrews also employs this term in describing Jesus' identification with us: 'Since the children have flesh and blood, he too shared in their humanity' (2:14). John twice addresses the recipients of his first letter as 'children (paidia)' (2:12, 18).

Another word for infant, although not used figuratively by Jesus for his disciples, occurs in the Gospel accounts. Brephos (baby) is used by Luke to describe Elizabeth's unborn child (Luke 1:41, 44), the newborn Jesus (Luke 2:12, 16), and the children brought to Jesus for blessing (Luke 18:15). This is the word chosen by Peter in his exhortation to new Christians: 'Like newborn babies (*hos artigenneta brephe*), crave pure spiritual milk, so that by it you may grow up in your salvation' (1 Peter 2:2). In this passage there is none of the tone of rebuke that accompanies the use of *nepios*.

An aspect of membership in God's family cited several times by the New Testament writers is the promise of an inheritance.[10] To be God's child is also to be his heir (*kleronomos*, Galatians 3:29; 4:7). In this position of privilege we are identified with Christ, says Paul, as 'fellow-heirs (*synkleronomoi*)' (Romans 8:17). This privilege is extended to the Gentiles together with Israel (Ephesians 3:6). The poor of this world, James reminds us, have been chosen by God to be heirs of the kingdom (James 2:15). Husbands, says Peter, are to treat their wives with sensitivity, realizing that they are 'heirs with you of the gracious gift of life' (1 Peter 3:7).

One other figurative expression for children is used in the New Testament in reference to followers of Jesus—*sperma* (descendants, literally 'seed'). The Jews of Jesus' day proudly referred to themselves as 'Abraham's descendants' (John 8:33), and even Paul identified himself in this way (Romans 11:1). Yet Paul suggested an extended meaning for the term, identifying the true offspring of Abraham as those who shared Abraham's faith in God's promise (Romans 4:16, 18). Thus, after describing how the promises of God are appropriated by faith (Galatians 3:14), Paul summarizes in Galatians 3:29: 'If you belong to Christ, then you are Abraham's seed, and heirs according to the promise.'[11]

Drawing from the technical legal vocabulary of his day, Paul introduces a term closely related to *hyios* (son), that is, *hyiothesia*, which refers to both the process and the state of adoption. The word appears seldom in classical Greek or the LXX (Braumann, DNTT, I:287). In Romans 9:4, Paul uses it for God's adoption of the nation of Israel, but in the other four passages, it refers to God's gracious act of making us his children:

> You did not receive a spirit that makes you a slave again to fear, but you received the Spirit of sonship (Romans 8:15);

> We wait eagerly for our adoption as sons, the redemption of our bodies (Romans 8:23);

> But when the time had fully come, God sent his Son, born of a woman, born under the law, to redeem those under the law, that we might receive the full rights as sons (Galatians 4:4–5);
>
> In love he predestined us to be adopted as his sons through Jesus Christ (Ephesians 1:5).

In these passages we see that adoption implies freedom from fear, intimacy with God, hope for the future, release from bondage to the law, and experience of the gracious love of God. It emphasizes that the relationship of sonship is an honor, a privilege, a blessing, something that we have no right to expect or to demand.

Meeks observes that adoption not only brings us into relationship with God, but also into relationship with a community:

> ... the image of the initiate being adopted as God's child and thus receiving a new family of human brothers and sisters is a vivid way of portraying what a modern sociologist might call the resocialization of conversion. The natural kinship structure into which the person has been born and which previously defined his place and his connections with society is here supplanted by a new set of relationships (1983:88).

The function of adoption terminology in the nurture of community is also explored by Robert Atkins (1987), who sees Paul's use of the term as a 'metaphor of inclusion', providing a rationale for why people of such diverse social levels and cultural backgrounds should all be included in the group. Atkins also suggests that Paul uses adoption terminology because it implies no social hierarchy, but rather expresses the spiritual equality of all the members of the believing community.

PARENTS

Corresponding to the metaphors related to sonship and childhood are the images concerning parenthood. Our focus in this context, of course, is not on God as the heavenly Father, but on followers of Jesus described figuratively as 'parents' of other believers.

Jesus did not use these metaphors for his disciples nearly as often as he described them as children. In fact, he specifically warned them against ascribing the honorary title of 'father' to any fellow-disciple (Matthew 23:9). In Mark 3, when he describes those who

80

do the will of God as his spiritual family, he refers to 'brother', 'sister', and even 'mother', but not to 'father.' Similarly, in Mark 10:29–30, when he encourages his disciples about the benefits they will receive in return for their sacrifices, he promises 'brothers, sisters, mothers, children', but not fathers. Whenever Jesus uses the term 'father', he is speaking either of literal biological descent, or of God as Father, but never of one disciple in relation to another.[12]

However, in the New Testament writings, the metaphor of parenthood is used fairly often, primarily by the apostle Paul. In 2 Corinthians 12:14, speaking of his readiness to sacrifice with joy for the Corinthian believers, Paul introduces the illustration of the parent (*goneus*) with children, saying that 'children should not have to save up for their parents, but parents for their children.' Spiritual leaders should not be a burden on their followers; they are called to be sacrificial servants, expending themselves joyfully for those whom they have helped to bring to spiritual birth, like parents with children.[13]

In 1 Timothy 5:1–2 Paul reminds Timothy to exhort an older man 'as if he were your father,' and to treat the 'older women as mothers.' Thus even the spiritual leader is to show respect for older members of the family of believers, just as would be appropriate in the ordinary household. Beyreuther remarks: 'A high estimation of motherhood and parenthood can be traced everywhere in antiquity' (DNTT III:1068).

In a beautifully tender passage in the first letter to the Thessalonians, Paul describes himself and his ministry team in maternal imagery. He says, 'We were gentle among you, like a mother (*trophos*) caring for her little children (*tekna*)' (1 Thessalonians 2:7). The word *trophos* refers to a woman nursing, whether her own children or someone else's;[14] but in this context, with the emphasis on love, and with the reference to the 'father' in verse 11, it is clear that the word should be taken as 'nursing mother' rather than 'wet nurse'. The emphasis on gentleness in leadership conveyed by this image is quite striking:

> In his [Paul's] world as in ours, gentleness was not always greeted as a wholly desirable quality. Some regarded it as mere flattery and believed that more radical surgery was needed if men were to be improved. Boldness and abusive scolding were considered essential by many of the wandering philosophers if their teaching was to have any impact (Tidball 1986:106).

The image of the spiritual leader as mother is also implied in 1 Corinthians 3:1–3, where Paul speaks of having to give them milk, not solid food,[15] as well as in Galatians 4:19, where he speaks of the agony he has endured in the process of bringing these believers to spiritual birth: 'I am again in the pains of childbirth until Christ is formed in you.'

More often than 'mother', however, we find the image of father (*pater*). Of course, in the passages we have already seen where apostles refer to others as 'son' or 'children,' the parental metaphor is implied. But several times the apostle Paul describes himself explicitly as spiritual father. For example, Paul commends Timothy, because, 'as a son with his father he has served with me in the work of the gospel' (Philippians 2:22). Note that Paul does not say, 'Timothy served me,' but rather that he served 'with me.' His description of himself as father in no way implies an inferior or servile status for Timothy. As Fernando observes: 'As far as status is concerned, our spiritual children are on an equal footing with us. We are brothers and sisters under a common Master and Father' (1985:18). In the passage already alluded to in 1 Thessalonians, Paul, Silas, and Timothy write: 'You know that we dealt with each of you as a father deals with his own children, encouraging, comforting, and urging you to live lives worthy of God' (1 Thessalonians 2:11–12). Here the emphasis of the illustration is on individualized care, on practical exhortation from the more experienced to the less experienced.

In 1 Corinthians 4:15 Paul makes his strongest assertion of spiritual fatherhood: 'Even though you have ten thousand guardians in Christ, you do not have many fathers, for in Christ Jesus I became your father through the gospel.' Implied in this image is Paul's authority. Only a few verses later he asks, 'Shall I come to you with a whip, or in love and with a gentle spirit?' (4:21). The obvious implication is that Paul can exercise his parental powers of discipline if he has to. Yet the overall tone of the passage is that of appeal, and loving persuasion, not of insistence on superior status or rights. Holmberg (1980:79), however, observes that in employing the image of father Paul is implying a relationship far more demanding than any ordinary obligation, for, 'When are you free from the obligation of respecting and obeying "father", and when have you repaid the debt of gratitude to the person who has given you life (eternal)?'

To what extent is Paul's use of the 'father' image parallel to the general associations of the word in the first-century world? And how is his employment of this term consistent with Jesus' command to 'call no man father?' Concerning the general role of the father in the ancient world, Hofius says:

> In the patriarchal societies of antiquity, the father figure is endowed with two particular characteristics. On the one hand, the father rules as head of the household and the person to whom most respect is due, having absolute authority over his family. On the other hand, he has the responsibility of guarding, supporting and helping other members (DNTT I:614).

In the Old Testament, we find the term 'father' used of Naaman by his servant (2 Kings 5:13), of the prophet Elisha by two kings of Israel (2 Kings 6:21; 13:14), and of a young Levite invited by different Israelites to be their priest (Judges 17:10; 18:19). In each case it is a title of honor given to one who has a role of spiritual leadership. Hofius also notes:

> In Rabbinic Judaism, where the title of father was frequently used of respected scribes, the metaphor of father and child is occasionally applied to the relation-ship between a teacher of the Torah and his pupil (DNTT I:617).

In the classical world as well, the title of 'father' was often used as a term of respect.

Yet the term 'father' is not used within the New Testament by one believer referring to another[16]—perhaps because the writings are by those in senior positions, but also, I believe, in obedience to the spirit of Jesus' exhortation in Matthew 23. Furthermore, when Paul refers to himself as father, he is pointing to the undeniable fact that he was used by God to bring those particular people to spiritual birth, to faith in Christ. Thus Tidball says: 'Paul does not usually use it [the idea of being a father] to signify his authority over them, but to mark his close relationship and his paternal love for them' (1986:105).

Furthermore, Paul treats his spiritual children as adults. He does not attempt to keep them weak and dependent on himself.[17] Stott emphasizes this theme strongly in his description of the preacher as a father:

> We are never to adopt toward a fellow man in the Church the attitude of dependence which a child has towards his father, nor are we to require others to be or to become spiritually dependent on us ... It is ridiculous for one Christian to claim the authority of a father over a fellow Christian and demand his subordination as a child if the two are in reality brothers ... It is, then, the authority of a father over dependent children which is forbidden to us (1961:82–84).

However, the image of father is certainly appropriate in speaking about the person used as the means of another's conversion, or as a symbol of affectionate concern.[18]

Members of a People

So far in this chapter we have been exploring terms related to the household or family, images that describe the interpersonal relationships between those who are born spiritually into the community of Christians through faith in Jesus Christ. Through this miracle of new birth they are adopted as children of God, and become brothers and sisters to one another.

As the gospel moves outside the confines of Palestine, and encounters more and more directly the influences of Greek and Roman culture, another set of metaphors emerges. Now the believing community is seen not only as a household, but also as a people, a nation. As long as the followers of Jesus were all Jewish, and as long as there was a prospect that Israel as a whole might embrace Jesus as true Messiah, there was no occasion for this imagery to take hold. But after the leaders of Jerusalem rejected Jesus' claims and engineered his execution at the hands of the Romans, and as the followers of Jesus became a persecuted sect within Judaism, a new consciousness began to grow. Samaritans and Gentiles began to come to faith, and soon the believers found themselves forming new bonds with those who had previously been strangers, while being pushed away by non-believers who had been their former associates. Under the leadership of the Holy Spirit, the early Christians began to see themselves as the true Israel, and to appropriate some of the terms used to describe God's people in the Old Testament. They realized that their true and permanent identity was not to be found in any human political structure. Instead, as citizens of heaven they would always be 'aliens and strangers,' never fully identified with any particular group of people except the community of faith. Therefore, the images for followers of Jesus described in the rest of this chapter arise several years after the earthly ministry of Jesus, and do not appear in Jesus' teaching in the Gospels.

IMAGES OF ASSOCIATION

A number of the terms are drawn from God's promise to Israel at Mount Sinai: 'Now if you obey me fully and keep my covenant, then out of all nations you will be my treasured possession. Although the whole earth is mine, you will be for me a kingdom of priests and a holy nation' (Exodus 19:5–6). Peter quotes these and other Old Testament phrases in describing followers of Christ: 'But you are a chosen people (genos eklekton), a royal priesthood (basileion hierateuma), a holy nation (ethnos hagion), a people belonging to God (laos eis peripoiesin), that you may declare the praises of him who called you out of darkness into his wonderful light. Once you were not a people (laos), but now you are the people of God; once you had not received mercy, but now you have received mercy' (1 Peter 2:9–11). All three of the key terms for this new people are brought together in these verses: genos, ethnos, and laos.

The term genos is derived from the stem gen- (C. Brown, DNTT II:35), and is related to words like gennesis (birth), gennema (offspring), and gennao (be father of). To distinguish it from the other two words, it is best translated as 'race.'[19] It emphasizes a line of descent, a lineage. Israel was a race chosen from among the other nations (Deuteronomy 7:6; 10:15; Isaiah 43:21) to be the arena of God's gracious actions in history, preparing for the birth of the Messiah. Christians have been adopted into this lineage, as spiritual descendants of Abraham, through following his example of faith (Galatians 3:14, 29).

The reference to believers as a holy nation (ethnos hagion) is taken from Exodus 19:6. An ethnos is a group of people held together by common customs and patterns of life. The church too is a people set apart, distinct from others. Although not physically or geographically separated, their habits and behavior should make clear that they belong specially to God, reserved for his service. To become a Christian, then, is in a sense to adopt a new 'culture', with a new worldview, a new system of values, and a new pattern of behavior.

Minear (1960:73) notes that this image of God's people as ethnos is used briefly by Jesus in Matthew 21:43, where he says: 'Therefore I tell you that the kingdom of God will be taken away from you and given to a people (*ethnei*) who will produce its fruit.' Such a statement must have been quite startling to Jesus' Jewish listeners, who referred to Israel as the people (*laos*) of God, while all the rest of mankind were called the 'nations' (*ethne*) (Bietenhard, DNTT II:790–791).[20]

Laos, we have just observed, is the word reserved in the Greek Old Testament for Israel as the people specially chosen by God. In classical Greek it is not a precisely defined word, but is associated with 'the language of high style and ceremony' (Bietenhard, DNTT, II:788). Israel is a people solely by God's gracious initiative, not by any merit of their own. As Minear says:

> Everywhere in the Bible we hear that the birth and survival of this people are due alone to God's gracious action in creating, calling, sustaining, judging, and saving it. They are a people only because he dwells within them and moves among them (1960:69).

Three other New Testament authors use this image as well. Insisting upon the necessity of the Christian's separation from everything that is evil, Paul conflates three Old Testament passages (Leviticius 26:12; Jeremiah 32:38; Ezekiel 37:27) that speak of God's relationship to his people: 'As God has said, "I will live with them and walk among them, and I will be their God, and they will be my people"' (1 Corinthians 6:16). The author of Hebrews speaks about the Sabbath rest that remains for the people of God (Hebrews 4:9). Then, finally, the promise of being God's people finds its fulfillment in the magnificent vision of John in the book of Revelation: 'They will be his people, and God himself will be with them and be their God' (21:3).

Each of these words *genos*, *ethnos*, and *laos* is, in Atkins' terms (1987:318), a 'metaphor of inclusion.' Each speaks of a place of belonging, with a new web of horizontal relationships. These words also imply a new and honorable identity, the privilege of belonging to God and being chosen by him for a special purpose. For the purposes of our taxonomy we will call them 'images of association,' that is, images that emphasize the new connections formed between God and the believer, and between the believers and one another.

Three more images of association introduced in the New Testament letters are drawn from the institution of the Greek city-state. Tidball says that the city-state (*polis*) was considered by the Greeks to be 'the best form by which an individual could associate with his fellow-man' (1984:76). Under Roman rule these city-states still continued to enjoy a considerable degree of freedom, as long as they did not antagonize the Roman authorities. Stambaugh and Balch offer this description:

> [The polis was] a community of relatively small size with temples to the Greek gods and an open air *agora* for public business. It was administered with some degree of autonomy by magistrates and a council, either recruited from a hereditary oligarchic élite or chosen through democratic election by the citizens who owned property (1986:14).

Note the reference to 'citizens'. Tidball elaborates on the importance of citizenship:

> For all their high ideals of democracy they functioned only because the privileges of membership were restricted. The high status and value of citizenship was preserved by excluding some from ever being able to acquire its status. Foreigners and slaves were two classes excluded by this ancient attempt at quality control (1984:78).

The early Christians in some cases could claim the privilege of citizenship (as for example, Paul did to great advantage more than once, e.g. Acts 16:37; 22:25; 25:11). But in many more cases, they had no such social advantage. Thus, to be described as citizens of a heavenly city brought great security and comfort.

The author of Hebrews speaks of the city (*polis*) to which Abraham and the other patriarchs looked forward, the place that lay at the end of their pilgrimage (11:10, 16). These sojourners became symbols of Christians, who also looked forward to a future place of belonging with God. The heavenly Jerusalem has both a present and a future aspect, representing the whole people of God, past and present, on earth and in heaven. Thus the author says: 'You have come to Mount Zion, to the heavenly Jerusalem, the city of the living God' (12:22). The future aspect of the city comes to the foreground once again in the next chapter: 'For here we do not have an enduring city, but we are looking for the city which is to come' (13:14). The church is a future-oriented community. Its real identity and significance will be revealed in the age to come. Its best days lie ahead.

Another metaphor related to the *polis* occurs once in Philippians 3:20, where Paul says: 'Our citizenship (*politeuma*) is in heaven.' Paul has been talking about straining toward the goal of God's heavenward call, and has been expressing sorrow over those whose minds are earthbound, and who can think only of their stomachs. In the following verses he speaks of waiting for a Savior from heaven who will transform our bodies. The citizenship metaphor thus pulls God's people upward and forward, inspiring them to live holy lives in the present.

Stambaugh and Baugh provide some helpful insights into the historical associations of the term *politeuma*. Noting that migrant traders and craftspeople sometimes moved to a city to live as non-resident aliens, they say:

> Normally, such artisans and traders lived under the laws and customs of the host city, with specific liabilities and privileges according to the individual situation. They organized themselves and met regularly for business and to celebrate their common heritage. In some cases it was convenient for the political authorities to recognize such a community of foreigners as an autonomous entity, known as a *politeuma* (cf. Phil.3:20). As such, the group could enjoy a certain amount of social independence, although always subject of course to the general political control of the state (1986:41).

Along similar lines, Meeks states that in certain cities where Jews were numerous, they were allowed to form 'a recognized, semi-autonomous body of residents in a city who, though not citizens, shared some specific rights with citizens' (1983:35–36). Thus, the term *politeuma* recognized a certain amount of identification with the present place of residence, while acknowledging that the primary focus of loyalty was somewhere else.

One other citizenship metaphor emphasizes not so much the connection with heaven, but the interrelationship with fellow-citizens. In Ephesians Paul describes how Jesus Christ has torn down the barriers that used to separate Jews from Gentiles. He says to the Gentiles: 'You are no longer foreigners and aliens but fellow-citizens (*sympolitai*) with God's people and members of God's household' (Ephesians 2:19).

One other term can be classified with these images of association, the word *plesion* (neighbor). It is a somewhat vague term, connected with the word *pelas* (near), and means 'one standing near, neighbor,

88

fellow man, nearest . . . the one with whom I have to do' (Falkenroth, DNTT, I:258–260). I place it here because it calls to mind the image of the one living next to me in community.

In most of the passages where *plesion* appears in the New Testament letters, the context deals with the treatment of fellow-believers, rather than the Christian's witness to the unbelieving community. In Romans 15:2, Paul summarizes his discussion about the strong and weak members of the fellowship by exhorting his readers: 'Each of us should please his neighbor for his good, to build him up.' 'Neighbor' is a word that bridges a barrier; it reminds us that we are near to someone from whom we might feel distant. Similarly in Ephesians 4:25, Paul rebukes the practice of lying on the basis that we are connected to one another: 'Each of you must put off falsehood and speak truthfully to his neighbor, for we are all members of one body.' James rebukes his readers for their attitudes of favoritism within the congregation, quoting the commandment, 'Love your neighbor as yourself' (2:8); later in his letter he deals with the problem of a judgmental spirit toward fellow-believers, asking, 'But you—who are you to judge your neighbor?' (4:12). Thus to be a neighbor is to be closely connected in God's eyes; and, therefore, we have no right to push one another away.

IMAGES OF DISASSOCIATION

Closely related to the community-oriented images of association are two 'images of disassociation', terms which describe the Christian as one who does not fully belong in the communities of this world. Both are used by Peter in his first letter. The first is *parepidemos* (temporary resident), used in Peter's opening greetings to his readers: 'Peter, an apostle of Jesus Christ, to God's elect, strangers in the world (*parepidemois*)' (1 Peter 1:1). This word means someone who lives for a short while in a foreign place as a stranger or alien (Bietenhard, DNTT I:690). Elliott says that the *parepidemoi* are 'the "temporary visitors, transients, immigrants or wanderers" who have no intention or opportunity to establish permanent residence where they currently live' (1981:36); he suggests that the word be translated as 'visiting strangers' (1981:47).

The second word, *paroikos* (resident alien), is introduced by Peter in 1:17: 'Live your lives as strangers (*tes paroikias*) here in reverent fear.' In contrast to the *parepidemos*, the *paroikos* (a compound from *para-*, 'by', and *oikos*, 'house') is a long-term resident of the community, enjoying its protection, yet lacking the rights of a citizen (Bietenhard, DNTT I:690). Elliott offers a definition of the word in the broad sense:

In this general sense *paroikoi* are strangers, foreigners, aliens, people who are not at home, or who lack native roots, in the language, customs, culture, or political, social, or religious allegiances of the people among whom they dwell... Whereas *oikos* connotes associations and impressions of home, belongingness, and one's proper place, *paroikos* depicts the 'DP', the displaced and dislocated person, the curious or suspicious-looking alien or stranger. Distinguished from *oik-* terms and combined in both secular and biblical literature with such words as *allos*, *allotrios*, *xenos*, and *parepidemos* all of which variously denote the stranger, foreigner or transient visitor, *paroikos* in a general sense implies social separation, cultural alienation and a certain degree of personal deprivation (1981:24–25).

Elliott also cites the more technical meaning of *paroikos*, which is 'the "resident alien" (with his attendant, though restricted, rights and civil status)' (1981:30). The restrictions on the resident alien in this sense included the inability to vote, own land, hold priestly offices or the primary public offices, receive certain public honors, or intermarry with full citizens. Although resident aliens received only partial legal protection, they were fully liable for military service, production quotas, and taxes; because of these restrictions their opportunities for social or economic advancement were quite limited (1981:68).

In 1 Peter 2:11, both words come together, in a further exhortation to distinctive, holy living: 'Dear friends, I urge you, as aliens (*paroikous*) and strangers in the world (*parepidemous*), to abstain from sinful desires, which war against your soul.' Elliott (1981) sees these references as having to do primarily with the actual social conditions of Peter's readers, and only secondarily as a figurative reference to their heavenly citizenship. In fact, the title of his book, *A Home for the Homeless*, expresses his thesis that Peter uses *oikos* (household) imagery in order to raise the group consciousness of a community formed largely of displaced people. Our interest here, however, is in the figurative use of the terms, as used to warn Christians, whose real home is elsewhere, against conformity to the patterns of this world.

Outside of 1 Peter, these images occur in two other places. The author of Hebrews describes the patriarchs as those who 'admitted that they were aliens (*xenoi*) and strangers (*parepidemoi*) on earth' (11:13). In the passage previously quoted from Ephesians, Paul says to the Gentiles: 'You are no longer foreigners (*xenoi*) and aliens (*paroikoi*), but fellow-citizens (*sympolitai*) with God's people (*ton hagion*) and members of God's household (*oikeioi tou theou*)' (2:19). Here the image is reversed—the Gentile believers are not seen as aliens, but as 'no longer aliens'. It all depends on the point of reference (a good example of the fluidity of images, and the importance of considering context in their interpretation).

Additions to the taxonomy

The terms discussed in this chapter can be grouped according to the following taxonomy. The regular typeface simply repeats the taxonomy of terms given at the end of Part One, the expressions Jesus used to describe his followers. Where there is an asterisk, it denotes that the term used by Jesus is also found in the teaching of the New Testament church. The italics (bold italics for Greek words) are used for terms not used by Jesus, but employed by the apostles and other New Testament writers. Each chapter in Part Two will conclude with a similar partial taxonomy. At the end of Part Two all of these will be combined into an expanded taxonomy.

1. People

    1.1. Emphasis on Relationships

        1.1.1. Relationship by birth
            1.1.1.1. Member of household (*oikiakos*) (***oikeios, oikos***)
                1.1.1.1.1. Sibling
                    1.1.1.1.1.1. Brother (*adelphos*)* (***adelphotes***)
                    1.1.1.1.1.2. Sister (*adelphe*)*
                1.1.1.1.2. Child
                    1.1.1.1.2.1. Child (*hyios*)*
                        1.1.1.1.2.1.1. Son (*hyios*)*
                        *1.1.1.1.2.1.2. Daughter (**thygater**)*
                    1.1.1.1.2.2. Child (*teknion*)*
                    1.1.1.1.2.3. Child (*teknon*)*
                    1.1.1.1.2.4. Child (*nepios*)*
                    1.1.1.1.2.5. Child (*paidion*)*
                    *1.1.1.1.2.6. Baby (**brephos**)*
                    *1.1.1.1.2.7. Heir (**kleronomos, synkleronomos**)*
                    *1.1.1.1.2.8. Descendant (seed) (**sperma**)*
                    *1.1.1.1.2.9. Child by adoption (**hyiothesia**)*
                *1.1.1.1.3. Parent (**goneus**)*
                    *1.1.1.1.3.1. Mother (**meter**)*
                      *1.1.1.1.3.1.1. Nursing Mother (**trophos**)*

*1.1.1.1.3.2. Father (**pater**)*
1.1.1.2. Member of a people
    1.1.1.2.1. Images of Association
        *1.1.1.2.1.1. Member of race (**genos**)*
        *1.1.1.2.1.2. Member of nation (**ethnos**)*
        *1.1.1.2.1.3. Member of people (**laos**)*
        *1.1.1.2.1.4. Citizen of heavenly city (**polis**,*
                                  sympolites, politeuma)
        *1.1.1.2.1.5. Neighbor (**plesion**)*
    1.1.1.2.2. Images of Disassociation
        *1.1.1.2.2.1. Temporary resident (**parepidemos**)*
        *1.1.1.2.2.2. Stranger (**paroikos**)*

Notes

1   Banks (1980:59–60) notes that prior to Paul, family terminology was not particularly common, either among the Jews or the mystery religions, to describe the community of the faithful.

2   Elliott (1981:169) argues that in 1 Peter 2:4–10, the other passage in which Peter uses *oikos*, the word should be taken in the sense of 'household' rather than 'building.' However, I believe that the close connection with the 'living stones' image in verses 4 and 5, and the references to Jesus as the cornerstone in verses 6 through 8, make it more likely that the 'spiritual house (*oikos pneumatikos*)' (v. 5) is a temple in which the priests serve. Therefore, the image of the spiritual house will be discussed later, in chapter fifteen.

3   Others so designated include Quartus (Romans 16:24), Sosthenes (1 Corinthians 1:1), Apollos (1 Corinthians 16:12), Titus (2 Corinthians 2:13), Tychicus (Ephesians 6:21 and Colossians 4:7), Epaphroditus (Philippians 2:25), Onesimus (Colossians 4:9), Apphia ('our sister', Philemon 2), Philemon (Philemon 7, 20), Silas (1 Peter 5:12), and two unnamed individuals (2 Corinthians 8:18, 22).

4   Cf. Acts 9:30; 15:40; 2 Corinthians 11:9.

5   Note that when Paul speaks to the hostile Jewish crowd in Jerusalem he nevertheless calls them 'brothers' (Acts 22:1); but when he addresses a predominantly Gentile group of non-believers aboard ship, he calls them simply 'men (*andres*)' (Acts 27:10, 21, 25).

6   Morris (1964:24) contrasts the hierarchical organization of the Qumran community with the Christian Church: 'There we discern no hierarchy, but a band of brethren united in common devotion to Christ.'

7   In this quotation Paul combines and modifies several Old Testament passages, taking God's promise to make us his children, and making explicit the reference to daughters as well as sons: 'you will be my sons and daughters;' this is the only example of figurative use of the term 'daughter' for a Christian believer in the New Testament

letters. But Jesus used this word to address the woman with the issue of blood: 'Daughter (*thygater*), your faith has healed you' (Mark 5:34; cf. Matthew 9:22).

8   Cf. Jesus' debate with the Jews in John 8:31–47, especially verse 36: 'If the Son sets you free, you will be free indeed.'

9   This word does not make distinction according to age or sex (Braumann, DNTT, 1:285), unlike *hyios*, which refers to a male descendant (although *hyios* is used more generically throughout the New Testament). Fernando (1985:16) suggests that *teknon* conveys more tenderness and endearment than the more common word *hyios*.

10   Jesus also uses the image of the *kleronomos* (heir) in his parables (Matthew 21:38; Mark 12:7; Luke 20:14), but not to describe his disciples. Rather he pictures himself as the rightful heir who is rejected and killed by the tenants of the vineyard. However, Jesus does use the related verb *kleronomeo* (inherit) in reference to his disciples: 'Blessed are the meek, for they will inherit the earth' (Matthew 5:5); 'Come, you who are blessed by my Father; take your inheritance, the kingdom prepared for you since the creation of the world' (Matthew 25:34); 'Everyone who has left houses or brothers or sisters or father or mother or children or fields for my sake will receive a hundred times as much and will inherit eternal life' (Matthew 19:29).

11   Verse 29 is a restatement of verse 26: 'You are all sons of God through faith in Christ Jesus.'

12   'Jesus' omission of 'fathers', his valuation of a child, and his practice of calling women followers differ significantly from the patriarchal structure and values of Greco-Roman cities' (Stambaugh and Balch 1986:106).

13   Cf. Fernando (1985:15–26) on 'Leadership as Parenthood'.

14   Bradley (1987:71–72) reports that wet-nursing, which could be performed by either free or slave women, 'was probably a widespread occupation for women of low social status throughout the Roman world'.

15   Best (1988:36) reminds us that babies were breast-fed, not bottle-fed.

16   Stephen, in his address to the Sanhedrin in Acts 7:2, follows the customary respectful usage of addressing the assembly as 'Brothers (*andres adelphoi*) and fathers (*pateres*)'; but Paul, later addressing the same body, says simply 'My brothers' (Acts 23:2).

17   Whitehead and Whitehead (1986:26–27) warn that the danger of fostering unhealthy dependency is present in the contemporary usage of the father image.

18   See also chapter twenty of Greenslade (1984:131–136) on 'Father' and chapter two of Best (1988:29–58) on 'Fatherly Care'.

19   'The term 'race' refers in the New Testament to biological continuity (e.g. Acts 13:26; Philippians 3:5)' (Minear 1960:72).

20   Bietenhard also observes that in classical usage *ethnos* had a derogatory connotation, in the sense of common people, or foreigners in contrast to Hellenists, similar to *barbaros* (non-Greek, barabarian).

7

Appointed and called

In the previous chapter we examined images drawn from relationships into which people are generally born, terms related to household and nation. Next we turn to words which indicate a relationship formed by special appointment or choice. Once again we find that expressions used by Jesus are taken up by the New Testament writers, but that new terms are also introduced.

Chosen

Jesus referred to his followers as 'chosen' (*eklektos*) by God, and as such, under God's special care and protection. Paul uses the term in the same way in Romans 8:33, when he asks, 'Who will bring any charge against those whom God has chosen (*eklekton theou*)?' God is the defender of those whom he has gathered by his grace. The fact that believers are chosen by God is their guarantee of security, in spite of their weakness or their sinfulness, both now and in the life to come.

In Romans 16:13, Paul sends his greetings to Rufus, addressing him as 'chosen in the Lord', a phrase which could have been applied to any Christian. In his pastoral letters Paul uses the term *eklektos* in reference to believers in general. In 2 Timothy 2:10 he says, 'I endure everything for the sake of the elect (*tous eklektous*),' and in Titus 1:1 he identifies himself as an apostle of Jesus Christ 'for the faith of God's elect'. For Paul, to see people as 'chosen by God' is no excuse for personal inaction. No, he sees himself as the means by which God's choice is realized. He gladly expends himself for the sake of those on whom God has placed such high value.

To be chosen by God is to enjoy a great honor. Elliott, in a section entitled 'Election and Eliteness', observes:

> Stress upon the group as 'elected by God' would also serve subsequently to reinforce the self-esteem of the group when challenged by outsiders as well as to provide a rationale for continued separation from the 'less honored' (1981:122).

Yet to be chosen by God is not only to enjoy privilege, but also to assume a responsibility. Peter addresses his first letter to 'God's elect (*eklektois*) ... who have been chosen according to the foreknowledge of God the Father... for obedience to Jesus Christ and sprinkling by his blood' (1 Peter 1:1–2). In bringing together the idea of God's choice with the responsibility for obedience, Peter reminds his readers of the purpose of their selection. The same ethical dimension appears in Paul's exhortation to the Colossians, where he urges them 'as God's chosen people (*eklektoi tou theou*), holy and dearly loved' to live lives of compassion, kindness, humility, gentleness, patience, forgiveness, love, peace, and thankfulness (Colossians 3:12–17).

Coenen notes that the word *eklektos* originated in a military context, but that by the time of Plato it was being used in a political sense, for electing people to a particular task or administrative office. He says:

> [Election] is always, however, accompanied by some kind of obligation or task concerned with the well-being of all the other members of the community of which the one elected forms part. Through its proper organs, the *polis* [city-state] gives the individual who has special gifts the opportunity to develop these for the benefit of all (DNTT, I:536).

This link between the privilege of being chosen and the call to responsible action on behalf of others is found in the biblical use of the term as well.

The Twelve

The idea of 'choice' is linked closely in the Gospels with Jesus' appointment of the Twelve (*dodeka*). They are the representatives of the new Israel, corresponding to the twelve patriarchs. Their selection not only implies a special position of leadership for them within the believing community, but also emphasizes the continuity between the people of God under the old covenant and the people of God under the new covenant.

Twice outside the Gospels the group of apostles are called 'the Twelve'. In Acts 6:2, we read that 'the Twelve[1] gathered all the disciples[2] together' to resolve the problem of equitable food distribution among the widows. Then in 1 Corinthians 15:5 Paul says that Jesus appeared to Peter 'and then to the Twelve.' Thus even

Paul recognizes the special identity of this original group of apostles.

In the book of Acts we see the Twelve forming a leadership team in the Jerusalem fellowship, not only taking the primary role in teaching of the Word and in prayer, but also providing overall direction to the community. Yet the Twelve do not remain long as an identifiable leadership group. In Acts 15 the decisions are made by the 'apostles and elders' (vv. 2, 4, 6, 22–23), and by Acts 21 only the elders are visible (v. 18), with James, not the apostle but rather the brother of Jesus, as the most visible leader. Thus after the initial phase of establishment of the Church, the Twelve begin to recede into the background; there is no attempt to perpetuate the group as such after the martydom of James the apostle in Acts 12:2. Raymond Brown observes:

> The symbolism of the Twelve is associated with the idea that the Christian movement represents the renewal of Israel... When the individual members die, they are not replaced; rather, as founders of the renewed Israel they are immortalized, with names written on foundations of the new Jerusalem (Rev. 21:14) (1970:55).

This term, then, as important as it is in the founding of the Church, is not one which can be applied to any believers or church leaders living today.

Saints

The next few terms appear rarely if at all in the Gospels, but become quite prominent in the other New Testament writings. *Hagios* (saint) is one of most frequently used terms for followers of Jesus, especially in the writings of Paul[3] and in the book of Revelation.[4] Yet, it is rarely used for members of the holy nation in the Old Testament (Seebass, DNTT II:227), and is not used at all by Jesus with reference to his disciples. Whenever it is used of Christians in the New Testament, it occurs in the plural. Although God is named 'the Holy One (*tou hagiou*)' (1 John 2:20), as also is Christ (Acts 3:14; Revelation 3:7), no individual Christian is called by this term.

However, the believers are frequently referred to as saints or holy ones (*hagioi*). This term speaks of the special relationship of the believer to God, as one who has been set apart for God's purposes (similar to *eklektos*). It reminds us of the distinctive calling, character, privilege, and mission of the Christian. Sometimes it is

used simply as a synonym for 'Christian', as when L[...]
Peter's visit to the 'saints' in Lydda and Joppa (Acts[...]
when Paul sends greetings to and from the 'saints' (R[...]
2 Corinthians 13:13; Philippians 4:21-22).

Quite a number of times the word *hagios* is used in connection with ministry, with reference to acts of service and love. For example, Paul refers several times to the offering for the relief of impoverished Christians in Judea as a 'service to the saints' (Romans 15:25-26, 31; 1 Corinthians 16:1; 2 Corinthians 8:4; 9:1, 12). He frequently commends those who have loved, helped, served, or refreshed the 'saints' (1 Corinthians 16:15; Ephesians 1:15; Colossians 1:4; 1 Timothy 5:10; Philemon 5, 7). In Ephesians 4 he describes how gifted individuals have been supplied to the church by Christ 'to prepare God's people (*ton hagion*) for works of service' (v. 12). Perhaps this word is used to express the special importance of these people to God, and therefore their value and worth as both recipients of ministry and agents of ministry.

Several other passages speak of the marvelous privileges that are available to the saints. They are called by God (Romans 1:7; 1 Corinthians 1:2). The Spirit intercedes for them (Romans 8:27). They will judge the world (1 Corinthians 6:1-2). They will receive a glorious inheritance (Ephesians 1:18; Colossians 1:12). The privileges of citizenship are theirs (Ephesians 2:19). They experience the love of God (Ephesians 3:18). Mysteries are disclosed to them (Colossians 1:26). They have been promised future glorification (2 Thessalonians 1:10). The matchless faith of the gospel has been entrusted to them (Jude 3).

Yet none of these benefits exempt them from suffering. Many of the references in the book of Revelation are to the suffering and warfare of the saints (13:7, 10; 14:12; 16:6; 17:6; 18:24). Nevertheless, their prayers are heard by God (5:8; 8:3-4) and their final triumph is assured (11:18; 18:20). To be a saint means ultimately to be rescued and rewarded by God, but not to be shielded from all pain and conflict in the meantime.

In only a few cases is the term *hagios* specifically associated with the call to holy living. In Ephesians 5:3 Paul urges Christians to avoid sexual immorality, impurity, and greed, because 'these are improper for God's holy people (*hagiois*)'. In Revelation 19:8, the bride of the Lamb is dressed in bright, clean, fine linen, representing 'the righteous acts of the saints.'

Freedmen

The writings of Paul contain many allusions to our being set free from bondage and slavery. For example, in Romans 6, Paul says that we have been freed from slavery to sin in order to offer ourselves willingly as servants of God. In 1 Corinthians 8 through 10 he discusses the proper use of Christian freedom, as related to the treatment of the weaker brother. In Galatians 4 and 5 he contrasts bondage to the law with freedom to serve one another. And in Colossians 2 he calls for freedom from mere human regulations. However, the actual word for the slave who has been set free, *apeleutheros*, occurs only in 1 Corinthians 7:22: 'He who was a slave (*doulos*) when he was called by the Lord is the Lord's freedman (*apeleutheros*); similarly, he who was a free man (*eleutheros*) when he was called is Christ's slave (*doulos*).'

Paul is explaining that no matter how enslaved a believer may be sociologically, there is still a far more fundamental freedom that he enjoys; on the other hand, no matter how free he may appear to be in the eyes of society, he is not free to do whatever he wants, but is responsible to the Lord as his master.

The other term used by Paul in this verse, *eleutheros*, refers to the person who was born free, who enjoys the full rights of citizenship in the *polis* (Blunck, DNTT I:715). Peter uses the same word in his exhortation in 1 Peter 2:16, with the same caution to remember that even the one who is free is still Christ's servant: 'Live as free men (*eleutheroi*), but do not use your freedom (*ten eleutherian*) as a cover-up for evil; live as servants (*douloi*) of God.'

The language of freedom, slavery, and manumission provided vivid metaphors for first-century believers. Roman citizens often set their slaves free, and the freed slaves became Roman citizens, usually adopting the status of their former masters. When such slaves were free, they did not always leave their masters, but sometimes chose to remain as members of the family (Stambaugh and Balch 1989:115; Tidball 1984:73). After being set free, however, the former slave did not escape all obligations or restrictions:

> The freedman was bound to his former master (who now became his patron) by certain legal obligations, and even the most successful freedman carried with him a certain stigma of his servile origin: His name proclaimed his status as a freedman; he could not hold public office or

Free but responsible

rise to the status of an equestrian; he could not marry a member of the senatorial aristocracy. On the other hand, any children born after manumission enjoyed complete social freedom and could even rise to the aristocracy (Stambaugh and Balch 1986:115; cf. K. Bradley 1987:81).

Although most of the Roman slaves never gained their freedom, and in spite of the limitations they continued to bear even after manumission, 'it is absolutely clear that slaves coveted freedom and were anxious to become whenever possible part of the great mass of ex-slaves' (K. Bradley 1987:81).

Thus when the early Christians spoke of the believer as *eleutheros* or *apeleutheros*, they employed terms that represented elevated status, with new dignity and privilege. Yet as Paul taught so clearly, no one was truly born free in the sense of the *eleutheros*. Rather, a person must be set free by the gracious act of God, thus becoming a freedman (*eleutheros*). And somewhat as the manumitted slave might return to voluntarily serve in the former household, so the Christian had been set free to serve freely in the household of a new master, the Lord Jesus.

Assembled and called

Sometimes terms become so familiar that we forget the imagery that originally lay behind them. Such may be the case with the next word, *ekklesia*, normally translated as 'church.' It is one of the terms used most frequently to describe the community of followers of Jesus, although it occurs only once on the lips of Jesus, in the well-known statement to Peter in Matthew 16:18: 'And I tell you that you are Peter, and upon this rock I will build my church (*mou ten ekklesian*), and the gates of Hades will not overcome it.'

The word is used in several senses. In the first place, it commonly refers to the gathering of Christians in a particular locality. Thus we find references to particular cities—the church at Jerusalem (Acts 8:1), at Antioch (13:1), in Cenchrea (Romans 16:1), and in Corinth (1 Corinthians 1:2; 2 Corinthians 1:1), as well as the church of the Laodiceans (Colossians 4:15), and of the Thessalonians (1 Thessalonians 1:1). There are specific references to the church in Priscilla and Aquila's house (Romans 16:4–5; 1 Corinthians 16:19), and in Nympha's house (Colossians 4:15), in addition to general geographic references to the church throughout Judea, Galilee, and Samaria (Acts 9:31), the churches throughout Syria and Cilicia (Acts 15:41), the Galatian churches (1 Corinthians 16:1), the churches in the province of Asia (1 Corinthians 16:19), the Macedonian churches (2 Corinthians 8:1), and the churches of Judea (Galatians 1:22).

In many other passages *ekklesia* has reference to a group (or groups) of Christians meeting together regularly in the same locality, even if the specific geographic reference is not stated, as in the following examples:

> ... what I teach everywhere in every church
> (1 Corinthians 4:17);

> ... when you come together as a church
> (1 Corinthians 11:18);

> show these men the proof of your love and the reason for
> our pride in you, so that the churches can see it
> (2 Corinthians 8:24);

> not one church shared with me in the matter of giving
> and receiving, except you only (Philippians 4:15);

> he should call the elders of the church to pray over him
> (James 5:14);

> they have told the church about your love (3 John 6).

Some passages use 'church' in a more general sense, to denote Christians in general, but still at a particular time and in identifiable places, as when Paul says, 'I persecuted the church of God' (1 Corinthians 15:9; Galatians 1:13). But there is an even broader and loftier usage of the term *ekklesia*, in passages like Ephesians 1:22, which states that Christ has been appointed 'head over everything for the church', and Ephesians 5:23–32, in which Paul compares the love of a husband for his wife to that of Christ for the church. In one of the most magnificent tributes to Christ in all of scripture, Paul says that Christ is 'the head of the body, the church' (Colossians 1:18). The author of Hebrews says that his readers 'have come to the church of the firstborn, whose names are written in heaven' (12:23).

Thus *ekklesia* has a broad range of references, from a specific group of Christians gathered in a home, to all of the assemblies in a given geographical area, to the entire group of believers in Chr..., past and present, on earth and in heaven, seen as a whole. But certain aspects of the term can be seen through all the usages.

In the first place, it is clear that *ekklesia* refers to people, not to buildings or to institutional structures. In New Testament usage, churches can decide, welcome, gather, pray, send greetings, enjoy peace, be grateful, enjoy hospitality, praise, choose, see, share, and suffer. They can also be destroyed, seized by fear, stumbled, despised, edified, persecuted, burdened, and imitated. These are all words that describe people, not bricks or organization charts.

The use of such verbs in connection with *ekklesia* also indicates that the church is a group of people connected together, acting in harmony, sharing feelings and experiences, not merely an abstraction or a theoretical way of grouping people, like saying 'all left-handed people' or 'those with March birthdays'. The church is comprised of people vitally interrelated with one another, because Christ has called them together.

Thus we come to the character of the word *ekklesia*, and its basic metaphorical meaning. Originally it was a military word, referring to a call for the army to assemble. Later it came to be used of a civic gathering, referring to a group of people called together to assemble. Coenen remarks:

> Thus *ekklesia*, centuries before the translation of the Old Testament and the time of the New Testament, was clearly characterized as a political phenomenon, repeated according to certain rules and within a certain framework. It was the assembly of the full citizens, functionally rooted in the constitution of the democracy, an assembly in which fundamental political and judicial decisions were taken... The word *ekklesia*, throughout the Greek and Hellenistic areas, always retained its reference to the assembly of the *polis* (DNTT, I:291).

Coenen also asserts that *ekklesia* was almost never used for guilds or religious fellowships. In fact, none of the words used by the Greeks for such religious assemblies (e.g. *heorte, synodos, koinos, synagoge*[5]) found their way into the New Testament language of community gatherings (DNTT I:291–292; cf. Stambaugh and Balch 1986:138).

In the Old Testament, there were two words for the gathering of the people. The general word for the community as a whole was *edah*, usually translated by *synagoge*. The other word, *qahal*, is 'the ceremonial expression for the assembly that results from the covenant'; whenever *ekklesia* appears in the Old Testament, it always translates *qahal* (Coenen, DNTT, I:292, 295). Meeks says that 'we have no evidence that [*ekklesia*] was ever applied to the Jewish community in a given place' (1983:80).

Thus the New Testament authors avoided the term which had become associated since the exile with the Judaistic practice of the synagogue, and instead employed a term which had Old Testament associations of the calling together of the covenant people, but also the assembly of free citizens of the Greek *polis*.[6] Thus *ekklesia* describes a group of people brought together not by their own initiative, but by God's, not by their voluntary decision to associate, but by their response to the prior call of God. And it describes those who enjoy the full rights and privileges of the community; there are no second-class citizens or outsiders in the *ekklesia*; all have the rights of citizens, all are under the covenant.

Furthermore, as Coenen asserts, the fundamental nature of the *ekklesia* is an event; it is an action which calls into being, and which continues to call into being, the assembly, centered around the anticipated presence of the living Christ (DNTT, I:299). Thus *ekklesia* is a dynamic concept, with strong verbal imagery underlying the noun, in a way that is not evident in the more static English word 'church.'

Closely related to the previous term (*ekklesia*, the community of those who have been called together) is the word 'called' (*kletos*). Whereas *ekklesia* focuses on the assembly of the group in response to the call, *kletos* emphasizes the personal summons itself. The word is passive. The actor is God. We are seen as responders, not as initiators, as those moving forward because of the summons.

A number of passages speak of Christians in general as being called. Thus Paul addresses the Romans as those 'called to belong to Jesus Christ (*kletoi Iesou Christou*)' (1:6) and 'called to be saints (*kletois hagiois*)' (1:7; cf. 1 Corinthians 1:2). In Romans 8:28 he affirms that 'in all things God works for the good of those who love him, who have been called according to his purpose'; the following verses spell out the purpose of that call: to be justified, glorified, and conformed to the image of God's Son. Thus the calling is not to a specific vocation, but to a pattern of holy living. Paul also refers to the Corinthians as 'those whom God has God has called' (1 Corinthians 1:24), and in the first verse of his letter, Jude addresses 'those who have been called', without further qualification or elaboration.

On two occasions Paul speaks of being called in a more specific sense. In Romans 1:1 he identifies himself as 'called to be an apostle (*kletos apostolos*).' In 1 Corinthians 1:1 he expands the same phrase as 'called to be an apostle of Christ Jesus by the will of God.' The addition of the reference to God's will further emphasizes that his ministry is a response to God's summons; the call comes from outside and above; his ministry is not a self-chosen vocation nor the expression of an inner urge to find his destiny.

Priests

The remaining image to be explored in this chapter is not used by Jesus, and is referred to only obliquely by Paul,[7] yet it has become one of the most important, and most controversial, in the later history of the church. This metaphor is expressed in two words: *hierateuma* (priesthood) and *hiereus* (priest).

The Book of Exodus introduces the idea of the corporate priesthood of the entire nation of Israel even before the appointment of the first Levitical priests. At the foot of Mount Sinai, before the giving of the Ten Commandments, God says to his people: 'You will be for me a kingdom of priests and a holy nation' (Exodus 19:6). The same promise is extended to Israel regathered by the Messiah in the Year of Jubilee, as pictured by Isaiah: 'You will be called priests of the LORD, you will be named ministers of our God' (61:6). Although the majority of references in the Old Testament concerning priests are specifically to the sons of Aaron and to their duties related to the tabernacle and the temple, these two passages speak of a more general function of standing between God and the rest of mankind which is part of their call to be a 'holy nation'.

Raymond Brown observes that: 'In Israelite theology the whole people was worthy of the title "kingdom of priests, holy nation" (Exodus 19:6), but that did not in any way prevent or conflict with the development of a specialized priesthood' (1970:7). Yet it is precisely this kind of 'specialized' terminology that the New Testament writers specifically avoid. When they speak of 'priests' and 'priesthood' they are referring to privileges that belong to all of God's people, not to an élite group of leaders or liturgical functionaries. In fact, given the great importance of the priestly functions in Israel's spiritual life, as well as the plethora of priests and temples in the

Hellenistic cities, it is remarkable that the writers of the New Testament did not make greater use of these metaphors. We must conclude that it was not a matter of oversight, but of conscious avoidance.

The explanation suggested by Brown is that 'the early Christians acknowledged the Jewish priesthood as valid and therefore never thought of a priesthood of their own;' thus, not until the temple was destroyed, and the Christians began to think of themselves as a distinct religion rather than simply a sect of Judaism, could the idea of a Christian priesthood emerge (1970:17–19).

No individual in the New Testament is ever called a 'priest.' The metaphor is always used in a corporate sense. The most extended development is found in 1 Peter 2. There Peter begins by describing believers as living stones being built together into a spiritual house, but then changes the image: 'to be a holy priesthood (*hierateuma hagion*), offering spiritual sacrifices acceptable to God through Jesus Christ' (2:5). In the next few verses he develops the metaphor of Jesus Christ as the cornerstone, and then returns in verse 9 to the theme of priesthood, quoting from Exodus 19 and other Old Testament passages: 'But you are a chosen people, a royal priesthood (*basileion hierateuma*), a holy nation, a people belonging to God, that you may declare the praises of him who called you out of darkness into his wonderful light.' The privileges of leading in worship, and of offering sacrifice, usually reserved for the priests, now belong to all of God's people. Nor are these functions given to a special class of people within the church. The image of priesthood is not used to imply special authority for the leader, or restricted performance of liturgical ceremonies, or any unusual measure of personal consecration or holiness. Rather the privileges described are open to all. Morris, however, wisely cautions:

> This refers not to 'the priesthood of each believer' but to 'the priesthood of all believers.' That is to say it is a corporate ministry, a ministry exercised by the whole church ... The New Testament makes it plain that the Church is a priestly body ministering constantly in Christ's name on the basis of what Christ has done. But it knows nothing of individual 'priests' within the priestly body (1964:31–32).

The book of Revelation also employs the image of priest on several occasions in describing the privileged position made available to Christians. In Revelation 1:6, John describes Jesus Christ as the one who 'has made (*epoiesen*) us to be a kingdom and priests to serve his God and Father (*hiereis toi theoi kai patri autou*).' Note that this priesthood is by God's appointment; in this context it is not a hereditary office nor a task for which one volunteers.

Again, in Revelation 5:9–10 the four living creatures and the twenty-four elders sing praise to the Lamb: 'You are worthy to take the scroll and to open its seals, because you were slain, and with your blood you purchased men for God from every tribe and language and people and nation. You have made them to be a kingdom and priests to serve our God, and they will reign on the earth.'

In view of the explicit mention of people from every tribe, language, people, and nation, it is clear that this new priesthood is not just for the exclusive few; not for the descendants of one priest, Aaron, or for one tribe, Levi, or even for one nation, Israel. The extraordinary value ascribed by God to the entire priestly people is implied by the price that was paid for them: the Lamb's own blood.

This section of Revelation also highlights another aspect of the priestly function: to share in God's rule, just as the priests taught the Law to God's people and helped to order the life of the community accordingly. Although all are on the same level as priests, this equality is not inconsistent with the exercise of authority (although the authority in view here is not authority within the community, but authority that will be exercised over the created order and/or over the unbelieving world). Once again, in Revelation 20:6, the idea of priesthood is associated with the function of ruling: 'Blessed and holy are those who have part in the first resurrection. The second death has no power over them, but they will be priests of God and of Christ and will reign with him for a thousand years.'

The words 'blessed' and 'holy' underscore the themes of joy and privilege that are associated with this priesthood.

Additions to the taxonomy

The next section of the taxonomy can now be expanded as follows:

    1.1.2. Relationship by appointment
        1.1.2.1. Chosen (*eklektos*)*
        1.1.2.2. Twelve (*dodeka*)*
        1.1.2.3. Saint (**hagios**)
        1.1.2.4. Freedman (**apeleutheros, eleutheros**)
        1.1.2.5. Member of assembly/church (**ekklesia**)
        1.1.2.6. One who is called (**kletos**)
        1.1.2.7. Priest (**hiereus**)

Notes

1   The original number of twelve, reduced through the loss of Judas, has been restored through the election of Matthias (Acts 1:15–26).

2   Note Luke's usage of 'disciple' in the broad sense, referring to all the believers in general, in contrast to the twelve apostles chosen by Jesus to leave everything to be with him and to be trained by him.

3   More than 35 times in Romans, 1 and 2 Corinthians, Ephesians, Philippians, Colossians, 1 and 2 Thessalonians, 1 Timothy, and Philemon.

4   At least twelve occurrences.

5   The one exception is James 2:2.

6   Banks (1980:49) asserts that Paul's understanding of *ekklesia* combines ideas of the voluntary association, the household, and the universal, eternal commonwealth, all of which expressed the ideas of community of the people at that time. Thus he shows how the metaphors related to the church overlap and blend together. In this section, however, we are focusing on the distinctive character of each metaphor, and for that purpose we must note carefully the existing associations of the word *ekklesia* at the time Paul and others began to use it.

7   See remarks in chapter 10 about *latreuo* and *leitourgeo*.

8

Friends and followers

In this chapter we consider terms of voluntary association. Many of the images discussed in the previous two chapters have highlighted God's initiative in the relationship that binds his people to himself, and them to one another. God is the heavenly Father who has adopted children and established a spiritual family. His gracious choice has produced the holy nation. He is the builder of the new Jerusalem in which believers have been granted citizenship. He has freed the slaves, called the assembly together, and appointed the priests.

The next group of terms continue to emphasize the dimension of relationships in the Christian community, more than the tasks to which they are called. But the roles used to describe these relationships are generally ones that people choose for themselves. That is, we have no control over who adopts us, or who our brothers and sisters are, or the race into which we are born, or the call extended to us. But we can choose our friends, our business partners, and the ones whom we will imitate. As we will see, the initiative of God is still prominent, even in these metaphors of voluntary association, but the dimension of human response becomes more important.

Friend

We noted in chapter two that Jesus used two words translated 'friend': *philos*, which has a warm and positive connotation, and *hetairos*, which conveys a more cool and distant tone. Since *hetairos* does not occur outside the Gospels, we turn our attention to the use of the term *philos*. Apart from Jesus' use of the term, and other occurrences of the word in ordinary social usage (e.g. officials in Ephesus described as 'friends' of Paul, Acts 19:31), the only appearance of *philos* as a term for Christians comes in John's third letter. In his closing remarks, John says, 'The friends (*hoi philoi*) here send their greetings. Greet the friends (*tous philous*) there by name' (v. 14). It is interesting that the Gospel writer who records Jesus' statement, 'I have called you friends' (John 15:15), should also be the New Testament writer to use this term for his fellow-disciples. With this word he expresses the love (*philia, phileo*), the bond of companionship and shared life in community, that ties believers together.

Philos was an ordinary word used for friends or relatives (Günther, DNTT, II:547). However, there was a more restricted use of the word current in the Hellenistic world as well, referring to someone who had been drawn into a specific relation of intimacy, and some measure of dependence, with a person in higher position, such as the head of a household. For example, Tidball remarks:

> To be a friend or client was not to be the recipient of passing affection... The new position [e.g. of a slave set free] is usually described as one of 'intimacy.' The master's affairs would become his affairs and they were in the joint enterprise together without secrets (1984:80).

The voluntary aspect of the 'friend' relationship is emphasized by Moltmann through a contrast with the term 'brother':

> Compared with the concept of the friend, the concept 'brother' implies the inescapable destiny to brotherhood even in conflicts. It makes brotherly love unnecessary. Compared with the concept of the brother, the concept 'friend' stresses freedom. Rightly understood, the friend is the person who 'loves in freedom' (1977:316).

Wedding participant

The imagery of the wedding, used a number of times by Jesus in his parables, is employed by other New Testament writers, but with somewhat different vocabulary. Instead of comparisons to friends of the bride or bridegroom, or to guests at the wedding banquet, the emphasis shifts to the bride (*nymphe*) herself, who now becomes a symbol of the church. The roots of this image are found in the Old Testament, where God's covenant with his people is often described as a marriage (Isaiah 54:5; Jeremiah 2:2; Ezekiel 16:8; Hosea 2:16; cf. Minear 1960:52), and where there is often associated a strong note of joy (Günther, DNTT, I:585).

In writing to the Corinthians, Paul compares himself to the father of the bride, promising the virgin daughter (the Corinthian church) to the future husband (Christ), in a manner typical of cultures in which marriages were arranged. He expresses concern over whether this daughter's affections have now been captured by another lover, and whether her purity is still intact. He says: 'I promised you to one husband, to Christ, so that I might present you as a pure virgin (*parthenon hagnen*) to him' (2 Corinthians 11:2). In the image of the church as a virgin, the consummation of the union is still future; the main focus of the image is pure devotion, exclusive allegiance.

Although *parthenos* means specifically a virgin, an unmarried woman, the word *nymphe* can equally be applied to a virgin, a young woman, and a young wife; it means bride or betrothed. 'The bride can also be called *gyne* because by Jewish laws of marriage the engaged woman was already regarded as wife' (Günther, DNTT, II:584). In Ephesians 5, Paul instructs husbands to love their wives just as Christ loves the church; yet in those verses, even though the image is certainly implied, Christ is not specifically called the bridegroom nor is the church called the bride.

The image of the bride is used repeatedly in the final chapters of Revelation. In chapter 19 the announcement is given: 'The wedding of the Lamb has come, and his bride (*he gyne autou*) has made herself ready' (v. 7); she is clothed in bright linen, representing the righteous acts of God's people. In chapter 21 one of the angels invites John, 'Come, I will show you the bride (*ten nymphen*), the wife (*ten gynaika*) of the Lamb' (v. 9); then the angel shows him the new city of Jerusalem in all its splendor; here the images of the bride and of the city (*polis*, v. 10) blend together. The book of Revelation closes with an invitation to the thirsty to come and receive the free gift of the water of life: 'The Spirit and the bride (*he nymphe*) say, "Come!"' (22:17). The image of the bride thus conveys ideas of beauty, purity, undivided devotion, joyful celebration, and intimate love. The main link with Jesus' usage of wedding imagery is the atmosphere of joy.

Follower

The Gospel of Mark records Jesus' call to the first disciples in these words: 'Come, follow me (*Deute opiso mou*) and I will make you fishers of men' (1:17; cf. Matthew 4:19). Immediately they left their nets and followed (*ekolouthesan*) him (Mark 1:18; Matthew 4:20, 22). Likewise Levi the tax collector was enlisted with the summons: 'Follow me (*Akolouthei moi*)' (Mark 2:14). The life of 'following' into which Jesus invited his disciples was not so much a matter of literal physical positioning, like sheep following a shepherd, as much as it was a commitment to close association with him and imitation of his life. Throughout this study we have frequently referred to Jesus' 'followers', in recognition of the image first implied in their call (even though the noun 'follower' does not occur in the New Testament, nor is *akoloutheo* ever used purely in a metaphorical sense).[2]

DISCIPLE

A number of New Testament terms can be included under the heading of those who have decided to 'follow' Jesus, identifying with his life and calling. First is *mathetes* (disciple), already discussed at length in chapter two. Outside of the four Gospels, all of the occurrences of this word are found in the book of Acts, beginning in chapter 6 and continuing through chapter 21. Never is the word used in the restricted sense for the Twelve (as it is sometimes in the Gospels). Rather it is Luke's general term for Christians, used in the same way as 'believer' or 'brother'. The identification between 'disciple' and 'Christian' is made explicit in Acts 11:26, where we read: 'the disciples were called Christians first at Antioch.'

Usually *mathetes* occurs in the plural, but a few individuals are also called 'disciple': Ananias (9:10), Saul (9:26), Tabitha (9:36), Timothy (16:2), and Mnason (21:16). The term is used for both new and established believers, and for both Jews and Gentiles. In general it refers to the rank and file of believers. Nowhere is a church leader or apostle explicitly called a 'disciple'. The verb *matheteuo* (to make disciples, cf. Matthew 28:19) occurs in Acts 14:21, where we read that in Lystra and Derbe Paul and Barnabas 'won a large number of disciples (*matheteusantes hikanous*)'; this passage, besides illustrating that the apostles' activities were in obedience to Jesus' Great Commission, indicates that believers could be called 'disciples' from the very onset of conversion. In addition to Luke's own use of the term as narrator in Acts, *mathetes* is also found in Peter's remarks to the Jerusalem Council in Acts 15:10, where he asks, 'Why do you try to test God by putting on the necks of the disciples (*ton matheton*) a yoke that neither we nor our fathers have been able to bear?'

Only twice in Acts is *mathetes* associated with any leader other than the Lord. In Acts 9:25 we read that '[Saul's] followers (*hoi mathetai*) took him by night and lowered him in a basket,' thus

110

enabling him to escape from Damascus. Notice that here the reference to these people as *mathetai* is Luke's expression, not Paul's. Then in Acts 20:30 Paul warns the Ephesian elders about false teachers who will emerge in their fellowship 'to draw away disciples after them'.

It is striking that a term used so frequently by the Gospel writers, and found so often on the lips of Jesus, should be so completely unused by the leaders of the early church in reference to those that they themselves brought to the Lord and nurtured in faith—especially in view of the popularity in today's church of the vocabulary of 'discipling' and references to 'my disciples'. Perhaps the reluctance of the New Testament writers to use this term arose because they associated it with apprenticeship to the Lord himself, not to any human leader. Thus when they heard the Lord's command to 'Go and make disciples' (Matthew 28:19), they understood the emphasis to be on persuading people to follow Jesus, rather than on gathering a group of followers around themselves.

The basic meaning of *mathetes* is 'learner.' Müller explains that in Greek usage:

> A man is called a *mathetes* when he binds himself to someone else in order to acquire his practical and theoretical knowledge. He may be an apprentice in a trade, a student of medicine, or a member of a philosophical school. One can only be a *mathetes* in the company of a *didaskalos*, a master or teacher, to whom the *mathetes* since the days of the Sophists generally had to pay a fee (DNTT, I:484).

The word *mathetes* is found very rarely in a few alternate readings of the Old Testament. The vocabulary of the Rabbi and his disciples emerged, then, not from the Old Testament, but from Judaism's contact with Greek philosophy. However, the usage of this term in the New Testament goes beyond the Greek concept, for in the Gospels *mathetes* 'is used to indicate the total attachment to someone in discipleship' (Müller, DNTT, I:486).

Tidball has observed that although the term 'prophet' was controversial when applied to Jesus in first-century Palestine, 'enemies and disciples alike... were willing to accept that Jesus was a Rabbi' (1984:39); he affirms that in a number of respects, the way that Jesus called and trained his disciples was typical of rabbinic practices of that day. However, Müller (DNTT, I:488) notes the differences between the role assumed by Jesus, and that of the ordinary rabbi or Greek teacher. For one thing, although ordinary disciples normally volunteered to join the 'school', Jesus issued a decisive call (and sometimes even discouraged those who tried to volunteer). Furthermore, disciples in the other schools expected to graduate and to become 'masters' themselves, but Jesus called people to a lifelong surrender and commitment to follow.

In the Book of Acts the radical commitment involved in the *mathetes* role is not made as explicit as it is in the Gospels, perhaps because Luke is assuming knowledge of his first treatise. However, the application of the term to the entire community of believers is a reminder that for anyone to follow Jesus is to enroll in a school from which one never graduates.[3]

IMITATOR

Four other words related to the idea of following can be added to Jesus' use of *mathetes*. Paul urges the Ephesian believers to 'be imitators (*mimetai*) of God, as dearly loved children' (5:1); specifically, they are exhorted to demonstrate the self-sacrificing love of Christ. The idea of imitation naturally arises from the image of a child following in the footsteps of a parent.

Another dimension of this imitation is introduced in Paul's first letter to the Corinthians where he says, 'I urge you to imitate me (*mimetai mou ginesthe*)' (4:16), and, 'Follow my example (*mimetai mou ginesthe*), as I follow the example of Christ (*kathos kago Christou*)' (11:1). In Philippians 3:17, Paul invites the church to 'join with others in following my example (*symmimetai mou ginesthe*).' Twice he commends the Thessalonian believers for their willingness to imitate the example of other believers as well as the Lord: 'you became imitators (*mimetai*) of us and of the Lord' (1 Thessalonians 1:6), and, 'you, brothers, became imitators of God's churches in Judea' (1 Thessalonians 2:14).

In classical Greek usage, the *symmimetes* is an imitator, 'especially a performer or an artist who imitates' (Bauder, DNTT, I:490). The Jewish rabbis spoke of imitating God, or the lives of outstanding people. DeBoer (1962), in a major study of this word group, notes that the Greeks understood how essential the process of imitation was in education and in character development. Therefore, Paul was drawing on a word with a rich background of usage and association. DeBoer emphasizes that Paul invited imitation only from those who were his spiritual children. Nor does Paul expect the believers to imitate him in all his personal idiosyncracies, but only in those respects in which he is modeling the character and mission of Jesus Christ.[4]

Paul's use of the term *mimetes* corresponds to Jesus' call to become a *mathetes*. In this way the importance of learning from human role models is not overlooked, but the central allegiance remains focused on Jesus Christ.

FOLLOWER OF THE WAY

In considering the image of following, we should also include the several references in the book of Acts to Christianity as 'the Way (*hodos*)', with Christians as followers of the Way. Luke reports in Acts 9:2 that Saul had letters from the high priest so that he could imprison any in Damascus 'who belonged to the Way.' In Ephesus, Luke reports, some of the Jews 'refused to believe and publicly maligned the Way' (19:9); later, in the same city, 'there arose a great disturbance about the Way' (19:23). In Acts 22:4, speaking to the crowd in Jerusalem, Paul recalls his earlier life, and says, 'I persecuted the followers of this Way.' In his testimony before Felix, Paul says, 'I worship the God of our fathers as a follower of the Way' (24:14); a few verses later Luke describes Felix as 'well acquainted with the Way' (24:22). This is a term, then, that believers chose for themselves, unlike 'Christian', which was coined for them.

A 'way' is a road or path. To describe Christianity as 'the Way' is to imply a distinctive manner of life, a pattern of behavior, and also to imply a destination and a goal. The Christian life is not merely a pattern of belief, or an act of mental assent, but a framework for action. To be a follower of the Way is also to give exclusive allegiance to Jesus, who spoke of the 'narrow road (*he hodos he apagousa*) that leads to life' (Matthew 7:13–14), and who said, 'I am the Way (*Ego eimi ho hodos*)' (John 14:6).[5]

BELIEVER

One of the most commonly used terms for followers of Jesus, especially on the part of Luke and Paul, is 'believers (*hoi pisteuontes* or *hoi pistoi*)'. Luke uses these words many times in Acts in general reference to followers of Jesus, whether Jew or Gentile (2:44; 4:32; 10:45; 15:5; 16:1; 19:18; 21:20, 25; 22:19). Paul uses the terms frequently in his letters as well (1 Corinthians 14:22; 2 Corinthians 6:15; Ephesians 1:1, 19; 1 Thessalonians 1:7; 2 Thessalonians 1:10; 1 Timothy 4:10; 5:16).

The verbal form, *hoi pisteuontes*, indicates that believing in Jesus is an ongoing state of trust and commitment. The noun, *hoi pistoi*, indicates the solid commitment of faith which describes these individuals. In both cases, the object of faith is the gospel, and more particularly, Jesus Christ himself. As Paul and Silas said to the Philippian jailor, 'Believe in (*pisteuson eis*) the Lord Jesus, and you will be saved—you and your household' (Acts 16:31). The distinguishing mark of the Christian is that he or she is a believer; it is this which ties Jews and Gentiles together, and which divides those who are truly in the church from those who are not. Belief in Jesus Christ forms the common bond which makes possible the remarkable sharing seen in Acts 2:44 and 4:32. It is what delivers us from the kingdom of darkness and ushers us into the kingdom of light (Acts 19:18; cf. 2 Corinthians 6:15, 1 Timothy 4:10). It is the distinguishing mark which causes some to be persecuted while others are left alone (Acts 22:19). It qualifies us to experience the resurrection power of Christ (Ephesians 1:19–20). No term more fully captures what it is to be a Christian.

CHRISTIAN

The term 'Christian (*Christianos*)' is another which can be classed under 'follower'. An interesting aspect of this term is that it arose not within the Christian community, but as a somewhat mocking nickname employed by outsiders; nevertheless, it was soon adopted by the early disciples as a badge of identification with their Lord. As first used in Antioch (Acts 11:26),[6] the nickname expressed the fact that the disciples were seen as followers of the 'Christ-sect', much like those loyal to Herod were called the 'Herodians (*Herodianoi*)' (Mark 3:6; 12:13; Matthew 22:16). Perhaps the term also indicated that, for better or for worse, depending on the perspective of the beholder, these people were speaking and behaving much like Christ. Stambaugh and Baugh (1986:149) propose that the disciples may have been called 'Christus people' in Antioch because it was there that they first stood out from Judaism as a distinct sect.[7]

In Acts 26:28, in a tone of mild sarcasm, Agrippa asks Paul, 'Do you think that in such a short time you can persuade me to be a Christian?' In his first letter, Peter encourages his readers: 'If you suffer as a Christian, do not be ashamed, but praise God that you bear that name' (1 Peter 4:16). In both cases, the term is introduced in contexts where believers are being scorned or persecuted for their identification with Jesus Christ.

Beloved

The next word of voluntary relationship, 'beloved (*agapetos*)', is an affectionate term of address, used often in the New Testament letters, and sometimes found in combination with other terms like 'children (*tekna*, *teknia*)' and 'brothers (*adelphoi*).' Since Jesus had said that the distinctive mark of his community of disciples would be their love for one another (John 13:34–35), it is not surprising to find this word used so frequently in their communication with one another. This term emphasizes that the church is not simply a group of co-workers or fellow-pilgrims, drawn together by a common task and destination, but rather it is also knit together at the level of affections.

Every one of the New Testament letter writers, except for James, uses this affectionate term.[8] John uses it six times in the five short chapters of his first letter. Thus the relationship of these spiritual leaders to the congregations to which they wrote, with whatever authority they exercised, was based on love. As Jesus explained in John chapter 10, the difference between the Good Shepherd and the hired hand is found in the loving concern that the shepherd bears for the sheep.

The same word used for the believers' love for one another is also used by Paul of God's love for the believer. He addresses his readers in Romans 1:7: 'To all in Rome who are loved by God (*agapetois theou*),' and exhorts the Colossian Christians: 'as God's chosen people, holy and dearly loved (*egapemenoi*)' (3:12). Thus in loving one another we are loving those on whom God has already set his love.

Partner

The next term of voluntary association is *koinonos* (partner). Paul describes Titus as 'my partner and fellow-worker among you' (2 Corinthians 8:23), and appeals to Philemon to welcome Onesimus by saying, 'if you consider me a partner' (Philemon 17). In the book of Revelation, the author John identifies himself as 'your brother and companion (*synkoinonos*) in the suffering and kingdom and patient endurance that are ours in Christ Jesus' (Revelation 1:9).

This word *koinonos* occurs in Luke 5:10 in connection with James and John, who were partners with Simon Peter in the fishing business. It also occurs in Revelation 18:4 where the followers of Jesus are warned to disassociate themselves from Babylon, the wicked trade center that symbolizes the world system, and not to be a 'partner' with her in her sins. Both of these passages illustrate the secular and commercial associations that help us to see the implications of this image.

Underlying the whole word group that includes *koinonos* and the frequently occurring *koinonia* (fellowship) is the phenomenon of voluntary associations in the Hellenistic world. As Tidball says:

> Voluntary associations proliferated, especially in Greek areas, in New Testament days... People would gather with a common interest; a social or philanthropic cause; a trade or philosophy (1984:86).

All of these associations had a religious dimension. They provided their participants with a depth of personal relationship and a sense of identity, based not on similar social status or background but on common goals. Their functions included common meals, caring for one another in sickness, and helping with burial expenses.[9] In fact, the bonds formed were so close that sometimes the authorities became uneasy about the potential power of these associations, and banned them:

> It is precisely the appeal across barriers of family, ethnic origin, and social status that aroused the hopes of the alienated as well as the anxieties of the privileged (Kee 1980:84).

Similarly, Sampley observes:

> To belong was a strong cultural drive and had been so since the disintegration of both the *polis* and the sense of identity it had offered. To counter insularity some people even resorted to membership in several associations at the same time (1980:6).

The parallels with the first-century Christian fellowships are obvious. When the apostles Paul and John spoke of partnership with fellow-Christians, they were invoking one of the most powerful images of intimate, interdependent relationship known in the world of their day.

Patroness/helper

One final term of voluntary relationship must be mentioned. In Romans 16:2, Paul sends greetings to Phoebe, saying, 'she has been a great help to many people (*prostatis pollon*), including me.' The word *prostatis* means protectress, patroness, helper, and corresponds to the masculine *prostates*, which was found in both Jewish and pagan religious circles (Bauer 1979:718). Stambaugh and Balch link this term with the voluntary societies just described:[10]

> The *thiasoi* that met in Greek cities and the *collegia* in Roman cities resembled Christian communities in several significant ways... Most of these societies depended on the generosity of one or several patrons to supplement the more modest contributions of ordinary members... The hosts of Christian house churches functioned in a way analogous to that of such patrons... [*Prostatis*] probably denotes a woman who functions as a patroness to some society (1986:140).

In this context, the term does not denote authoritative leadership, but rather a ministry of generous care for the congregation (Malherbe 1983:98).

Additions to the taxonomy

The following additions can now be made to the section of the taxonomy entitled 'Relationship by voluntary association':

> 1.1.3. Relationship by voluntary association
> > 1.1.3.1. Friend
> > > 1.1.3.1.1. Friend (*philos*)*
> > > 1.1.3.1.2. Friend (*hetairos*)
> > 1.1.3.2. Wedding participant
> > > 1.1.3.2.1. Friend of bridegroom (*hyios tou nymphonos*)
> > > 1.1.3.2.2. Friend of bride—virgin with lamp
> > > 1.1.3.2.3. Guest at wedding banquet
> > > *1.1.3.2.4. Virgin engaged (**parthenos**)*
> > > *1.1.3.2.5. Bride (**nymphe, gyne**)*
> > 1.1.3.3. Follower
> > > 1.1.3.3.1. Disciple (*mathetes*)*
> > > *1.1.3.3.2. Imitator (**mimetes**)*
> > > *1.1.3.3.3. Follower of the way (**hodos**)*
> > > *1.1.3.3.4. Believer (**pistos**)*
> > > *1.1.3.3.5. Christian (**Christianos**)*
> > *1.1.3.4. Beloved (**agapetos**)*
> > *1.1.3.5. Partner (**koinonos, synkoinonos**)*
> > *1.1.3.6. Patroness/helper (**prostatis**)*

Notes

1   Cf. parallel expression in 1:20: *apelthon opiso autou*.

2   Blendinger, DNTT, I:480–483. For this reason 'follower' was not included in the typology of terms used by Jesus in Part One; but it will be used as a heading in the expanded typology of Part Two.

3   Dulles (1987) suggests that the most appropriate contemporary model for the church is a 'community of disciples', a term which suggests an 'alternative society' (p. 207).

4   Cf. Tidball (1986:108–109), who draws heavily on DeBoer.

5   Cf. Minear (1960:148–150).

6   In this verse and those immediately surrounding, we find several of what have become the most common terms for the followers of Jesus: church, disciples, Christians, brothers.

7   Rengstorf (DNTT, II:343) observes that for the term to arise, *Christos* must have taken the meaning of a proper name, perhaps because of its similarity to the common name Chrestos.

8   Thus Paul (1 Corinthians 10:14; 2 Corinthians 7:1; 12:19; Philippians 2:12; 4:1; Colossians 4:14; Philemon 1); Peter (1 Peter 2:11; 4:12; 2 Peter 3:1, 8, 14, 17); author of Hebrews (6:9); Jude (vv. 3, 17, 20); and John (1 John 2:7; 3:2, 21; 4:1, 7, 11; 2 John 1–2, 5).

9   Cf. Banks (1980:49); Cobble (1988:78–79, 96, 101); Malherbe 1983:88–89); Meeks (1983:31–32); and Sampley (1980), who provides a full discussion of the whole concept of partnership in the Greco-Roman world.

10 So also Malherbe (1983:98) and Meeks (1983:60).

9

Serving under authority

In the previous three chapters we have examined terms and images based on people—family members, citizens, freedmen, priests, friends, patrons, and so on—where the emphasis is on the relationships that link followers of Jesus to the Lord and to one another. We now turn to human images which focus our attention instead on the task. In Part One we saw that Jesus invited his disciples to be 'with him', that is, to enter a personal relationship, but also sent them out to teach and to serve in his name, that is, to engage in a task. Of course it is not always possible to make hard and fast distinctions between terms which stress the relationship and those which emphasize the task, because images by their very nature are so fluid, and also because the reality to which these images point, the life of discipleship, necessarily involves both relationship and task dimensions.

Servant

In this chapter we will explore the terms which describe those who function under the authority of another, including the many words that deal with servanthood. As we noted in Part One, the two most prominent clusters of images in Jesus's description of his followers have to do with family (especially 'child of God', and 'brother/sister'), and with servanthood. The same emphasis continues throughout the writings of the early church.

SERVANT (DOULOS)

The most general word for servant or slave is *doulos*, with the related words *syndoulos* (fellow-servant), *douleuo* (to serve) and *douloo* (to make someone a slave). The word group has a strong emphasis on being under the authority of another—most often, the authority of God.

There were a good number of slaves in the early churches, but these were exhorted to serve their masters as if they were serving the Lord (Ephesians 6:5–7; Colossians 3:22–23). Even menial work took on a new dignity, and found a new and higher standard of excellence, when seen as service offered to Christ himself.

But the term *doulos* was also applied figuratively to the whole community of believers, no matter what their social status. Peter urged all his readers to 'live as servants of God *(theou douloi)*' (1 Peter 2:16). Throughout the book of Revelation, John referred to believers as servants *(douloi)* and fellow-servants *(syndouloi)* of God (1:1; 2:20; 6:11; 7:4; 19:2, 5; 22:3, 6). Paul commended the Thessalonians for turning from idols 'to serve *(douleuein)* the living and true God' (1 Thessalonians 1:9); this phrase summarizes the whole intent and purpose of the Christian life.

In particular, the leaders of the early church gladly applied this term to themselves. Paul introduces himself to the Romans as 'a servant of Jesus Christ' (1:1); in Galatians 1:10 he says that if he were still trying to please men he would not be a 'servant of Christ'; in writing to Titus, he calls himself a 'servant of God' (1:1). In their salutation to the Philippians, Paul and Timothy refer to themselves as 'servants of Christ' (1:1). Similarly, James calls himself a 'servant of God' (1:1), Peter introduces himself as a 'servant and apostle of Jesus Christ' (2 Peter 1:1), and Jude identifies himself as a 'servant of Jesus Christ' (v. 1).

Paul expresses thankfulness for Timothy as one who served *(edouleusen)* with him in the work of the gospel, like a son serving with his father (Philippians 2:22). He also commends Epaphras as 'our dear fellow-servant *(agapetou syndoulou hemon)*' (Colossians 1:7), and as a 'servant of Jesus Christ' (Colossians 4:12). He refers to Tychicus as a 'fellow-servant in the Lord' (Colossians 4:7). When writing to Timothy, Paul reminds him that 'the Lord's servant must not quarrel' (2 Timothy 2:24). Thus both apostles and their co-workers are described as *douloi*. Those in the highest positions of leadership do not hesitate to picture themselves in the lowest status of servanthood, following the Master, who said, 'Whoever wants to be first must be your slave *(hymon doulos)*' (Matthew 20:27).

The apostle Paul spoke of himself not only as a *doulos* of the Lord Jesus, but also of the Lord's people. Both times he used this image it was in writing to a proud, self-centered church, preoccupied with matters of status and fractured with competition and rude behavior. To them Paul wrote about his willingness to forfeit his rights, and his desire to 'make [himself] a slave *(edoulosa)* to everyone,' (1 Corinthians 9:19) to bring more people to Christ. In his second letter he says even more directly, 'We do not preach ourselves, but Jesus Christ as Lord, and ourselves as your servants *(doulous hymon)* for Jesus' sake' (2 Corinthians 4:5). His ultimate accountability is still to Christ; but Christ has assigned him the task of serving the

Corinthians, like the master of a household who assigns certain slaves to attend to the honored guests.

For us who live in a society where slavery as a social institution has long since been abolished, it is difficult to appreciate how startling this imagery must have been to people in the Hellenistic world. The Romans had more slaves than any previous society. During the relatively peaceful years in which the New Testament was written, the slave trade was less active, and the majority of slaves were born and raised in captivity. Slaves worked in all sorts of circumstances—in miserable condition in the fields and in the mines, and sometimes in relative comfort as managers of households, as physicians, or as educators. Yet in spite of the widespread acceptance of the practice, and the relatively humane conditions in which many household slaves lived, slavery was viewed by the Greeks and the Romans as a despicable condition:

> It remained peculiar to Greek thought that man found his true worth only in being conscious of himself and in the free development of his potential. Hence *douleuein* in the sense of dependence and subordination in service is debasing and contemptible (Tuente, DNTT III:593).

> Greek philosophers considered [the slave] something less than human. Roman law regarded him as a piece of property, and the thousands of slaves who worked as chattel gangs on ships, farms, road construction, or mining were treated as nothing but a commodity. On the other hand, the obvious fact that many slaves were intelligent, resourceful, clever human beings made somewhat ambivalent the position of those who were entrusted with the supervision of a farm or an urban workshop, with entertaining the family or educating its children (Stambaugh and Balch 1986:113).

> The distinction between slavery and freedom was not meaningless, and no matter how relatively privileged some slaves might have been they nevertheless remained the juridical peers of those less fortunate ... No slave, in other words, was exempt from the forces of social and economic exploitation, a notion which is inextricably bound up with the Roman practice of slavery as whole (K. Bradley 1987:17).

The ability to be sold was the slave's most compelling reminder of his status as a sheer commodity (K. Bradley 1987:52).[1]

Yet this was the image that became the dominant metaphor for Christian service and leadership.[2] More than anything, it emphasized that the Christian did not belong to himself or herself. The follower of Jesus was under authority, to go where he commanded, to do the tasks that he assigned, to serve whenever the Master spoke and whomever the Master wished.

A number of other words related to servanthood highlight various aspects of the task to which the servant of the Lord may be assigned. Several of the terms used by Jesus in the Gospels (misthios, pais, paidiske, and therapeia) are not used of Christians in a metaphorical sense later in the New Testament, but other words do reappear.

HOUSEHOLD SERVANT (OIKETES)

Paul refers to the household servant (oiketes)[3] in Romans 14:4, in his discussion of differing attitudes toward doubtful practices. He asks, 'Who are you to judge someone else's servant (oiketen)? It is to his own master he stands or falls.' To be a servant of the Lord, then, is to have a clear line of accountability to him that frees us from bending to every opinion of others who would evaluate us. To call a fellow believer a servant of the Lord is likewise to give that one the freedom to follow the dictates of his or her own conscience.

ASSISTANT (HYPERETES)

Another word for servant, hyperetes, used by Jesus of his disciples in John 18:36, is applied literally to John Mark in Acts 13, where he accompanies Barnabas and Saul as their 'helper.' The word originally referred to a rower, a galley slave (Hess, DNTT III:546), one of the most miserable and difficult tasks that could be assigned.

Paul says that this term was first applied to him by the Lord himself. When recounting the story of his conversion, before Agrippa, Bernice and Festus, Paul tells how the risen Lord Jesus met him on the Damascus road, and commissioned him: 'I have appeared to appoint you as a servant (hypereten) and as a witness of what you have seen of me and what I will show you' (Acts 26:16). In speaking of the roles that he, Apollos, and Cephas play in the church, Paul employs the same metaphor, saying, 'So, then, men ought to regard us as servants of Christ (*hyperetas Christou*) and as those entrusted (*oikonomous*) with the secret things of God' (1 Corinthians 4:1). In this verse Paul combines two servant words from opposite ends of the spectrum—the lowly galley slave on the one hand, and the household manager on the other. Yes, he and the other apostles have been given great responsibility by the Lord, but in essence they remain nothing more than humble servants of the one who assigned them the task.

MANAGER (OIKONOMOS)

In the following verses, Paul mentions that the most important qualification for the *oikonomos* is faithfulness, and that only the Lord has the right to evaluate who has been faithful and who has not (1 Corinthians 4:2–4). When listing the qualification for an overseer in the church, Paul says that since the overseer is entrusted with God's work (*hos theou oikonomon*), that is, since he functions as a steward or manager, he must be blameless (Titus 1:7). In each case we see the strong emphasis on accountability that underlies all of the servant words, and especially the *oikonomos* image.

Although the two passages mentioned use the *oikonomos* metaphor for Christian leaders (apostles and overseers), Peter chooses the term for an exhortation intended for all of his readers: 'Each one should use whatever gift he has received to serve others (*diakonountes*), faithfully administering (*hos kaloi oikonomoi*) God's grace in its various forms' (1 Peter 4:10). Thus Peter sees each Christian as an *oikonomos*, equally responsible to make use of the gifts and ministry opportunities that God has provided.

A large household could have more than one *oikonomos*. In the Greek world, *oikonomos* meant:

> ... the house-steward, and then by extension the managers of individual departments within the household, e.g. the porter, the estate manager, the head cook, the accountant, all domestic officials, who were mostly recruited from among the slaves (Goetz, DNTT II:254).

Thus we can appreciate why Peter could speak of each Christian as a 'steward', because each one carried a certain amount of leadership responsibility within God's household, implied in the gift assigned to him or her.

Elliott (1981:172) asserts that *oikonomia* (household management) was a familiar metaphor for political statesmanship in the first-century world, and that it was therefore quite easy to speak of the leader as an *oikonomos*.[4] Whitehead and Whitehead explain why this term might be especially valuable in the contemporary church:

> 'Steward' designates authority without superiority. While responsible for important decisions in a household, the steward is neither a king nor a father, neither a prophet nor a political leader. Yet the steward is authoritative in the group, exercising both power and service... The steward is emphatically not the owner. Not possessing any ultimate authority, this type of leader helps to interpret the owner's wishes for the community. The steward's authority is thus dependent, a 'guest authority' (1986:29).

SERVANT (DIAKONOS)

The most common set of terms for service in the New Testament are the cluster consisting of *diakonos* (servant), *diakonia* (service), and *diakoneo* (to serve). As we saw earlier in this chapter, the verb is used for the ministry of all Christians in 1 Peter 4:10: 'Each one should use whatever gift he has received to serve others.' The noun *diakonia* is applied to quite a variety of different ministries in the New Testament, including the role of apostle within the circle of the Twelve (Acts 1:25) as well as Paul's apostolic calling (Acts 20:24; 1 Timothy 1:12), the new covenant ministry exercised by Paul and Timothy (2 Corinthians 4:1), the offering collected for impoverished Christians in Judea (2 Corinthians 8:4; 9:1, 12–13), and the ministry of the whole church (Ephesians 4:12). In Acts 6, both the administration of the funds for the widows (v. 1), and the apostles' work in the Word and prayer (v. 4), are referred to as *diakonia*.

So then, the word *diakonia* is quite general and comprehensive. It includes apostolic leadership, proclamation of the gospel, relief of the needs of the poor, and the individual ministries of all the members of the church. Both the highest responsibilities of leadership and the most humble forms of helpfulness are included under the term 'service.' The ground is level for all. No function is so exalted that it ceases to be essentially 'service', nor is any task so small or lowly that it cannot be dignified by the same term. As Eduard Schweizer notes:

124

As a general term for what we call 'office', namely the service of individuals within the Church, there is, with a few exceptions, only one word: *diakonia*. Thus the New Testament uniformly and thoughout chooses a word that is entirely unbiblical and non-religious and never includes association with a particular dignity or position (1961:173–174).

Similarly, Leon Morris contrasts the Christian concept of service with the hierarchical emphases so characteristic of other religious groups of that day:

Christianity was no slick imitation of existing ecclesiastical organizations. It made no attempt to set up a hierarchy modeled on previously existing institutions. It was well aware of the kind of thing that was common in the world at large. But it preferred *diakonia*, lowly service, to the grandiose ideas of the Gentiles (Lk 22:25f). It took a term in common use for the most ordinary kind of service and made that its characteristic term for ministering. And it used it very widely. It did not transform it into a term of great dignity aimed at flattering a superior order of ministers. It used it for ministers, but it continued to use it also of the service of ordinary Christians (1964:35).

As we have noted in chapter two, the basic meaning of *diakonos* is one who serves at table. It becomes one of Paul's favorite terms for describing himself and his co-workers. The individuals who are identified as *diakonos* or *syndoulos* by Paul include Phoebe (Romans 16:1), Tychicus (Ephesians 6:21; Colossians 4:7), Epaphras (Colossians 1:7), Timothy (included in the 'we' of 2 Corinthians 3:6 and 6:4), and Apollos (1 Corinthians 3:5). Paul designates himself as a servant of Christ in 2 Corinthians 11:23, as a servant of the gospel in Colossians 1:23, and as a servant of the church in Colossians 1:25.

It is interesting to observe how Paul employs this word when his ministry is under attack, or when he is being compared unfavorably to other leaders. Instead of insisting on his superiority to Apollos, he reminds the Corinthians that even the greatest leaders are no more than 'servants (*diakonoi*), through whom you came to believe as the Lord has assigned to each one his task' (1 Corinthians 3:5). He

125

defends the integrity of his ministry by pointing to the sufferings which he has gladly endured as a 'servant of God' (2 Corinthians 6:3–11) and 'servant of Christ' (2 Corinthians 11:23–33). In the same spirit of humility in Ephesians 3, after calling himself a 'servant of the gospel' (v. 7), Paul says that he is 'less than the least of all God's people' (v. 8). In Colossians 1, he links his role as 'servant of the church' with participation in Christ's sufferings (vv. 24–25).

Thus the term *diakonos* may be used to describe a church leader, but the emphasis is on humility and on helpfulness, not on authority or status. New Testament leadership begins with the recognition that even the leader with the greatest responsibilities is no more than a humble table waiter, expected to endure suffering as part of the call to service in Christ's name. This leadership means service to Christ, to the gospel, and to the church; there is no place for personal aggrandizement or kingdom-building.

On two occasions Paul uses *diakonos* to describe a specific group of individuals within the church. He addresses his letter to the Philippians: 'to all the saints in Christ Jesus at Philippi together with the overseers and deacons (*diakonois*)' (1:1). Here the *diakonoi* are plainly leaders of the church, engaged in particular areas of service, perhaps like the seven who were appointed in Acts 6 (even though the seven are never actually called *diakonoi*). In 1 Timothy 3, after defining the qualifications for overseers, Paul lists the requirements for the *diakonos*, which include the same standards of exemplary life, but do not include the requirement of teaching skill.[5]

The specific responsibilities of the *diakonoi* are not spelled out in the New Testament, perhaps because the office was still relatively new, or perhaps because the structure was intended to be fluid, adaptable to changing needs and local circumstances. That is, each congregation, as it grew large enough, might appoint individuals to administer certain areas, but there was nothing fixed about the position or the responsibility. It was basically a function established in response to a particular need, rather than a permanent office.[6] It focused and organized the ministry of service that was still the task of every believer and every leader.[7]

ONE WHO SERVES GOD

The next three servant terms are not used by Jesus in the Gospels, but rather are introduced by Paul in his letters. The first is not a noun, but since it is sometimes translated as 'serve', it is included here. The verb *latreuo* (to serve) refers to 'the service of God by the whole people and by the individual, both outwardly in the cultus and inwardly in the heart' (Hess, DNTT, III:550). It speaks of serving in the context of worshiping. In Romans 1:9, Paul speaks of 'God, whom I serve (*latreuo*) with my whole heart.' Kruse (1985:126) notes: 'Here for the first time Paul uses liturgical terminology in relation to his own apostolic ministry.' Then in Romans 12:1, where he urges his readers to offer their bodies as living sacrifices, as their 'spiritual act of worship (*ten logiken latreian hymon*)', Paul 'draws upon the same imagery to depict every Christian's service to God' (Kruse 1985:129). Paul uses the verb *latreuo* again in 2 Timothy 1:3, where he says, 'I thank God, whom I serve, as my forefathers did...'

Paul is not the only New Testament writer to use this term for Christian service. In Revelation 7:15 the white-robed multitude, from every nation, tribe, people, and language, are said to be before the throne of God to 'serve him day and night in his temple.' Later, in his vision of the new Jerusalem, John pictures the throne of God and of the Lamb, saying, 'his servants (*douloi*) will serve (*latreusousin*) him' (22:3). Here then is an image of service which will continue to be appropriate into all eternity, even after all earthly tasks are accomplished, and when service on the human level may no longer be necessary or even possible.

PUBLIC SERVANT

The closely related term *leitourgeo*, also translated as 'serve', with the related noun *leitourgos*, has a broader frame of reference. In classical Greek, it means to do public work at one's own expense, but from the narrow political sense it becomes broadened to refer to almost any type of service. In the Old Testament, *leitourgeo* is used exclusively for the service of priests, unlike *latreuo*, which can also refer to the people in general (Hess, DNTT III:550–551). The word *leitourgos* is applied to government officials in Romans 13:6, and to Epaphroditus in his role of rendering help to the apostle Paul in Philippians 2:25, 30. In neither case is the image used in a religious sense. However, in Romans 15:16, Paul thanks God for the grace given to him to be:

> ... a minister (*leitourgon*) of Jesus Christ to the Gentiles with the priestly duty (*hierourgounta*) of proclaiming the gospel of God, so that the Gentiles might become an

offering (*prosphora*) acceptable to God, sanctified (*hagiasmene*) by the Holy Spirit.

The collocation of all of these metaphors related to priestly service plainly show that here *leitourgos* is not being used in the broader sense of 'public servant', but rather of service in public worship.

The cultural background of the word *leitourgos* is described by Stambaugh and Balch:

> The members of the ruling classes, who had the financial resources and the honor of municipal office, were expected to contribute from their own wealth for the benefit of the entire community. In Greek cities, wealthy men were assessed certain *leitourgiai* ('liturgies', literally 'people works') (1986:75).

> The upper classes took great pride in this service, and on their tombstones they listed the offices held, commissions undertaken, public buildings erected, and public games sponsored (1986:117).

Thus Paul seems to employ this metaphor in both the cultural and the religious sense, describing Epaphroditus as a public benefactor sent from the Philippians, and describing himself as a priest offering public service to God through his mission to the Gentiles. The link between the two usages appears to be the public nature of the service.

GUARDIAN (*PAIDAGAGOS*)

The remaining servant role, the *paidogogos*, describes the one who acted as the custodian or guide for the children. His role was to conduct the children to and from school, and respect was due to him as well as the father (Bauer 1979:603). In Galatians 3:24–25, Paul describes the Law as a *paidagogos* conducting us to Christ. In 1 Corinthians 4:15–16, he uses the image in a different way: 'Even though you have ten thousand guardians (*paidagogous*) in Christ, you do not have many fathers, for in Christ Jesus I became your father through the gospel. Therefore I urge you to imitate me.' The Corinthians had had many who had assisted them and watched over them in their Christian life like guardians, leaders who had come along after Paul, some as eminent as Peter and Apollos. But there remained a special relationship with the one who had brought them to birth.

128

Shepherd

Next we turn to some other images of people who work under authority. Three of the terms were employed by Jesus—shepherd, worker, and apostle. Although Jesus clearly described himself in shepherd terminology in John 10, he applied this term only indirectly to his disciples. However, after the ascension, when Jesus was no longer present to give personal leadership to his flock, the shepherd metaphor became more prominent.

Paul exhorts the elders of the Ephesian church in Acts 20:28: 'Be shepherds (*poimainein*) of the church of God, which he bought with his own blood.' The function of shepherding which Paul emphasizes in this passage is that of guarding the flock from the 'savage wolves', the false teachers who will try to come in and draw away disciples. In his first letter, also speaking to elders, Peter says: 'Be shepherds (*poimanate*) of God's flock that is under your care' (5:2). In both cases, the flock belongs to God, not to the shepherd. The shepherd is a servant, assigned the task of caring for God's people; but the shepherd must remember that the flock belongs to God, not to him. The New Testament writers continue to describe Jesus as the Chief Shepherd, who provides the role model for all under-shepherds (e.g. Hebrews 13:20; 1 Peter 2:25; 5:4; Revelation 7:17).

In 1 Peter 5, no specific duties for the shepherd are described; it is probably assumed that the functions of feeding, leading, nurturing, protecting, and so forth would be evident from the observation of actual shepherds, or from passages like Psalm 23 or Ezekiel 34 that develop the analogy more fully. In Ephesians 4, Paul cites another function for the human shepherd, along with several other types of leaders in the church, i.e. apostles, prophets, evangelists, and teachers, who are grouped under a single definite article with the 'pastors/shepherds' as *tous de poimenas kai didaskalous*, indicating that we should speak of pastor-teachers, rather than of two separate groups. These leadership gifts, says Paul, are given 'to prepare God's people for works of service' (v. 12), with the result that the whole community becomes unified and mature.

The shepherd image is one of the few that is applied exclusively to leaders, and not to members of the community as a whole. Therefore, it becomes a very important image for understanding what is distinctive about the role of leadership. Although many other images, like 'brother' or 'fellow-servant', express the equality of every member of the fellowship, a term like 'shepherd' reminds us that even on the human level, some are responsible to lead while others follow, some have authority while others are called to respond to that authority. Christ is not the only shepherd; he has appointed human shepherds to assist him. The shepherd image conveys ideas of tenderness, nurture, and devotion; but it also implies discipline (the rod and the staff), the setting of limits (protection against wolves), and the right to establish direction (leading to pasture). In fact, the verb *poimaino* is sometimes translated as 'rule' (Revelation 2:27; 12:5; 19:15; cf. Psalm 2:9). Gibbs reminds us that although the pastor is to be a servant-leader, he is still primarily a servant of God, not of the sheep:

> If a pastor sees his role in terms of meeting every need and responding to every demand, he will end up becoming a follower of the sheep, rather than their leader. Within a biblical context the shepherd goes ahead of the flock to guide his animals to water and pastures and to look out for any dangers lurking ahead (1987:20).

Yet, as important as the images of the shepherd and the sheep are in the Old Testament, where the setting is mostly rural, and although the patriarchs as well as Moses and King David are known as shepherds, we notice that as the church moves into a more urban setting, the pastoral imagery is not employed as frequently. Nevertheless, the image of the leader as shepherd has remained popular through the history of the church, and continues so today.[8] In answer to the question of whether shepherding is an appropriate analogy for modern society, Oden replies:

> We are well served by a central image of ministry that is nurturant, life-enabling, and non-combative except in extreme emergency, when the sheep are endangered. Modern stereotypes that portray shepherds as always males fail to grasp the fact that in primitive pastoral societies, women as often as men were active in caring for valued animals, the source of wealth in nomadic families (1983:53).

McFague also observes that:

> ... characteristics associated with shepherding are very similar to those associated with maternal imagery for

God in the Old Testament: renewal, comfort, physical nurture, care, guidance, compassion (1982:135).

Worker

Jesus urged his disciples to pray that the Lord of the harvest would send out workers (*ergatai*) into his harvest field (Matthew 9:38). The image of the disciple as 'worker (*ergates*)' or 'fellow-worker (*synergos*)' is also a favorite of Paul's. In 2 Timothy 2:15 he urges Timothy to present himself approved to God as a 'workman (*ergaten*) who does not need to be ashamed and who correctly handles (*orthotomounta*) the word of truth.' The verb *orthotomeo*, used in the Greek translation of Proverbs 3:6 and 11:5, means to cut a straight path; it conveys the image of a road-builder cutting through a thick forest, or a traveler trying to make his way through thick underbrush.

In his letters Paul makes frequent reference to those who have collaborated in ministry with him as his 'fellow-workers'. He applies the term *synergos* to Priscilla and Aquila (Romans 16:3), Urbanus (Romans 16:9), Timothy (Romans 16:21; 1 Thessalonians 3:2), Titus (2 Corinthians 8:23), Epaphroditus (Philippians 2:25), Clement (Philippians 4:3), Mark (Colossians 4:10; Philemon 24), Jesus called Justus (Colossians 4:11), Philemon (Philemon 1), Aristarchus, Demas, and Luke (Philemon 24).

The term fellow-worker implies a dimension of equality. The emphasis is not on one person being over while the other is under; rather, both are laboring toward a common goal. Thus in addressing the Corinthian spirit of favoritism for one leader over another, Paul says of himself and Apollos, 'We are God's fellow-workers' (1 Corinthians 3:9). In his second letter to the Corinthians, Paul speaks sadly of the disciplinary function he had to perform on a previous visit, softening his tone by saying, 'Not that we lord it over your faith, but we work with you (*synergoi esmen*) for your joy' (1:24). Before God, who commissioned the task, all the workers stand on the same level.

Yet there can still be a dimension of authority in the expression 'God's fellow-worker.' When the focus is on being fellow-workers with other Christians, the emphasis is on equality. But when the focus is on working together with God, then the ones who speak on behalf of God convey God's authority in their words. Thus Paul exhorts the Corinthians later in his second letter: 'As God's fellow-workers we urge you not to receive God's grace in vain' (6:1).

In Jesus' parables, the word *ergates* often has reference to an agricultural worker. Stambaugh and Balch explain the context of this image:

> The great majority of the Roman empire's work force was engaged in farming and herding... Some small private farms were tended by their owners, with help from their families and perhaps a couple of slaves... At some places, the holdings of the wealthy landowner would be divided into small individual plots to let out to tenant farmers or some kind of lease arrangement... At others, large tracts were farmed directly by gangs of slaves, under the supervision of one or more stewards; these stewards were themselves slaves who had demonstrated loyalty and skill at organization (1986:68).

In the New Testament letters, some new words for workers are introduced, drawn from the world of agriculture. In 2 Timothy 2:6, Paul urges Timothy to be like a farmer (*georgos*)[9] who works hard and therefore deserves a share of the crops. The reference to the 'share' implies that the farmer is working for someone else: the crops are not his to gather and store as he wills. In 1 Corinthians 3:6–8, Paul describes himself as the one who plants (*ho phyteuon*) and Apollos as the one who waters (*ho potizon*), while God is the one who causes the growth. Some workers initiate a new work; others maintain it and nurture it. But the credit for the results belongs to God alone, who assigns the different tasks to each one. When there is growth and fruit, God is the only explanation.

Apostle

Another task-oriented term Jesus uses for his disciples is *apostolos* (apostle). As we have seen, this word can be used in a more general sense of one who has been sent by another, or in the more restricted sense to refer to the twelve disciples who were specifically commissioned by Jesus. In the rest of the New Testament, most of the occurrences of *apostolos* refer explicitly to the Twelve (e.g. Acts 1:2, 26; 6:2; 8:1), and to the apostle Paul (e.g. Romans 1:1; 11:13), who received his special call from the risen Jesus on the road to Damascus. However, the circle of reference is also enlarged to include Barnabas (Acts 14:4, 14), Silas and Timothy

(1 Thessalonians 1:1; 2:6–7), and possibly Andronicus and Junias (Romans 16:7).[10]

Several passages refer to the group of apostles in a general sense, as a class of leaders within the church. In 1 Corinthians 12:28–29, the apostles are listed first among the spiritual gifts. Similarly, in Ephesians 4:11–12 they are cited first among those who who were given by Christ to the church in order to 'prepare God's people for works of service'. In Ephesians 3:5, Paul says that the mystery of Christ has been revealed by the Spirit to 'God's holy apostles and prophets'.

A related word, *apostole* (apostleship), is introduced in Acts and the letters. In each case it refers to the person who has received authoritative commissioning by Jesus. The first followers of Jesus in Jerusalem pray for wisdom to select an individual to fill Judas's vacancy in 'this apostolic ministry (*tes diakonias tautes kai apostoles*)' (Acts 1:25). In his letter to the Romans, having introduced himself as one 'called to be an apostle' (1:1), Paul says that he has received 'grace and apostleship' to call the Gentiles to faith in Christ. To the Corinthians, who questioned his credentials, Paul insisted, 'You are the seal of my apostleship in the Lord' (1 Corinthians 9:2).

The ministry of apostle is not one for which a person volunteers. Rather, Paul's emphasis is on being called to be an apostle (Romans 1:1; 1 Corinthians 1:1), being appointed as an apostle (1 Timothy 2:7; 2 Timothy 1:11), and being an apostle by the will of God (2 Timothy 1:1) and at the command of God (1 Timothy 1:1). God is the one who commissions authoritative leaders for his church; they do not appoint themselves.

To be an apostle is to suffer. Paul compares the apostles to gladiators brought last into the arena to fight to the death (1 Corinthians 4:9ff). Leadership in Christ's church is not a position of luxury and ease, but the privilege of leading the way into suffering, to be the first to die, to be made a spectacle, to be seen as weak, foolish, and dishonored in the eyes of the world.

The true apostle is known not only by his willingness to suffer (cf. 2 Corinthians 11), but by a number of other authenticating marks. The apostle has seen the risen Lord (1 Corinthians 9:1; 15:7–9; Acts 1:21–22). The proof of his ministry can be seen in unbelievers converted and churches established (1 Corinthians 9:1–2). He performs signs, wonders, and miracles in the power of the Spirit (2 Corinthians 12:12). When the later letters of the New

Testament speak of the apostles, they refer to those who laid the foundations in the early days of the church (Ephesians 2:20; 2 Peter 3:2; Jude 17; Revelation 21:14). Although there are functions in the church today which parallel the first-century apostles' work of church-planting and pioneering in new areas, the New Testament usage of the term seems generally to focus on a specific group of early leaders who had no successors in the strict sense.

Attempts have been made to understand the role of the apostle in terms of the Jewish institution of the *shaliach*. For example, Campenhausen insists that:

> ... the very word 'apostle' is nothing other than a literal translation of a Jewish legal term with a definite meaning, namely *shaliach*, which denotes the plenipotentiary representative, whose task it is to conduct business independently and responsibly for the one who has assigned him these powers for a particular service (1969:22).

However, others have disputed this identification. For example, Schmithals (1969) is convinced that the model is drawn from the Gnostic apostle, not the *shaliach*. Müller (DNTT I:126–136) contrasts the Christian apostle, whose duty includes mission to the Gentiles, with the *shaliach*, who never functioned outside the Jewish context; he feels that not enough attention has been paid to the verb *apostello* (to send) itself as the starting point, noting that in secular Greek it was being used 'as a technical term for divine authorisation', and that the corresponding noun was used in the sense of messenger (as in 2 Corinthians 8:23 and Philippians 2:25).[11] He asserts that:

> The term [*apostolos*] does not denote a continuing office, important in itself, but the exercise of a function limited in scope and duration by a definite commission, and terminating on its completion.

Even if the apostolic office in the strict New Testament sense has not existed since the first century, the apostolic function of opening new territories for the gospel and planting new churches among previously unreached peoples is certainly continuing. As George and Logan express it:

> Apostles are the people with itchy feet: they have to go beyond where they are, because they've been wired that

way. God doesn't let them sit still. They move into territory that lacks a viable body of believers, and they plant new churches (1987:21).

Whether or not we accept such a flexible, informal definition of 'apostle', it is clear that *apostolos* is not one of those terms that is, or should, be applied to every follower of Jesus. Rather it describes a particular initiating leadership role, a specific pioneering function, as well as a distinctive divine calling, which go beyond the general mandate for every disciple to bear witness to Jesus.[12]

Messenger

Two words are used in the New Testament which describe a messenger. The first, *euanggelistes* (evangelist), means someone who brings good news. Although the related verb, *euanggelizo*, is found frequently in the New Testament, the noun occurs only three times in the reference to Philip in Acts 21:8, in the list of equipping gifts in Ephesians 4:11, and in Paul's exhortation to Timothy to 'do the work of an evangelist' (2 Timothy 4:5). In classical Greek usage, the *euanggelos* is a messenger 'who brings a message of victory or other political or personal news that cause joy' (Becker, DNTT II:107). George and Logan propose that an effective evangelist 'knows who is ripe' (1987:22).

The other type of messenger, the *keryx* (herald), in classical Greek 'denotes the man who is commissioned by his ruler or the state to call out with a clear voice some item of news and so to make it known' (Coenen, DNTT III:48). He was used to announce judicial verdicts. Stott compares the role of the herald to that of the steward:

> Although both steward and herald are go-betweens, the steward standing between householder and household, and the herald between sovereign and people, the herald seems in the New Testament to possess a more direct authority and to represent his master more closely (1961:35).

Twice Paul applies this metaphor to himself, saying that God had appointed him as 'a herald' (1 Timothy 2:7; 2 Timothy 1:11).[13] The corresponding verb is used of Jesus in Mark 1:14: 'Jesus went into Galilee, proclaiming (*kerusson*) the gospel (*to euanggelion*) of God.'

Both words, *euangellos* and *keryx*, indicate the delivery of a message on behalf of someone else. Neither the evangelist nor the herald make up their own announcements. They function under the authority of the one who sent them. Coenen (DNTT III:50) distinguishes between the emphasis of the two words:

> The binding, commanding, and settling nature of this proclamation distinguishes *kerysso* and its cognates from *angello* and its compounds, which refer rather to the imparting of information, or making an offer.

Ambassador

Another New Testament word picturing an authorized representative is 'ambassador', expressed through the verb *presbeuo* (to be an ambassador, or to work as an ambassador). The ambassador both represents the people who send him and negotiates for them (Coenen, DNTT I:193). Thus the ambassador role goes beyond the delivery of a message, but is more like that of the apostle, who also takes action on behalf of the sender.

In 2 Corinthians 5:20, Paul writes: 'We are therefore Christ's ambassadors (*hyper Christou oun presbeuomen*) as though God were making his appeal through us.' In Ephesians 6, Paul invites the Corinthians to pray that he will be able to proclaim boldly the gospel, 'for which I am an ambassador (*hyper hou presbeuo*) in chains' (v. 20). As a prisoner in Rome, to which foreign delegates came from far and wide, Paul thinks of himself as an ambassador from the King of Kings. The status of the ambassador is generally related to the status of the ruler that he represents. This high honor is therefore a privilege available to the humblest of willing believers.

Soldier

One other image of a person performing a task under authority is introduced by the apostle Paul: the soldier (*stratiotes*) and fellow-soldier (*systratiotes*). All three occurrences of this term are found in letters that Paul wrote from prison, surrounded by Roman soldiers. He refers to Epaphroditus (Philippians 2:25) and to Archippus (Philemon 2) as his fellow-soldiers. He urges Timothy in 2 Timothy 2:3–4: 'Endure hardship with us as a good soldier (*stratiotes*) of Christ Jesus. No one serving as a soldier (*strateuo-*

menos) gets involved in civilian affairs—he wants to please his commanding officer (*stratologesanti*).'

The image of the soldier implies a life of discipline, struggle, and hardship. It implies strict accountability to one's superior. Notice that Paul does not compare himself to the general, with his fellow-Christians as the troops. No, he describes the others as fellow-soldiers, all under the same commanding officer, Jesus Christ.

Other passages also refer to the image of warfare for the Christian life, though not employing the noun *stratiotes*. For example, in 2 Corinthians 10:3–4 Paul speaks of waging spiritual warfare (*stratiometha*) with divinely powerful weapons (*hopla tes strateias*). In 1 Timothy 1:18 he exhorts Timothy to 'Fight (*strateuei*) the good fight (*strateian*).' Of course, there is also the well-known passage in Ephesians 6 where Paul describes the full armor of God (*ten panoplian tou theou*, v. 11) which the Christian is to wear in the struggle against the devil (cf. 1 Thessalonians 5:8). The apostle Peter also uses the military image in 1 Peter 2:11 where he warns against the sinful desires 'which wage war (*strateuontai*) against your soul' (cf. James 4:1).

Additions to the taxonomy

Here then is the expansion on the section of the taxonomy related to performing a task under the authority of another.

    1.2. Emphasis on Tasks

        1.2.1. Task executed under the authority of another
            1.2.1.1. Servant (*doulos*)* (**syndoulos, doule**)
                1.2.1.1.1. Relationship words
                    1.2.1.1.1.1. Hired servant (*misthios*)
                    1.2.1.1.1.2. Low status servant
                        1.2.1.1.1.2.1. Manservant (*pais*)
                        1.2.1.1.1.2.2. Maidservant (*paidiske*)
                    1.2.1.1.1.3. Member of household (*oiketes*)*
                1.2.1.1.2. Function words
                    1.2.1.1.2.1. Personal helper (*therapeia*)
                    1.2.1.1.2.2. Assistant for tasks (*hyperetes*)*
                    1.2.1.1.2.3. Server for meals (*diakonos*)*
                    1.2.1.1.2.4. Manager (*oikonomos*)*
                    1.2.1.1.2.5. One who serves God (*latreuo*)
                    1.2.1.1.2.6. One who renders public service (**leitourgos**)
                    1.2.1.1.2.7. Guardian (**paidagogos**)
        1.2.1.2. Shepherd (*poimen, poimaino*)*

1.2.1.3. Worker (*ergates*)* (**synergos**)
    1.2.1.3.1. Farmer (**georgos**)
        1.2.1.3.1.1. One who plants (**phyteuon**)
        1.2.1.3.1.2. One who waters (**potizon**)
    1.2.1.3.2. Yokefellow (**syzygos**)
1.2.1.4. Apostle (*apostolos*)* (**apostole**)
1.2.1.5. Messenger
    1.2.1.5.1. Messenger with good news (*evangelist*)

                                              (**euaggelistes**)

    1.2.1.5.2. Herald (**keryx**)
1.2.1.6. Ambassador (**presbeuo**)
1.2.1.7. Soldier (**stratiotes, systratiotes**)

Notes

1   Bradley provides a thorough treatment of the abuses of slavery in the Roman world, arguing against those who imply that the condition of slaves was not really all that unpleasant.

2   A number of helpful works on servanthood in ministry have been published in recent years, dealing with the key passages in the Gospels and the epistles, and drawing out practical implications for contemporary ministry. Among these are Barber and Strauss (1982:109–114); Barnett (1981); Cedar (1987); Dale (1986:25–35); Dulles (1987); Dunn (1975:249–253); Engstrom (1983:56–65); Fleming (1989); Getz (1984); Green (1964); Greenslade (1984); Hanson (1962); Harper (1977:72–86); Hian (1987:13–24); Kraemer (1958:138–155); Kruse (1985); Küng (1967:495–502); LePeau (1983:15–31); Lim (1987); McCord (1966); McKenna (1989); Messer (1989:97–115); Moltmann (1977:102–104); Price (1989); Richards and Hoeldtke (1988:102–112); R. Stevens (1987:131–134); Stott (1961:100–124); Swindoll (1986); Van Proyen (1985:141–144); Wagner (1984:113–116); White (1986:87–89); Whitehead and Whitehead (1986:28–30); and Wimber (1987). Zimmerli and Jeremias (1965) treat the Old Testament background of the servant image, especially as applied to Jesus as the 'Servant of the Lord'.

3   Elliott (1981:69) observes that in the first century slaves were used primarily as household servants, more than for agriculture or industry, and that they were a very important part of the whole economic system based on the *oikos* (household).

4   On the church leader as steward, see also Campbell and Reierson (1981:44–58); Dibbert (1989:32); Greenslade (1984:115–119); Hian (11987:25–30); B. Jones (1988:29, 61); Sawyer (1986:6); Stott (1961:11–32); and Whitehead and Whitehead (1986:29–32).

5   It is not clear whether the reference to *gynaikas* in 1 Timothy 3:11 means the wives of the deacons, or women who function as deaconesses. Nor is it certain whether Phoebe (Acts 16:1) held an official position as deaconess in the church at Cenchrea, or whether Paul was using *diakonos* in the more general sense,

commending her as one who engaged in acts of service, as he does with Tychicus and Epaphras.

6   Description of the historical development of the office of the deacon can be found in Barnett (1981) and McCord (1966). Practical comments on the modern-day role of the deacon are found in Green (1964:51–57), Harper (1977:174–183), Morris (1964:81–90), and Oden (1983:66–68).

7   Kraemer (1958:152) suggests that this concept of service is so central to the ministry of Jesus Christ (along with the concept of shepherd) that the traditional *munus triplex*, three-fold office, of Christ should be expanded to *quintuplex*, with Christ as *diakonos*, prophet, priest, king, and shepherd.

8   Quite a number of recent authors draw heavily from the shepherd image in their discussions of Christian leadership, including Adams (1975), Cedar (1987:99–126), Greenslade (1984:106–110), Hian (1987:31–46), Purkiser (1969:104–120), Tidball (1986), Oxenrider (1982:215–346), and Youssef (1986:27–36).

9   Jesus uses this word in his illustration of the vine, describing God the Father as the 'gardener (*georgos*)' (John 15:1).

10   Depending on whether the phrase 'outstanding among the apostles' means that these individuals were outstanding as apostles, or whether they were commended as outstanding by the circle of the apostles. The latter explanation seems more plausible, in that Paul's approach is not to hold one leader in greater esteem than the rest (cf. his references to 'those who seemed to be important' in Galatians 2:2, 6).

11   So also Meeks (1983:131), who notes that *apostolos* 'meant at its simplest level "agent" or "envoy", and Paul could use the word ambassador or its verb as a synonym.'

12   Discussions of the role of the apostolic ministry in the New Testament and in the church today include Campenhausen (1969), Green (1964:58–75), Greenslade (1984:138–143), Kruse (1985), Lampe (1948), Morris (1964:39–61), and Schmithals (1969).

13   Both Stott (1961:33–59) and Purkiser (1969:74–103) explore the implications of this image for the preacher.

10

Athletes and leaders

The next set of task-related words are based on various social roles and activities that are performed more or less independently, that is, without specific reference to the direction of someone in authority. The words in the previous chapter each emphasize that the follower of Jesus is accountable to the Master, and is under his authority. The words to be discussed in this chapter suggest insights about the nature of the ministry tasks themselves and the conditions under which they are performed.

Only one of these words is an illustration used by Jesus of his disciples: the witness (*martys*).[1] The others are introduced in Acts or the New Testament letters. Most of the terms mentioned thus far can be applied to Christians in general. However, many of the terms discussed in this chapter are appropriate only for leaders in the Christian community.

Witness

In his final words to his disciples, Jesus uses the word *martys* (witness). In Acts 1:8 he tells them: 'You will be my witnesses in Jerusalem, and in all Judea and Samaria, and to the ends of the earth.' The book of Acts gives many illustrations of the continued usage of this term. Matthias is appointed to replace Judas because, as Peter says, 'one of these must become witnesses with us of his resurrection' (1:22). Again and again in his preaching Peter continues to insist that he and others are witnesses of the resurrection (2:32; 3:15; 5:32; 10:39, 41). According to Paul, both Ananias and the risen Jesus had told Paul that he was being appointed as a witness (22:15; 26:16). Two other individuals are called witnesses; Paul refers to Stephen as the Lord's witness (Acts 22:20); and Jesus, addressing the church the church at Pergamum in John's vision, alludes to 'Antipas, my faithful witness' (Revelation 2:13). In each of the latter two cases, the idea of witness is associated with someone who remained faithful to the point of death for Christ's sake. But the basic idea of the word *martys* is not someone who lays down his life, but rather someone who reports what he has personally seen and heard. In each of the references in the book of Acts, those described

when I read the statements by Bennett about being a "witness" it didn't come into my mind about "martys". It's about the willingness to be "witness" as 'witnesses' are those who actually saw the risen Christ—including Stephen, who saw the heavens opened and Jesus as the Son of Man standing at the right hand of God (7:56), as well as Paul, who met Jesus on the road to Damascus (9:3–6).

The same emphasis on personal observation is maintained in the other New Testament uses of the word. Paul alludes to the confession that Timothy made 'in the presence of many witnesses' (1 Timothy 6:12) and later urges him to pass on what he heard from Paul 'in the presence of many witnesses' (2 Timothy 2:2). In his first letter Peter makes his appeal to the elders as a fellow-elder and as 'a witness of Christ's sufferings' (1 Peter 5:1).

The word *martys* originally comes from the legal arena, and means one who gives evidence in a trial, both in classical Greek and in Old Testament usage.

> One is a witness for something one has experienced, or one is enlisted as such for an event . . . The idea of testimony or of witness derived from uncertifiable subjective convictions is not known in the Old Testament, and also has no place in Judaism (Coenen, DNTT, III:1042).

A closely related term is used by Peter in 2 Peter 1:16 when he says, 'We did not follow cleverly invented stories when we told you about the power and coming of our Lord Jesus Christ, but we were eyewitnesses (*epoptai*) of his majesty.' The term *epoptes* (eyewitness), derived from the verb *epopteuo* (to look at), was used in the contemporary Greek mystery religions:

> In the language of the mystery religions the highest grades of the initiates, who had seen the holiest, bore this title. So *epopteuo* came to be associated with the highest human good fortune (Coenen, DNTT, I:189).

In the New Testament, when the image of the witness is used to describe followers of Jesus, it always refers to people who have personally experienced Jesus. Thus the metaphor strongly emphasizes the aspect of personal identification; it gives no room for second-hand reporting.[2]

Athlete

Terms related to athletics, although not used by Jesus, became very popular in the writings of the early church, starting with the writings

141

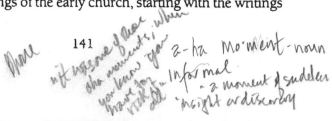

of the apostle Paul, who spent much of his time ministering in Hellenistic cities where the stadium was one of the most prominent and popular public places. According to Stambaugh and Balch, 'The most distinctive institution of Greek cities in the Hellenistic-Roman period was the gymnasium,' where boys and girls received instruction, and where the young and the wealthy spent long hours exercising (1986:121).

Of the various athletically-oriented words, the most general term is the verb *athleo*, which means to compete in an athletic contest in the arena. Paul urges the Philippians to stand firm in one spirit, 'contending as one man (*miai psychei synathlountes*) for the faith of the gospel' (Philippians 1:27). His use of the verb *synathlountes*, meaning 'contending together', evokes the image of an athletic team, a group with a common goal and a common opponent, whose victory depends not just on individual performance but on co-ordination of effort. He uses the same word later in his letter when he pleads for Euodia and Syntyche to live in harmony with one another, reminding them that they have 'contended at my side (*synathlesan moi*) in the cause of the gospel' (Philippians 4:3). These two women had forgotten that they were teammates, and had started to treat one another as opponents and competitors. They had lost sight of the real enemy.

In 2 Timothy 2:5, Paul uses the image of the athlete to motivate Timothy to accept the disciplines that are needed to ensure victory: 'Similarly, if anyone competes as an athlete (*athlei*), he does not receive the victor's crown unless he competes (*athlesei*) according to the rules' (2 Timothy 2:5). The author of Hebrews uses the related noun *athlesis* (contest): 'Remember those earlier days after you received the light when you stood your ground in a great contest (*pollen athlesin*) in the face of suffering' (10:32).

This dimension of struggle implied in the athletic contest becomes even more focused in the words *agonizo* (to contend) and *agon* (contest). Paul encourages the Philippians who have suffered through the same struggle (*ton auton agona*) that Paul has had with those who oppose the gospel. At Thessalonica, as in Macedonia, Paul experienced the same strong opposition (*polloi agoni*, 1 Thessalonians 2:2). He urges Timothy to 'fight the good fight (*agonizon ton kalon agona*) of faith' (1 Timothy 6:12), and expresses confidence that he, Paul, has already 'fought the good fight (*kalon agona agonismai*)' (2 Timothy 4:7). Paul speaks of struggling (*agonizomenos*) with all his energy to help believers to become mature in Christ (Colossians 1:29), and, again, of struggling (*agona echo*) for their unity, encouragement, and understanding (Colossians 2:1–2). At the end of the same letter he commends Epaphras as one who is 'always wrestling (*agonizomenos*) in prayer for you' (4:12). The author of Hebrews exhorts his readers to run with perseverance 'the race (*agona*)' marked out for them (12:1).

So then the image of the contest implies opposition, suffering, and hardship. It speaks of the need for endurance and the willingness to bear pain if the goal is to be achieved. It also implies discipline and the willingness to sacrifice personal comfort and short-term gratification for the sake of long-term goals. Paul reminds the Corinthians that 'Everyone who competes in the games (*ho agonizomenos*) goes into strict training' (1 Corinthians 9:25). The contest imagery reminds us that we are in a contest where there are winners as well as losers. The struggle is not against fellow-Christians, but against the forces of darkness that oppose the gospel.

Although the image of the contest can be used in association with athletic events like races (e.g. 1 Corinthians 9:24, 26; Hebrews 12:1), the primary reference is to combat sports like wrestling and boxing, which played such a prominent part in the Greek athletic contests. That is why the reference to Epaphras' struggle in prayer in Colossians 4:12 is translated by the NIV as 'wrestling'. Paul also uses the more specific vocabulary of these sports in his description of the struggle and disciplines of the Christian life. In Ephesians 6:12, he says, 'Our struggle (*pale*) is not against flesh and blood.' The word *pale* refers to a wrestling match. As Paul further develops the image of struggle in that chapter, he transforms it into the soldier involved in hand-to-hand combat. In 1 Corinthians 9:26 Paul uses the image of the boxer, saying, 'I do not fight (*pykteuo*) like a man beating the air.' His action is purposeful, intent on victory.

The other type of athletic contest frequently pictured is the footrace. Twice in the passage just cited from 1 Corinthians 9, Paul compares the Christian to a runner: 'Do you not know that in the race (*stadioi*) all the runners (*trechontes*) run (*trechousin*), but only one gets the prize? Run (*trecho*) in such a way as to get the prize' (v. 24); also, 'I do not run (*trecho*) like a man running aimlessly' (v. 26). He challenges the Galatians: 'You were running (*etrechete*) a good race—who cut in on you and kept you from obeying the truth?' (Galatians 5:7). The author of Hebrews urges his readers to 'run (*trechomen*) with endurance' the race marked out for them (12:1).

One of Paul's favorite images for a ministry completed is the image of finishing a race (*dromos*), not dropping out from exhaustion or getting disqualified along the way. In his sermon in the synagogue at Pisidian Antioch, he describes John the Baptist as 'completing his work', literally, 'finishing the race (*eplerou... ton dromon*)' (Acts 13:25). A few chapters later in Acts, encouraging the Ephesians elders, Paul says that all the sufferings and hardships of his ministry will be worthwhile if only he can 'finish the race (*teleiosai ton dromon mou*)' (20:24). Near the end of his life, Paul is finally able to say triumphantly, 'I have finished the race (*ton dromon teteleka*)' (2 Timothy 4:7).

Through all of these athletic images run several themes. One is that the Christian life requires effort and exertion simply to keep moving forward, let alone to complete the task; it is not going to be easy; there will be pain and suffering, even the shedding of blood and possibly the loss of life. Second, there are disciplines to observe and rules to keep, just as an athlete has in both training and competition. Third, there will be opposition; the chief opponent is the devil, not just a competitor but a deadly enemy. Fourth, there is a goal to be attained which will make all the sacrifices worthwhile. And fifth, the Christian does not struggle alone; he or she is part of a team, striving together to achieve what they could never attain independently.

The themes are certainly parallel to those which Jesus enunciated through other images. But the athletic metaphor continued to grow in popularity and to be used widely in the early decades of the church.

> In early Christendom the image of the *athletes*, contestant, found such favor that the word was taken over into the vocabularies of the Latin and Coptic churches... In the Acts of Thomas Christ is called 'our athlete' (Ringwald, DNTT, I:646).

Leader/director

Of the various terms drawn from leadership roles in the first-century world, most are applied to corresponding leadership roles within the church. As we will see, some are used more broadly. The most striking feature of this group of terms, however, is that none of them is used by Jesus in the Gospels to describe his followers, even though several of these terms became very prominent in reference to leaders in the early church. This seems to reinforce the observation made in Part One that even though Jesus was training his disciples for leadership roles in the church, he was much more concerned that they see themselves through images that stressed their accountability to God, and their commonality with one another, rather than in terms of the special functions of oversight and direction which they would be given within the community after Jesus ascended to heaven. Brotherhood and servanthood were the two dominant images that Jesus wanted to plant in the minds and hearts of his followers. In the early church these metaphors continued to form the context within which all specialized leadership functioned.

EXPERT BUILDER

Although the Greek language is full of *arch-* compounds, the New Testament authors avoid these terms almost entirely when describing followers of Jesus.[3] The one exception is Paul's comparison of himself to an *architekton* (expert builder) in 1 Corinthians 3:10, who laid the foundation at Corinth upon which others were building. In secular Greek, *tekton* meant 'a craftsman or builder in wood, stone, or metal' and *architekton* referred to 'a head builder, masterbuilder, contractor, or director of works' (Packer, DNTT, I:279). It is used in Isaiah 3:3 where God speaks of the judgment in which all the the leaders and specially skilled people of the nation will be removed.

Some leadership roles precede others, just as Paul has referred earlier in 1 Corinthians 3 to the one who plants and the one who waters; some begin the work that others continue. The *architekton* is one of those initiating and founding leadership roles.[4] Yet, says Paul, even the contribution of the *architekton* has no permanence unless it is used to establish a work on the foundation of Jesus Christ himself (3:11). The *architekton* is not a totally independent agent; rather his ministry, like every other, comes about as a response to the prior call of God, and must be conducted according to God's design. Paul further acknowledges that he laid the foundation 'by the grace God has given me' (3:10); just as the ministry of leadership originates in the grace of God, it also depends on the grace of God for its execution.

ROYAL RULER

The book of Revelation speaks of believers sharing in Christ's rule as members of his kingdom (*basileia*). The first chapter contains a doxology to Jesus Christ as the one who 'has made us to be a kingdom (*basileian*) and priests to serve his God and Father' (1:6). Chapter five records a song of praise to Jesus, the Lamb, who has purchased with his own blood people for God from every corner of the earth. In language similar to that of 1:6, the four living creatures and twenty-four elders sing: 'You have made them to be a kingdom (*basileain*) and priests to serve our God, and they will reign (*basileusousin*) on the earth' (5:10).

Similarly, those who participate with Christ in the first resurrection will reign (*basileusousin*) with him for a thousand years (20:4, 6). The servants of God described in Revelation 22:5 are said to reign (again, *basileusousin*) with him for ever and ever. A related metaphor is the picture of believers sitting on thrones (e.g. 3:21; 20:4; cf. Matthew 19:28; Luke 22:28–30; Revelation 4:4).

The apostle Paul extends the encouraging promise: 'If we endure, we will also reign with him (*symbasileusomen*)' (2 Timothy 2:12). In the kingdom, all of God's people are destined to rule, to exercise dominion, a destiny far more glorious than even the creation mandate given to humankind in Genesis 1:28. Jesus promised the disciples that they would sit on thrones judging the twelve tribes of Israel in the coming kingdom (Matthew 19:28; Luke 22:28–30), but a similar promise is extended to every follower of Jesus as well. Unlike social systems in which some are perpetual rulers and others form a permanent underclass, in the community of the King all share his rule with him.

OVERSEER

However, in the life of the church in its present historical form, various leadership roles are focused in particular individuals. The fact that all will someday reign with Christ does not mean that no one is needed to lead in the present. The word *episkopos* (overseer) is one of the words that is applied to leaders within the church fellowship. The letter to the Philippians is addressed to 'all the saints in Philippi, together with the overseers (*episkopois*) and deacons' (1:1). In 1 Timothy 3:1, Paul says that 'If anyone sets his heart on being an overseer (*episkopes oregetai*), he desires a noble task,'[5] and then lists the qualifications that should be expected of an overseer (*episkopon*, v. 2ff). A similar list for the overseer's qualifications is given in Titus 1, where the term *episkopos* and *presbyteros* (elder) are used for the same person (1:5, 7).[6]

In both Acts 20 and 1 Peter 5, it is evident that the three primary terms for church leader (elder, overseer, shepherd/pastor) were used interchangeably in the early church. In Acts 20, Paul is addressing the elders of the church at Ephesus (v. 17); he charges them to 'keep watch over the flock of which the Holy Spirit has made you overseers (*episkopous*),' and to 'be shepherds (*poimainein*) of the church of God.' All three terms describe the identical set of leaders. In the same way, in his first letter Peter addresses elders (5:1) and urges them to 'be shepherds (*poimanate*) of God's flock that is under your care, serving as overseers (*episkopountes*)' (5:2).

The verb *episkopeo* stresses 'active and responsible care'; in secular Greek the noun *episkopos* is used to describe a deity keeping watch over a country (especially concerning treaties and markets), men with responsible positions with the state, and officials of religious communities (Coenen, DNTT, I:189). Although there are no direct connections that can be drawn between leadership roles in the Old Testament and the Christian office of the *episkopos* (Coenen, DNTT, I:190), there are a number of parallels between the *episkopos* and the 'Supervisor of the Many' (*mebaqqer/paqid*) in the Qumran assembly (R. Brown 1970:67–69). Meeks (1983:80) holds that *episkopos* is likely to have been taken from the leadership of the Greek voluntary associations, and that it was the only such term borrowed from them. It is far more likely that the term Paul used in Hellenistic cities like Ephesus was borrowed from local political and social institutions than from the Qumran sect. In any case, the term *episkopos* implies overall supervising, ordering, evaluating, and setting of direction.[7]

LEADER (*HEGEMONOS*)

A term for leader used mainly by the author of Hebrews is *hegemonos*, a present participle based on the verb *hegeomai* (to lead or guide). In Luke 22:26, Jesus says to his disciples, 'the greatest among you should be like the youngest, and the one who rules (*ho hegemonos*) like the one who serves (*ho diakonon*).' The term *hegemonos* is used of kings of Israel (Ezekiel 43:7), military commanders (1 Maccabees 9:30; 2 Maccabees 14:16), rulers of Judah (Matthew 2:6), and Joseph's position as ruler of Egypt (Acts 7:10). Thus it is a word used for broad and authoritative leadership roles. In Acts 15:22, Judas and Silas, chosen to help convey the decisions of the Jerusalem Council to the Gentile believers, are described as 'leaders (*andras hegoumenous*) among the brothers'; thus, even among 'brothers' there can be leaders; the fact that all are brothers does not invalidate the leadership function within the community.

In the last chapter of the book of Hebrews, the author refers to the role of *hegemonos* three times. The leaders are described as 'those who spoke the word of God to you' (13:7), that is, those who first preached and established churches among them. In the first place, the believers are exhorted to 'remember' their leaders, to 'consider the outcome of their way of life,' and to 'imitate their faith' (13:7); the leaders in view here are primarily teachers and role models. Second, they are told to 'obey' their leaders and to 'submit to their authority' with willing spirits that will enable the leaders to do their work with joy (13:17); in this case, the leaders are described as those who 'keep watch over you'; these may or may not be the same leaders who originally brought the word of God to them; but the leadership role described here seems to imply the general supervisory role implied in the word 'ruler' in the other contexts already cited. Finally, the author instructs his readers to 'greet' their leaders as well as all God's people (13:24); thus the 'leaders' are an identifiable group, distinguishable from the membership of the community as a whole. Yet notice that *hegemonos*, as also *episkopos*, occurs in the plural when the reference is to a particular local situation. The picture we see in the New Testament is of a team of individuals working together, not of one strong individual dominating all the others.

PILOT

A very colorful leadership word, used only once in the New Testament, is *kybernesis* (administration), based on the word *kybernetes*, which means the captain, pilot, or steersman of a ship (Bauer 1979:456). In 1 Corinthians 12 Paul is listing the spiritual gifts that God has appointed in the church. First he lists apostles, prophets, and teachers as a group; after that he lists 'workers of miracles, also those having gifts of healing, those able to help others, those with gifts of administration (*kyberneseis*), and those speaking in different kinds of tongues' (12:28).

The related verb *kybernao* probably came at first from the language used by Mediterranean sailors; but very early it came to be used in a metaphorical sense as well; Plato used the associated noun of leading political rulers, and others used the word group in reference to divine guidance and rule (Coenen, DNTT I:193). In the Greek Old Testament, *kybernesis* is given as the function of rulers (Proverbs 1:5; 11:14). The term *kybernetes* is used for sailors in Ezekiel 27:8, 27–28 (translating the Hebrew *hobel*).

In the New Testament, *kybernetes* occurs at Acts 27:11 and Revelation 18:17 as the one who steers the ship, who pilots it to its destination; this person's reponsibilities, of course, would include the direction of the activities of the other crew members. From Acts 27:11 it is clear that the owner of the ship and the pilot are two different people. This observation contributes a useful insight into the illustration: the owner of the ship determines where it is to go, but the pilot determines the best route and method to get there. In the same way, the overall goal of the church has been defined by the Lord, the 'owner'; but the role of the administrator, the 'ship's captain', is to establish the specific direction and to coordinate the activities of the other members toward that end. Coenen defines *kybernesis* as 'a mediating function of keeping order within the whole life of the church' (DNTT, I:198).[8]

ELDER

The term used most frequently for leaders of the New Testament congregations is *presbyteros* (elder). The basic meaning of the term denotes someone who is older. Unlike most of the other terms for leadership, this one comes from well-known patterns within the Jewish community. As Coenen says: 'Elders are an established part of the patriarchal clan and tribe system, where an authority which was scarcely challenged, though variously qualified, belonged to the heads of families' (DNTT I:194). The elders in Israel were responsible for judicial, political, and military decisions. At first, all the members of the Sanhedrin were called *presbyteroi*, until later a distinction was made between lay and priestly members of the Council.

Stambaugh and Balch describe the pattern of leadership in the synagogue at the time of the New Testament:

> An executive committee attended to the secular affairs of the community; its members were called 'elders' or, like the chief magistrates of a Greek city, 'archons.' The inscriptions also refer to a secretary, who would keep records and handle correspondence. An attendant (*hy-*

peretes in Greek, Luke 4:20; cf. John 7:32) took care of the building, kept order during the service, made announcements, led in prayer if necessary, and administered corporal punishment in accordance with the law (1986:49).

Lightfoot (1901:18) observes that the concept of elders is so familiar that Luke doesn't even take any effort in the Book of Acts to explain it: 'When he first mentions presbyters, he introduces them without preface, as though the institution were a matter of course.' Lampe proposes how elders were appointed in the early church:

> Presbyters are evidently people who, for various reasons are men of high standing in the community... In the new churches, the traveling missionaries, such as Paul and Barnabas, appointed elders to take the leading position, selecting them, no doubt, as the modern pioneer on the mission field would, on the ground of age and secular status... An elder might, while enjoying that status, exercise a particular function or ministry, such as *episkope*. St. Peter, as an apostle, can properly speak of himself as a fellow-elder (1949:17).

It was the elders at Jerusalem who received the gift for famine relief from the church at Antioch (Acts 11:30), and who helped to decide the basis on which Gentiles should be received into the church (Acts 15:2, 4, 6, 22–23; 16:4). Paul and Barnabas appointed elders for each of the churches they established on their first missionary trip (Acts 14:23); later Paul instructed Titus to do the same for the churches of Crete (Titus 1:5). Paul requested a special gathering with the elders of the church at Ephesus on his way back to Jerusalem (Acts 20:17). In his first letter to Timothy Paul gave instructions about the treatment of elders; those who directed the affairs of the church well, especially those working at preaching and teaching, were to be given 'double honor' (5:17; in the context, a reference not only to respect, but also to reimbursement); accusations were not to be treated casually, but handled carefully with proper attention to witnesses, and willingness to give public rebuke when necessary (5:19). James called for the involvement of the elders in prayers for the sick (James 5:14). Peter instructed elders about proper attitudes and motivation (1 Peter 5:1–3), calling himself 'a fellow-elder (*sympresbuteros*)', and John the apostle referred to himself as 'the elder' in his second and third letters (2 John 1; 3 John 1).

As with elders in the Jewish community, the elders of the first-century church always appear as a group. References to elders in particular churches are consistently plural (e.g. Acts 14:23; 15:4; 20:17; James 5:14), the same pattern noted with *episkopos* and *hegemonos*. Thus the life of community and teamwork is expressed within the leadership of the church as well as within the life of the congregation as a whole.[9]

Greenslade attempts to capture the essential character of the role of the elder:[10]

> [The elder] is less 'work-orientated' and more 'value-orientated.' He gathers people and is concerned for their attitudes... He is interested in [the church's] inner health, in the climate or environment in which the members live and which will radically alter their growth and effectiveness... An elder seeks to maintain the body as a life-support system for believers (1984:183–184).

LEADER (*PROHISTAMENOS*)

The remaining words for leader to be discussed are based on the verb *prohistemi*, the basic meaning of which is to set before or over someone or something. In secular Greek the participle *prohistamenos* was used to refer to leadership in an army, a state, or a party; 'a position of this sort involves the task of guarding and responsibility for and protection of those over whom one is placed,' so that the verb can refer to supporting, caring, and showing concern for someone (Coenen, DNTT I:193). Hian (1987:117) says that it 'conveys the picture of someone presiding over others. The position of an executive president is a good modern equivalent.' Greenslade (1984:191) develops the idea of going before, linking *prohistamenos* with *poimen* (shepherd): 'Like an eastern shepherd [the leader] will lead the flock from the front not nag them from behind. This suggests the courage to take initiative and make decisions.' Malherbe (1983:99) says that the verb may mean to manage, but that it also carries the element of personal care.

Paul uses this word a number of times in reference to church leadership. He exhorts the Thessalonians to 'respect those who work hard among you, who are over you in the Lord (*prohistamenous hymon*) and who admonish you,' and to 'hold them in the highest regard in love because of their work' (1 Thessalonians 5:12–13). In 1 Timothy 5:17 he urges proper respect and/or compensation for elders who 'direct the affairs of the church well (*kalos proestotes*).'

In reviewing the qualifications for overseers and deacons in 1 Timothy 3, Paul says that the ability to lead a household is an important indicator of ability to lead in the church. Paul insists that the overseer must 'manage (*prohistamenon*) his own family well and see that his children obey him with proper respect' (v. 4), for 'If anyone does not know how to manage (*prostenai*) his own family, how can he take care of God's church?' (v. 5). Similarly, the deacon must demonstrate the ability to 'manage (*prohistamenoi*) his children and his household (*oikon*) well' (v. 12). The word *prohistemi* plainly carries a note of exercise of authority, as well as the demonstration of personal care. Both respect and obedience are expected from those who are under the direction of the *prohistamenos*.

In Romans 12, Paul urges the believers to exercise the capacities Christ has given to them. He lists seven spiritual gifts, of which the sixth is leadership: 'if it is leadership (*ho prohistamenos*), let him govern diligently.' Note that leadership is seen as a gift of the Spirit, not simply an office to which one is elected or appointed.[11]

Teacher

Another very common task-related role described in the early Christian community is that of the *didaskalos* (teacher). Tidball (1986:107) remarks that 'Paul's writings are permeated with the language of the classroom.' The leadership of the Antioch church was apparently comprised of 'prophets and teachers (*didaskaloi*)' (Acts 13:1). This word appears in two of the lists of spiritual gifts; in 1 Corinthians 12:28 it is cited third, grouped with the apostles and prophets; in Ephesians 4:11, it appears after apostles, prophets, and evangelists, in a sort of 'hyphenated' form with 'pastors', thus 'pastor-teachers (*tous de poimenas kai didaskalous*).' Twice Paul says that he himself was appointed as a teacher (1 Timothy 2:7; 2 Timothy 1:11). James 3:1 warns that 'not many of you should presume to be teachers' because teachers will be evaluated more stringently by the Lord.

Each of the references cited so far views the role of *didaskalos* as a function performed not by everyone in the church, but only by those who are gifted and appointed to do so. However, the author of Hebrews points to a broader application of the teaching role. In 5:12 he scolds his readers for their immaturity, saying, 'though by this time you ought to be teachers (*didaskaloi*), you need someone to teach (*didaskein*) you the elementary truths of God's word all over again.' In this context every believer is expected to become a teacher, able to communicate the basic truths of the Christian message to others; thus the ability to teach is an index of maturity.

In secular Greek, *didaskalos* as a widely used word and 'covers all those regularly engaged in the systematic imparting of knowledge or technical skills'; yet in the Septuagint it occurs only twice; Wegenast (DNTT, III:766) offers this explanation:

> It is clearly not just the word but the whole idea of 'teacher' which is foreign to the Old Testament since the latter is more concerned with obedience than with the imparting of information.

Even in the Gospels, where Jesus is often called *didaskalos*, the emphasis is not on mere acquisition of knowledge but on prompt application of the truth that has been heard (e.g. Matthew 7:24–27; Mark 3:35; Matthew 28:20). So then, although the teacher in the early church 'had the task of explaining the Christian faith to others and of providing a Christian exposition of the Old Testament' (Wegenast, DNTT, III:768), the teacher could never be content with accumulation of facts unaccompanied by changes in attitude and behavior.

Another word used for teaching in the Christian community is *katecheo*, which means to pass on information about something. The word does not occur in the Septuagint. Luke opens his Gospel by explaining that he wants Theophilus to 'know the certainty of the things you have been taught (*katechethes*)' (1:4). In Acts 18:25 Luke describes Apollos as one who 'had been instructed in the way of the Lord.' In Romans 2:18 Paul rebukes the pride of the person who brags that he has been 'instructed (*katechoumenos*) by the law.' Galatians 6:6 contains instructions about how the community should provide for its teachers: 'Anyone who receives instruction in the word (*ho katechoumenos ton logon*) must share all good things with his instructor (*toi katechounti*).'

Prophet

The one remaining term to be discussed in this part of the taxonomy is *prophetes* (prophet). Of course, the prophet role was very familiar because of its prominence in the Old Testament:

> The Old Testament prophet is a proclaimer of the word, called by God to warn, exhort, comfort, teach, and counsel, bound to God alone and thus enjoying a freedom that is unique (Peisker, DNTT III:79).

John the Baptist was commonly acknowledged as a prophet (Matthew 11:9; 14:5), and some of Jesus' listeners saw him in the same category as well (Matthew 16:13–14; 21:11).[12] But Jesus did not use this term to describe himself, or his followers. However, very early in the history of the church, people known as prophets were recognized and given leadership in the community. Some of the prophets had an itinerant ministry (Acts 11:27–28; 21:10), as did teachers like Apollos (18:24) and evangelists like Philip (8:5). In other cases, prophets apparently functioned as part of the ongoing leadership of the congregation. For example, prophets and teachers at Antioch commissioned the first missionary team (13:1); Judas and Silas, leaders in the Jerusalem church (15:22), were also known as prophets (15:32); and Paul gave detailed instructions to the Corinthian congregation about the regulation of the prophetic gift in their regular services (1 Corinthians 14).

The functions of prophets specifically detailed in the New Testament include warning the Christian community of impending difficulties (Acts 11:28; 21:10–11); speaking to encourage, strengthen, comfort, and instruct believers (Acts 15:32; 1 Corinthians 14:3, 31); bringing people under personal conviction of sin (1 Corinthians 14:24–25); and preparing God's people for works of service (Ephesians 4:11–12).

The congregation at Corinth is assumed to have more than one person with the gift of prophecy, for all the prophets are instructed to weigh carefully the messages given by the two or three who are allowed to speak in any given meeting (1 Corinthians 14:29–31). The prophets are to speak in an orderly manner, and are to acknowledge not only the discipline of the group, but also the authority of Christ's apostles (14:32–33, 37–38). Even the most inspired public ministries are designed to serve the needs of the fellowship, and are to be expressed within its overall order.

Prophets are often mentioned together with apostles as playing the foundational leadership roles in the church. In 1 Corinthians 12:28, Paul says that God has appointed in the church 'first of all apostles, second prophets.' Similarly, in Ephesians 4:11, he says that Christ gave 'some to be apostles, some to be prophets', and so forth. The church, says Paul in Ephesians 2:20, is 'built on the foundation of the apostles and prophets.' In John's vision, in the chorus of praise over the downfall of Babylon, we find a threefold division of the church: 'Rejoice, saints and apostles and prophets!'

David Hill summarizes the conclusions of his study of New Testament prophecy with this definition:

> A Christian prophet is a Christian who functions within the Church, occasionally or regularly, as a divinely called and divinely inspired speaker who receives authoritative revelations or messages which he is impelled to deliver publicly, in oral or written form, to Christian individuals and /or the Christian community (1979:8).

Greenslade defines the prophet more informally as the 'eye-opener' of the church (1984:144–154), while George and Logan (1987:21) describe the prophet as one who 'listens to know what God has in mind for the people.'

As with the ministry of the apostle, a distinction should be made between the uniquely authoritative ministry of the first-century prophet in the foundation of the early Christian church, and the broader function of prophetic ministry that continues in the church today. When we say that the church is built on the foundation of the apostles and the prophets, we are referring to a ministry that cannot be duplicated or repeated. The church expresses its continuity with the apostolic tradition through its response to the authority of the canonical scriptures, which it holds to be complete; it evaluates the teaching and mission of its contemporary leaders in the light of this norm.

Additions to the taxonomy

With this chapter we complete the additions to the first half of the taxonomy.

1.2.2. Task executed independently
1.2.2.1. Witness (martys)*

                  1.2.2.1.1. *Eyewitness* (**epoptes**)

          1.2.2.2. Fisherman (*alieus*)

          1.2.2.3. *Athlete* (**athleo**)

               1.2.2.3.1. *Contestant* (**agonizomenos**)

                    1.2.2.3.1.1. *Wrestler* (**pale**)

                    1.2.2.3.1.2. *Boxer* (**pykteuo**)

                    1.2.2.3.1.3. *Runner* (**trecho**)

                        1.2.2.3.1.3.1. *One who finishes the race* (**dromos**)

          1.2.2.4. *Leader/Director*

               1.2.2.4.1. *Expert builder* (**architekton**)

               1.2.2.4.2. *Royal ruler* (**basileia, basileuo**)

               1.2.2.4.3. *Overseer* (**episkopos**)

               1.2.2.4.4. *Leader* (**hegemonos**)

               1.2.2.4.5. *Pilot* (**kybernesis**)

               1.2.2.4.6. *Elder* (**presbyteros**)

               1.2.2.4.7. *Leader* (**prohistemi**)

          1.2.2.5. *Teacher* (**didaskalos**)

               1.2.2.5.1. *Instructor* (**katecheo**)

          1.2.2.6. *Prophet* (**prophetes**)

Notes

1   The other image in this category used by Jesus is the fisherman (*halieus*), but this illustration does not appear again outside the Gospels.

2   Stott (1961:60–79) has a chapter on the preacher as witness.

3   However, Jesus himself is called *archegos* (founder or prince; Acts 3:15; 5:31; Hebrews 2:10; 12:2), *archiereus* (high priest; Hebrews 2:17; 3:1; 4:14; 5:10; 6:20; 7:26; 8:1; 9:11), *archipoimen* (chief shepherd; 1 Peter 5:4; Hebrews 13:20), and *archon* (ruler; Revelation 1:5).

4   Luecke and Southard (1986:93–103) provide an extended development of the 'architect' metaphor, viewing the pastor as the one who shapes the design of congregational life. Greenslade (1984:136–137) also touches briefly on the *architekton* image.

5   Tidball (1984:130) emphasizes that the Greek text does not include the word 'office', even though that word is often supplied by the English translators [though not by the NIV].

6   Oden (1983:71–72), however, insists that based on these verses from Titus that there is a distinction between the *episkopos* and the *presbyteros*, rather than the two words simply highlighting different aspects of the same person's function.

7   The role of the overseer in the first century and in the present-day church is discussed in Campbell and Reierson (1981:84–102), Green (1964:42–50), and Purkiser (1969:121–143).

8   Several recent authors focus on the application of the image of the *kybernetes* to church leadership today, including Gangel (1974:19–21), Greenslade (1984:194), Hian (1985:117–118), Luecke and Southard (1986:49–50), and Tidball (1986:110). Campbell and Reierson (1981:35) use this image as their basic metaphor for understanding the work of the pastor.

9   Stabbert (1982) argues strongly for plurality of eldership as the normative pattern for all churches; in particular, he believes that no single individual should be in charge as the head or leader. Writing in the context of Brethren churches, Oxenrider (1985) provides more room for an elder/pastor to give some measure of direction within the group of elders, through suggestions and persuasion.

10   Useful discussions of the role of the elder in the church today are found in Campbell and Reierson (1981: 59–83), Green (1964:33–41), Greenslade (1984:183–188), Harper (1977:174–183), Morris (1964:70–80), Oden (1983:68–71), Oxenrider (1982:15–65), Stabbert (1982), and Van Proyen (1985).

11   Engstrom (1983) calls this item in the list in Romans 12 the 'gift of administration', and uses it as the basis for his book on Christian administration. This usage is a bit confusing, since *kybernesis* is generally the word translated 'administration'. Dibbert (1989:32) cites *prohistemi* and *oikonomia* as two biblical words that closely correspond to the concept of 'manage', which he takes as the theme for his book.

12   Tidball (1984:34–35) applies Weber's analysis of the Old Testament prophet to the ministry of Jesus.

11

Humility, honor and unity

In the preceding five chapters, we have examined terms and images drawn from people: their occupations, political roles, religious activities, family relationships, recreational pursuits, and so forth. In the next two chapters we will consider the terms based on 'things', including animals, plants, buildings, and household objects. In the previous chapters, some of the terms for followers of Jesus referred to familiar and easily applicable social roles, such as 'disciple' or 'elder', such that there was hardly any metaphorical aspect at all to the words. In the coming chapters, however, since people are being compared to things, all of these terms are 'images' or 'metaphors'; in each case, of course, only certain aspects of the objects are being suggested as points of comparison.

In this chapter we will look at images that describe the relationships of followers of Jesus to the Lord, to one another, and to the world. First we will examine those that portray the followers of Jesus in their weakness, dependency, and suffering; then, at terms that express the special honor and dignity enjoyed by the Christian; and finally, the words that point to the interconnections between believers.

Images of weakness/dependence

Among Jesus' favorite descriptive terms for his followers were 'sheep (*probaton*)' and 'flock (*poimne/poimnion*)'. He used these images to express the disciples' vulnerability to attack and their proneness to wander into danger, but also to affirm the depth of his sacrificial love for them as the Good Shepherd.

The same terms are used, with similar associations, by the New Testament writers in the passages already cited in the discussion of *poimen* (shepherd) in chapter nine. In both passages where the word *probaton* is used, the focus is on Christians under the shepherding care of Jesus. The author of Hebrews refers to Jesus as the 'Great Shepherd of the sheep (*ton poimena ton probaton ton megan*)' (13:20). Peter focuses on the tendency of sheep to wander, and reminds his readers: 'You were like sheep (*hos probata*) going astray, but now you have returned to the Shepherd and Overseer of your souls' (1 Peter 2:25).

158

In the passages which speak of the flock (*poimnion*), however, the references to shepherds point to human leaders of the congregation. In Acts 20:28–29, Paul urges the Ephesian elders to keep watch over 'all the flock', and to guard against the savage wolves that 'will not spare the flock'. In his first letter, likewise addressing elders, Peter urges them to 'be shepherds of God's flock', and to be 'examples to the flock' (1 Peter 5:2–3). The first passage speaks of the sheep's need for protection; the second focuses on their need for instruction in right behavior.

The image of the 'flock' also underscores the corporate nature of the Christian life. The shepherd attends to the needs of the individual sheep, but also deals with them as a group, leading them to pasture and protecting them from marauders.

Another image that reminds us of our vulnerability and weakness appears once in James: 'You are a mist (*atmis*) that appears for a little while and then vanishes' (4:14). In view of the brevity and uncertainty of life, says James, we should not boast about our plans for the future, but should humbly acknowledge that, 'If it is the Lord's will, we will live and do this or that' (4:15). This is an appropriate caution, especially in view of the popularity in some quarters of the image of the Christian leader as the person who 'makes things happen', the manager or administrator who plans, organizes, and directs the community into the future. We must remember that the leader too is only a 'mist', here for a little while, then gone, dependent entirely on the grace of God for every breath.

Images of suffering/rejection

Although a number of biblical terms are often associated with suffering and rejection, such as the *diakonos* (servant) and the *martys* (witness), Paul introduces two images which express this dimension of the Christian life in the strongest possible terms. In 1 Corinthians 4:13, he says, 'Up to this moment we [apostles] have become the scum (*perikatharmata*) of the earth, the refuse (*peripsema*) of the world.' As Kee observes:

> [Paul] contrasts his own miserable clothing, inferior status, and social impotence with that of his well-heeled, socially powerful critics. The words he uses to describe himself and his immediate associates are the first-century equivalents of 'scum' and 'trash' (1980:97).

The first word, *perikatharma*, is compounded from the verb *kathairo* (to make clean) and the preposition *peri* (around). It describes the result of a very thorough scouring, that is, the dirt that is removed through intense scrubbing. Packer calls it 'a term of contempt for the kind of persons who volunteered as victims—"human rubbish"' (DNTT, I:479). The voluntary, sacrificial lifestyle of the follower of Jesus is a puzzle to those who see life's goals only in terms of the achievement of honors or possessions.

The second word, *peripsema*, comes from the verb *peripsao*, which means to wipe all around, to rub clean, and refers to the scum which is thereby removed. Packer describes a recurring Greek custom in which communities placated the angry gods by offering the 'scum' of society—that is criminals, the destitute, the deformed—as a human sacrifice (DNTT, I:479). Thus the term connotes rejection, and is well suited for identification with Christ's sufferings as the rejected Messiah.

Images of honor/dignity

One of the characteristic features of Roman society was its obsession with honor and prestige. Roman society was highly stratified, and people were very much aware of who was 'under' and who was 'over.'[1] Yet few of the early Christians came from the upper strata of society. In the early community of believers were many of the poor, including widows, orphans, slaves, and people of no particular social standing. Some of those who had previously enjoyed wealth or honorable positions in society had been forced to abandon those privileges after they became followers of Jesus, and persecution began (Hebrews 10:32–34). Others voluntarily surrendered much of their wealth as part of the spirit of sharing with a new spiritual family of brothers and sisters (Acts 4:32–35).

In this context the New Testament writers employed a number of images that pointed to the true dignity and high status that believers enjoyed in the eyes of God. Although several words related to 'building' will be discussed later, the word *naos* (temple), which is derived from *naio* (to dwell), is used in contexts which focus on the indwelling presence of the Spirit of God. It refers more specifically to the sanctuary, whereas the other word translated 'temple', *hieron*, denotes the whole complex of temple buildings in Jerusalem (von Meding, DNTT, III:781). Minear comments further on the difference in usage:

Of the two Greek words for 'temple', early Christian writers commonly chose to use *naos* rather than *hieron*, probably because they wanted to safeguard their conviction that God's temple is not something made with hands (Acts 17:24). *Hieron* referred primarily to the visible structure on Mt. Zion. *Naos* also made easier the typological reference to the tabernacle in the wilderness (*skene*) as well as to Solomon's masonry (1960:96).

The temple metaphor is used by Paul, especially in the Corinthian correspondence. In 1 Corinthians 3, Paul is teaching about the need for unity, rebuking the divisive spirits of those who want to rally around different leaders. He speaks of the Corinthians as 'God's building' (v. 9), then describes the differences in role between the one who lays the foundation and the others that build upon it. Next he asks:

> Don't you know that you yourselves are God's temple (*naos theou*) and that God's Spirit lives in you? If anyone destroys God's temple, God will destroy him; for God's temple is sacred, and you are that temple (3:16–17).

The community as a whole is of immense value to God. It is set apart as the place where his Holy Spirit dwells. Therefore, to do anything to disrupt the unity and peace of that sanctuary is to incur the judgment of God. The place where God has chosen to live must be treated with respect.

A few chapters later, Paul warns against sexual immorality, saying: 'Do you not know that your body is a temple (*naos*) of the Holy Spirit, who is in you, whom you have received from God? You are not your own; you were bought at a price. Therefore honor God with your body' (6:19–20).

The repetition of the accusing question, 'Do you not know?' implies that these are elementary teachings of which even the newest Christian should be aware. Again, the focus of the temple image is that God lives there. The great value that God ascribes to his people is implied in the price that was paid for their redemption. This image also points to the believer's accountability to God; the body is God's temple; it must be used only in ways appropriate to the presence of a holy God.

In 2 Corinthians 6 Paul introduces the image of the temple once again, this time as the basis for a warning not to be 'yoked with unbelievers', but rather to live lives of separation from the world. He asks: 'What agreement is there between the temple of God and idols? For we are the temple of the living God' (6:16). Then he alludes to some Old Testament passages (Leviticus 26:12; Ezekiel 37:27) which speak of God living and walking among his people. Thus, once again the image of the temple is associated with the presence of God, and hence with the need for complete holiness.

The other reference to the temple (naos) of God occurs in Ephesians 2. There Paul describes the church as a building founded on the apostles and prophets, with Jesus Christ as the cornerstone, which 'rises to become a holy temple (naon hagion) in the Lord' (v. 21), a 'dwelling in which God lives by his Spirit' (v. 22). Again, the presence of God is the key distinctive of the naos. It is the indwelling and purifying presence of God which gives dignity to the life of the individual believer, and which makes the community of believers worthy of respect, no matter how much the world may demean them, reject them, or persecute them.

A second image that ascribes an honorable status to the believer is that of the new creation (ktisis). Paul says in 2 Corinthians 5:17: 'If anyone is in Christ, he is a new creation (kaine ktisis).' Paul's omission of a second verb ('he is') in the Greek sentence make the phrase 'new creation' stand out even more dramatically—thus, 'If anyone is in Christ new creation!' Paul seems to recall God's work of creation in Genesis 1, where God spoke, and it came to be! Creation is something that only God can do. The only source for the Christian's new life is God himself.[2]

In Galatians 6:15, Paul says to the Galatians, who were so obsessed with human effort and activity as the path to holiness and acceptance with God: 'Neither circumcision nor uncircumcision means anything; what counts is a new creation (kaine ktisis).' The only righteousness which God accepts is that which he himself creates. The person who has thus been made new by God has a higher status than any human achievement or nobility of birth can possibly confer.

The third image of honor and dignity is based on the Hebrew word segullah, which referred to personal property, and in particular, to a king's treasure (David's 'personal treasures of gold and silver' in 1 Chronicles 29:3; Solomon's 'treasure of kings and provinces' in Ecclesiastes 2:8). This is the word which the Lord used to describe Israel as his treasured possession (e.g. Exodus 19:5; Deuteronomy 7:6; 14:2; 26:18; Malachi 3:17). Most often it is translated in the Greek Old Testament as *periousios* (rich possession), but sometimes as *peripoiesis* (possession, property). Both Greek words are used by New Testament writers to describe the special relationship of God to his people.

In Ephesians Paul describes the Holy Spirit as a seal, 'a deposit guaranteeing our inheritance until the redemption of those who are God's possession (*peripoieseos*)' (1:14). The whole passage is filled with descriptions of the riches and privileges that are ours in Jesus Christ, because of God's love and gracious choice. In the second chapter of his first letter, where he lists all the terms formerly descriptive of Israel but now applied to Christians, Peter says that believers are 'a people belonging to God (*laos eis peripoiesin*)' (1 Peter 2:9). Several times in this letter, written to Christians who were suffering insults and ostracism from their society, Peter speaks of God's choice of them, and uses terms like this to remind them of their value in the eyes of God. In Titus 2:14, Paul employs the other word, *periousios*, reminding Titus that Jesus Christ 'gave himself for us to redeem us from all wickedness and to purify for himself a people that are his very own (*laon periousion*), eager to do what is good.'

Images of interconnection

Some of the most important and frequently used metaphors are those which describe how the individual believers are linked together, and formed by God into an interdependent and unified whole.

BUILDING

First we will consider the image of the building. Again we return to Ephesians 2, a passage rich in images, especially compounds and derivatives of *oikos*. In verse 20 Paul shifts from the metaphors of citizenship and membership in a household, to the image of a building—an easy transition, in view of the double meaning of *oikos* as either the house or the people who inhabit it. He describes the apostles and the prophets as the foundation, Jesus Christ as the cornerstone, and then individual Christians as the building materials. In verse 21 he says that in Christ 'the whole building (*oikodome*) is joined together and rises to become a holy temple (*naos*) in the Lord.' Then in verse 22 he says that 'you too are being built together (*synoikodomeisthe*) to become a dwelling (*katoiketerion*) in which God lives by his Spirit.'

In 1 Corinthians 3, another passage where a number of metaphors mix together, Paul says, 'You are God's field, God's building (*oikodome*)' (v. 9). Then he describes himself as the *architekton* (expert builder) who laid the foundation for the building.

Individual parts of the building are also used as metaphors. For example, in 1 Timothy 3:15, after giving instructions about the appointment of church leaders, Paul describes the community of believers as 'God's household, which is the church of the living God, the pillar (*stylos*) and foundation (*hedraioma*) of the truth.' To the church is committed the truth of the gospel, upon which all other truth must build. It is not simply one repository of truth among many truths, but it proclaims the truth in which is found the key to the unity of all of knowledge, whether historical, scientific, aesthetic, or philosophical. Blunck (DNTT I:662) observes that the adjective *hedraios*, from which *hedraioma* is derived, always refers to 'something secure and permanent in itself'.

The other word for foundation, *themelios*, is used of the foundation Paul laid for the church in Corinth, the one foundation which is Jesus Christ (1 Corinthians 3:10–11); Paul uses the same word for the apostles and prophets as the foundation of the church in Ephesians 2:20. In 2 Timothy 2:19, when Paul says, 'God's solid foundation (*stereos themelios*) stands firm,' the reference may be again to the church, as in 1 Timothy 3:15.

The word *stylos* (pillar), which Paul applies to the church in 1 Timothy 3:15, is used for individual leaders of the Jerusalem church in the book of Galatians. When describing his visit to Jerusalem to explain his ministry among the Gentiles, Paul says that he met privately with 'those who seemed to be leaders (*tois dokousin*)' (Galatians 2:2). A few verses later he says that 'those who seemed to be important (*ton dokounton einai ti*)' (2:6) added nothing to his message. Then in verse 9, he reports that 'James, Peter, and John, those reputed to be pillars (*hoi dokountes styloi einai*), gave me and Barnabas the right hand of fellowship when they recognized the grace given to me.' A pillar holds up the building; the whole structure depends on the pillars. However, Paul's reluctance to say that Peter, James, and John really were 'pillars' is shown in his usage three times of the verb *dokeo*, which means to seem to be, or to appear to be. His reluctance to overstate the importance of the roles of these leaders in Jerusalem must be understood in the context of the dispute that occasioned both his trip to Jerusalem and his later letter to the Galatians; for, in the matter of understanding that the gospel abolished all walls between Jew and Gentile, Paul was apparently farther advanced than the Jerusalem church and its leaders. No church leaders should ever be elevated so high by the congregation that they rise above the possibility of correction and rebuke. Nor should any individual leader ever become such a 'pillar' to a congregation that his or her removal would mean the collapse of the whole building.

The term *stylos* also appears in the promise of the Spirit of Jesus to the overcomer in Revelation 3:12: 'Him who overcomes I will make a pillar in the temple of my God.'

Another part of the building is the stones that comprise it. In 1 Peter 2, Jesus is described as 'the living Stone (*lithon zonta*)' (v. 4), the cornerstone (v. 6), the capstone (v. 7), and the stumbling stone (v. 8). In verse 5 Peter describes believers as 'living stones (*lithoi zontes*)' who come to Jesus to be built into a spiritual house (*oikos pneumatikos*).[3] It seems that 'stone' is not a sufficiently dynamic image to capture the phenomenon of growth and the pulse of new life that energizes the community of believers. Hence Peter speaks of 'living' stones.

The metaphor of the building speaks not only of the believers' special relationship to God as his dwelling place, as those who belong to him, and as those who are built upon Jesus the cornerstone and foundation, but also of their relationship to one another. They have been fitted together with the same skill employed by a stonemason, each stone carefully placed in relation to the ones around it, each one doing its part to hold up the entire structure, together fulfilling the purpose of providing a dwelling place for the Holy Spirit.

BRANCHES OF THE OLIVE TREE

The next two images are drawn from living organisms—the olive tree, and the human body. Both convey the ideas of unity in the midst of diversity. In Romans 11:16–24 Paul employs an extended metaphor, describing the people of God as a cultivated olive tree whose branches are broken off so that wild shoots can be grafted in. The roots of the tree are the patriarchs; the cultivated tree is the Jews; and the wild olive is the Gentiles. Because of unbelief, branches are broken off, whether natural or grafted; and by belief, both can be grafted in again. So then, the church as a whole grows together as one tree, but the one basis for inclusion, as well as for continuance, is faith, not any natural merit. This image highlights the gracious action of God, as well as the active human response of faith, in the formation of the community.

MEMBERS OF THE BODY

One of the best-known and widely used images of the church introduced by the apostle Paul is that of the human body, the *soma*. Although he develops the image at some length in Romans 12, 1 Corinthians 12, Ephesians 4, and several passages in Colossians, Paul is the only New Testament writer who uses it. In three of the passages, the references to the body are linked with discussion of spiritual gifts. In Romans 12, following the exhortation to surrender their bodies to God as living sacrifices, Paul gives a concise summary of this aspect of the body image: 'Just as each of us has one body (*heni somati*) with many members (*polla mele*), and these members do not all have the same function, so in Christ we who are many form one body, and each member belongs to all the others. We have different gifts, according to the grace given to us' (12:4–6).

Several features of the body image are visible in these verses. First, the body consists of those who are 'in Christ'; it is their relationship to him which makes them part of the body. Second, there is only one body; each individual member is in some way identified with and connected to the one body. Third, the body is very diverse; it is comprised of many different parts. Fourth, these different parts have special capacities, spiritual gifts, which are intended to be used for the welfare of the body and to enable the body to perform the functions for which it was designed. Fifth, the parts of the body are interdependent; they comprise a system; each can function properly only as it is operates in coordination with the whole.

These same basic features can be seen in the other passages where spiritual gifts and the body are discussed. In 1 Corinthians 12, Paul states that the body is a unit, even though there are many parts (v. 12, 20). The body is comprised of those who are part of Christ (v. 12, 27), who have been baptized by his Spirit (v. 13). Each different function is essential to the welfare of the body (vv. 14–25). The parts are interconnected such that the experience of the part affects the whole; they suffer together and rejoice together (v. 26).

In Ephesians 4, Paul again stresses the oneness of the body (v. 4), based on vital union with Christ, who is the source of life and growth (vv. 15–16). Each part has essential work to do (v. 16). The purpose of the spiritual gifts of apostle, prophet, evangelist, and pastor-teacher is to prepare God's people for service, in order to contribute to the building up of the body toward unity, knowledge, and maturity (vv. 11–13). The oneness of the body is also expressed in 1 Corinthians 10:17, in the context of instructions about the Lord's Supper: 'Because there is one loaf, we, who are many, form one body, for we all partake of the same loaf.'

The intimate connection of the parts of the body to one another is the basis for Paul's exhortation to truthfulness in Ephesians 4:25: 'Each of you must put off falsehood and speak truth to his neighbor, for we are all members of one body (allelon melon).' It is also the ground of the appeal for peace in Colossians 3:15: 'Let the peace of Christ rule in your hearts, since as members of one body (en heni somati) you were called to peace.' Because believers are in fact connected to one another through their common participation in Christ, they must do nothing that would tend to drive a wedge between them.

In his discussion of the new oneness that Christ has made possible between Jews and Gentiles, Paul says that God has created (ktisei) 'one new man', reconciling them both to God 'in this one body (en heni somati)' (Ephesians 2:15–16), a reference both to Christ's body tortured on the cross, and to the new fact of union in the community of Christ; then in the next chapter he speaks of the 'mystery' that Gentiles and Jews are 'members together of one body (syssoma)' (3:6).

One primary theme, then, of the body metaphor is unity in diversity. But another recurrent aspect of this image is the vital connection of the believers individually as well as corporately to Christ, who is the head of the body. In Ephesians 1:22–23, Paul says that God appointed Christ to be 'head (kephalen) over everything for the church, which is his body (to soma autou),' placing him above every rule and authority, and putting all things under his feet. The image of headship in this context is plainly one of rule and authority. Christ is head over everything, not just the church.

Other passages focus on Christ's headship over the church in particular. Ephesians 4:15–16 speaks of growing up into Christ, who is the head, from whom the whole body grows; here the head is the source of growth. In Ephesians 5, where Paul calls wives to submit to their husbands, that is, to come willingly under their authority, he grounds his exhortation in the observation that 'the husband is the head of the wife as Christ is the head of the church, his body, of which he is the Savior' (v. 23). In view of the parallel between these paragraphs and the ones that follow concerning parents with children (6:1–4), and masters with slaves (6:5–9), it is clear that headship here again is an image of authority.

But later in the passage about husbands and wives, Paul draws out another implication of the body metaphor in our relationship to Christ—that Christ feeds and cares for his church, just as a person does his own body (5:29). Paul also points to the parallels between Christ's loving sacrifice for the church, and the selfless love which husbands are to show to their wives (5:25–28, 33). Thus the authority which Christ possesses as head is exercised in love, for the benefit of the members of the body.

In the book of Colossians, in a section on the supremacy of Christ over the whole created order, Paul again speaks of Christ as the 'head of the body (he kephale tou somatos), the church' (1:18), and as the 'head over every power and authority' (2:10). He describes the false teacher as one who has 'lost connection with the Head, from whom the whole body, supported and held together by its ligaments and sinews, grows as God causes it to grow' (2:19).

Minear summarizes the various ideas connected with Christ's headship:

> Christ's headship is thus a way of pointing to his status as first principle, as first-born, as primal image, as the source and goal of all things, and as the legitimate ruler of all other spiritual rulers ... Whatever truth concerning divine authority may be seen fractionally elsewhere may be seen here totally in their head (1960:205).

The image of the body with Christ as head thus stresses the total authority of Christ in the community of disciples, and the total dependence of the disciples on Christ for life and growth. The headship of Christ also puts human leadership in right perspective, for no human being is ever called 'head' of the church; Christ is the authority to whom all human authority is responsible.

The use of the body as a metaphor for community life was not unique to Paul. However, Paul's use of the term was unique in several respects. First, as Banks notes:

> While the term 'body' did not originate with him, Paul was apparently the first to apply it to a community within

the larger community of the state, and to the personal responsibilities of people for one another rather than for more external duties (1980:70).

Meeks makes some additional observations:

> The use of the human body as a metaphor for society was a commonplace in ancient rhetoric, a favorite of the late Stoics, and was readily adopted by Jewish writers to speak of Israel. What makes the Pauline usage so extraordinary, and what has attracted so much theological comment, is the fact that 'the body of Christ' or its equivalent is used with a concrete allusion to the human body of Jesus, crucified and raised from the dead (1983:89).

BATCH OF DOUGH

One other metaphor can be placed in the category of 'images of interconnection.' In 1 Corinthians 5 Paul appeals to the congregation to deal decisively with sin that has been tolerated openly among them, so that the problems do not become even more widespread. He says: 'Don't you know that a little yeast works through the whole batch of dough (*phyrama*)? Get rid of the old yeast that you may be a new batch (*phyrama*) without yeast—as you really are' (5:6–7). The members of the church are so connected to one another that the sin in the life of one can soon spread to become sin in the life of many. Impurity in a part can endanger the integrity of the whole. Thus the interrelatedness of the community of believers is a great strength, but it also opens the community to great risk.

Additions to the taxonomy

The expansion of this section of the taxonomy makes evident how many new images were introduced by the New Testament writers. The only one of this set that was used by Jesus was that of sheep/flock.

2. Things

    2.1. Emphasis on Relationships

        2.1.1. Images of weakness/dependence
            2.1.1.1. Sheep/flock (*probaton, poimnion*)*

*2.1.1.2. Mist (**atmis**)*

2.1.2. Images of suffering/rejection
    *2.1.2.1. Scum (**perikatharma**)*
    *2.1.2.2. Refuse (**peripsema**)*

2.1.3. Images of honor/dignity
    *2.1.3.1. Temple (**naos**)*
    *2.1.3.2. Creation (**ktisis**)*
    2.1.3.3. Treasure
        *2.1.3.3.1. Special possession (**peripoiesis**)*
        *2.1.3.3.2. Treasured possession (**periousios**)*

2.1.4. Images of interconnection
    *2.1.4.1. Building (**katoiketerion, oikodome**)*
        2.1.4.1.1. Foundation
            *2.1.4.1.1.1. (**hedraioma**)*
            *2.1.4.1.1.2. (**themelios**)*
        *2.1.4.1.2. Stone (**lithos**)*
        *2.1.4.1.3. Pillar (**stylos**)*
    *2.1.4.2. Branches of olive tree (**elaia**)*
    *2.1.4.3. Members (**mele**) of body (**soma**)*
        *2.1.4.3.1. Members together (**syssomos**)*
    *2.1.4.4. Batch of dough (**phyrema**)*

Notes

1   See Elliott (1981:122); Malherbe (1983:86); Malina (1981:25–50); Stambaugh and Balch (1986:110).

2   Barber and Strauss (1982) emphasize that it is only through Christ's work of new creation that our needs for acceptance, self-worth, and competence are met (pp. 36–37), thus enabling the Christian leader to overcome 'repressive-compulsive' and 'emotional-impulsive' styles, and to demonstrate the maturity of 'rational-congruent' behavior.

3   The image of the 'spiritual house' in 1 Peter 2 will be discussed in the next chapter, because of the emphasis of that passage on the tasks of worship and witness.

12

Growth, dispersion, and service

The final set of images turn our attention to the tasks to which the follower of Jesus is called. There is work to be done, goals to be accomplished, a world to be won. The community of disciples is not simply to enjoy its loving fellowship with one another, or to revel in the privileges God has bestowed upon them, or to take pride in its separation from the world. No, the church is intended to grow, to influence its world, to engage in acts of service and proclamation.

Images related to growth

Agricultural metaphors do not play nearly as important a role in the rest of the New Testament as they do in the Gospels. Jesus' images of fields, seeds, vines, ripening crops, weeds, and bountiful harvests are no longer the primary ones used to communicate with the urban congregations. But, when these metaphors are used, the emphasis is still, as it was with Jesus, on what the field produces. The key question is, 'How is the harvest?'

FIELDS

For example, in Hebrews 6:7–8 the author pictures two types of land (*ge*). As in Jesus' parable of the soils, the contrast is between land that produces and land that does not. Both drink in the rain that falls on them; and both are intended to be useful to those for whom they are being farmed. In the first case, the land produces a useful crop and receives the blessing of God. But in the second case, the land produces only thorns and thistles; it is worthless, in danger of being cursed (though still not abandoned as utterly worthless), and in the end is burned (a common farmer's solution for dealing with a weed-infested field, in order to prepare it for the next planting season). Similarly, the believer receives blessings from God for a purpose; he or she is expected to produce something useful for the Lord with these resources and opportunities; something of value is supposed to grow in and through his or her life.

A similar but slightly more specific word than *ge* (soil/land) is used by Paul in 1 Corinthians 3, where Paul speaks of planting the seed at Corinth, Apollos watering it, and God causing the growth; he says, 'you are God's field (*georgion*, cultivated land)' (v. 9). The field belongs to God, and the fieldhands are servants assigned their tasks by him (v. 5). The field is the context for growth and development; it is full of possibilities; with proper cultivation a great harvest can be obtained. The focus of the illustration is found in the phrase in verse 6: 'God made it grow.' That is the one matter of consequence—not the names of the fieldhands, but the fact that the crop actually grew and flourished.

FIRSTFRUITS

An agricultural metaphor used a number of times by the New Testament writers is *aparche* (firstfruits). The basic meaning of the word is the first portion, the part set aside for God before the remainder could be used. In Exodus 23 God instituted the Feast of Harvest (also called Feast of Weeks, and later, Pentecost), to be celebrated 'with the firstfruits of the crops you sow in your fields' (23:16). In verse 19 God asks for the 'best of the firstfruits of your soil': not only the first, but also the best.[1] The offering of the firstfruit implies that there is more harvest to come; the first of the crop is given to the Lord, in full confidence that just as he has brought the crops to their initial ripeness, so he will continue his providential care until the whole harvest has been gathered in.

In 1 Corinthians 16:15 Paul refers to the household of Stephanas as 'the first converts (*aparche*) in Achaia.' Their conversion was the promise of many more to come, as the Lord encouraged Paul during his initial days in Corinth: 'I have many people in this city' (Acts 18:10). Paul also extends the illustration of the firstfruits by noting that the household of Stephanas had 'devoted themselves to the service of God,' just like a sacrificial offering.

James, writing to Jewish believers, said that God 'chose to give us birth through the word of truth, that we might be a kind of firstfruits (*aparchen*) of all he created (*ktismaton*)' (1:18). God is here described as the creator of life, the author of new birth. In that the gospel first came to the Jews, these Jewish believers are appropriately called the 'firstfruits' of the whole community of Jews and Gentiles who together comprise the church. Furthermore, as the first generation of believers, they are the 'firstfruits' of those who will be brought to birth in years to come.

In his vision of the 144,000 in the book of Revelation, John describes them as 'offered as firstfruits to God and to the Lamb' (14:4). This symbolic number has been variously interpreted. But the reference to them as 'firstfruits' should be related to the passages in Revelation about 'the multitude that no one could count, from every nation, tribe, people, and nation' (7:9) who remain faithful during the great tribulation, and to the proclamation of the gospel to 'every nation, tribe, language, and people' (14:6); thus the 144,000 represent the first of a much greater number of believers to be gathered to Christ from all over the world.

The image of the firstfruit, also used of Christ as the first to rise from the dead (1 Corinthians 15:20), turns our attention toward the final harvest. It reminds us of the great worldwide mission of the church, and the task of making disciples from every nation before the Lord returns. It is an image of hope, assuring us that there are still many peoples yet to be represented around the throne of the Lamb, and that many fields are becoming ripe for harvest. Paul Minear says:

> This idea reflects a strong sense of the church's mission to the world. It locates the historical present of the church as lying between what God has done and what he surely will do (1960:112).

NEW PLANTING

Another kind of growth is implied in the one other agricultural image used by the apostle Paul. He warns Timothy that the person appointed as overseer must not be a *neophytos* ('recent convert', 1 Timothy 3:6). Literally, he must not be 'newly planted', like a tender young tree just set into the soil. A young believer must have opportunity to grow, to develop strength, to attain some measure of maturity. The ability to bear good fruit must be demonstrated. If such growth has not had time to occur, there is considerable risk that the appointment to leadership will foster pride, and will make the new believer vulnerable to spiritual attack (3:6). Potential leaders need time to grow.

Images related to dispersion/influence

Two of the most familiar illustrations Jesus used in the Sermon on the Mount are 'salt' and 'light.' Both speak of the disciples' powerful influence on their world. Although salt is used as an image of words that have impact (Colossians 4:6), it does not otherwise appear outside the Gospels. The image of light, however, is more common.

LIGHT

Paul reminds the Thessalonian believers: 'You are all sons of the light (*hyioi photos*) and sons of the day' (1 Thessalonians 5:5), and that therefore they should be alert, self-controlled, and ready for Christ's coming. He exhorts the Ephesians: 'You were once darkness, but now you are light (*phos*) in the Lord; live as children of light (*tekna photos*)' (5:8). In the following verse Paul explains what that life of 'light' involves: goodness, righteousness, and truth. Continuing the metaphor, he urges them to expose the darkness of the world around them (5:11–14), bringing hidden things into the light. Thus the image of light is not only a symbol of the moral purity to which Christians are called, but also a call to confront the world with the reality of God's truth.

The same combination of the call to moral purity and the summons to proclaim God's truth to the world is conveyed by Paul's use of the image of the star (*phoster*) in Philippians 2:

> Do everything without complaining or arguing, so that you may be blameless and pure, children of God without fault in a crooked and depraved generation, in which you shine like stars (*phosteres*) in the universe as you hold out the word of life (2:14–16).

AROMA

Several new illustrations are introduced by Paul to describe the influence of believers on those around them. In 2 Corinthians 2 he describes the Christian life in terms of the triumphal procession of a victorious general, accompanied by the burning of aromatic spices. The bystanders have two very different reactions to the aroma. Some find it pleasing and life-giving; others find it nauseating and deadly. Paul uses two words for odor—*euodia* (fragrance) and *osme* (aroma, which can be either positive or negative). He says:

> Thanks be to God, who always leads us in triumphal procession in Christ and through us spreads everywhere the fragrance (*ten osmen*) of the knowledge of him. For we are to God the aroma (*euodia*) of Christ among those who are being saved and those who are perishing. To the one we are the smell (*osme*) of death; to the other, the fragrance (*osme*) of life (2:14–16).

Flender (DNTT III:599) notes that in the ancient world 'smell was considered to contain, quite literally, a life-giving force.' Odors are also noteworthy for the powerful associations they convey; they have the ability to awaken memories and emotions. Furthermore, odors are pervasive. Just as the fragrance of the ointment poured on Jesus' feet filled the house (John 12:3, *osme*), so the fragrance from the procession penetrates 'everywhere (*en panti topoi*)' (2 Corinthians 2:14). Whether it is perceived as pleasant or repulsive, the odor cannot be ignored. In the same way, the Christian witness in the world will evoke a variety of responses, but if it is truly the 'fragrance of Christ', people will be unable to disregard it.

LETTER

In this same letter to the Corinthians, Paul pictures them as a letter (*epistole*) of recommendation written from Christ, by Paul, with the Holy Spirit, on the hearts of Paul and Timothy (2 Corinthians 3:1–3). It is an open letter, displayed for anyone to read, providing proof of the authenticity of Paul's ministry, in that the letter describes lives that have been changed by the gospel. Christ is the author of the letter; Paul is only the scribe. The point of the illustration is that the very existence and life of the Corinthian church gives public evidence to the power of Christ, and to the effectiveness of the apostolic ministry.

In choosing this image, Paul was drawing on a very familiar practice in the first-century world. Letter-writing was such a common means of communication that standard formats were developed for various kinds of letters. The letters were often written by secretaries, and were sent through slaves, friends, and even strangers who happened to be traveling in the right direction (Stambaugh and Balch 1986:39–40; Malherbe 1983:101–103).

MODEL

One other term in this category is the word *typos*, which means a model, or pattern. The original meaning is that of a form, and in particular, a hollow mold, which leaves an impression when pressed against another object (Müller, DNTT III:904–905). This word is found in several of the New Testament letters in reference to believers setting a pattern of life for others to imitate. Paul commends the Thessalonians for becoming imitators of the apostles and the Lord, and subsequently becoming 'a model (*typon*) to all the believers in Macedonia and Achaia' (1 Thessalonians 1:7), known for their faith and for their decisive turning from idols to

God. In his second letter to them, Paul recalls how he and his team worked constantly in order to provide for their own needs, 'in order to make ourselves a model (*typon*) for you to follow (*mimeisthai*)' (2 Thessalonians 3:9); the need for such a model is evident from the surrounding verses, in which Paul rebukes those who are unwilling to work for a living (3:6, 11–12).

Paul invites the Philippian believers: 'Join with others in following my example (*symmimetai*), brothers, and take note of those who live according to the pattern (*typon*) we gave you' (3:17). Similarly, he urges Timothy, though he is relatively young, to 'set an example (*typos*) for the believers' (1 Timothy 4:12), and Titus also to set an example for the young men in everything, by doing what is good (Titus 2:7). Peter encourages the elders not to be domineering in their leadership, but rather to be 'examples (*typoi*) to the flock' (1 Peter 5:3). Each of these passages highlights the special responsibility of the spiritual leader to set the pace, and to provide a pattern of life that is worthy of imitation.[2] DeBoer explains that:

> Within the whole complex of ideas expressed by *typos*, that of personal example has a natural place. In the world of the New Testament and in the New Testament itself it was a well-established and well-accepted usage. The fact that upon occasion in the New Testament it is very closely connected to the idea of imitation serves as a further confirmation of this usage (1962:23).

As Price puts it succinctly, 'Basically to become a disciple is to become a duplicate' (1989:36); to be a follower of Jesus is to be conformed to his image, and to become a leader is to participate in the molding process.

Images related to service

The final set of images express various aspects of our service to God. None of them is used by Jesus in the Gospels to describe his followers.

VESSEL

The first word is *skeuos* (vessel). In Acts 9:15 the Lord tells Ananias that Paul is 'my chosen instrument (*skeuos ekloges*) to carry (*bastasai*) my name before the Gentiles and their kings and the people of Israel.' Paul says to the Corinthians that 'we have this treasure in jars of clay (ostrakinos skeuesin) to show that this all-surpassing power is from God and not from us' (2 Corinthians 4:7). The 'treasure' is the life of Jesus in us (v. 10); the containers are our weak, fallible bodies and human natures. Paul contrasts household articles used for noble purposes with those used for ignoble purposes, and urges Timothy to be an 'instrument (skeuos) for noble purposes, made holy, useful to the Master and prepared to do any good work' (2 Timothy 2:21). In each case the emphasis of this image is on the task. The Christian has a job to do; it may be 'any good work', or more specifically, the task of proclaiming the gospel. Although the image of the vessel is applied specifically to Christian leaders in two of the passages, it is equally appropriate for any believer.

SPIRITUAL HOUSE

The image of 'spiritual house' (oikos pneumatikos) from 1 Peter 2 is included in this section because its focus is the activity that takes place in the 'building', that is, 'offering spiritual sacrifices acceptable to God through Jesus Christ' (v. 5). Here the community of Christ is seen both as a temple, a place of worship, and as the priesthood that serves in the temple.[3] The 'spiritual sacrifices' would include expressions of thanksgiving and praise, as well as acts of obedient service (cf. Hebrews 13:15–16; Romans 12:1).

WORKMANSHIP

Another term linked closely with service to God is Paul's description of Christians in Ephesians 2:10: 'For we are God's workmanship (poiema), created (ktisthentes) in Christ Jesus to do good works, which God prepared in advance for us to do.' The purpose of God's creative artistry is that we might do the good works that have been assigned to us.

CROWN

Twice Paul refers to believers as his crown (stephanos). He tells the Philippians that he loves them and longs for them, that they are his 'joy and crown' (4:1). To the Thessalonians he writes: 'What is our hope, our joy, or the crown in which we will glory in the presence of our Lord Jesus Christ when he comes? Is it not you?' (1 Thessalonians 2:19).

The usual meaning of stephanos throughout the Greek world was 'crown' or 'wreath', especially the wreath of leaves bestowed to victors in athletic events; the state also awarded wreaths worked in gold as a mark of high honor; the stephanos was associated with victory, celebration, worship, royalty and public honor (Hemer, DNTT

I:405). When Paul calls these two churches, with whom he has such affectionate relationships, his 'crown', he is using a symbol of accomplishment, of victory won, of mission fulfilled. The establishment of a healthy church validates the ministry of the church-planter. The 'crown' metaphor also implies that a struggle has been won, that the goal has been achieved in spite of opposition and obstacles.

Another possible set of associations for the Thessalonian passage is described by Hemer:

> At the official visit (Gk. *parousia*) of a human potentate it was the custom to present him with a crown as a token of allegiance... Perhaps in 1 Th. 2:19 the Thessalonians are seen as Paul's joyful tribute to the coming Christ (DNTT I:406).

SEAL

The final metaphor is the seal (*sphragis*). This noun refers 'both to the tool that seals (e.g. a signet ring), the stone set in it (the gem) and the engraving on it (an image or name) as well as its imprint' (Schippers, DNTT III:497). In Mesopotamia, says Schippers, everyone had a staff and seal in order to mark personal property, to symbolize authority, and to serve as a guarantee or sign of protection.

Paul says to the Corinthians that he should not have to defend his position as a true apostle of Christ, because, 'you are the seal (*sphragis*) of my apostleship (*apostoles*) in the Lord' (1 Corinthians 9:2). Here the seal is used as a symbol of the genuine article; the Corinthians are the proof that Paul is not an impostor; their spiritual life and existence as a community testify to the integrity and effectiveness of Paul's apostolic work in preaching the gospel and establishing churches.

Additions to the taxonomy

The final modifications can now be added to the taxonomy of images. Once again, the majority of images discussed in this chapter are not found in the Gospels, even though they underscore the same themes emphasized by Jesus.

2.2. Emphasis on Tasks

2.2.1. Images related to growth
2.2.1.1. Soil (*ge*)*
2.2.1.1.1. Field (*georgion*)

2.2.1.1.1.1. Productive soil
2.2.1.1.1.2. Unproductive soil
   2.2.1.1.1.2.1. Pathway
   2.2.1.1.1.2.2. Rocky soil
   2.2.1.1.1.2.3. Thorny soil
2.2.1.2. Branch of vine (*klema*)
   2.2.1.2.1. Fruitful
   2.2.1.2.2. Unfruitful
2.2.1.3. Wheat (*sitos*)
   2.2.1.3.1. Seed (*sperma*)
2.2.1.4. *Firstfruits* (**aparche**)
2.2.1.5. *Something newly planted* (**neophytos**)

2.2.2. Images related to dispersion/influence
   2.2.2.1. Salt (*halas*)
      2.2.2.1.1. Savory
      2.2.2.1.2. Lost savor
   2.2.2.2. Light (*phos*)*
      2.2.2.2.1. Lamp in a house
         2.2.2.2.1.1. On lampstand
         2.2.2.2.1.2. Under a bowl
      2.2.2.2.2. *Star* (**phoster**)
   2.2.2.3. *Aroma*
      2.2.2.3.1. *Fragrance* (**euodia**)
      2.2.2.3.2. *Aroma* (**osme**)
   2.2.2.4. *Letter* (**epistole**)
   2.2.2.5. *Model/pattern* (**typos**)

2.2.3. *Images related to service*
   2.2.3.1. *Vessel* (**skeuos**)
   2.2.3.2. *Spiritual house* (**oikos**)
   2.2.3.3. *Workmanship* (**poiema**)
   2.2.3.4. *Crown* (**stephanos**)
   2.2.3.5. *Seal* (**sphragis**)

Notes

1   Cf. Abel's gift of the 'fat portions' from 'some of the firstborn' of his flock (Genesis 4:4). Various other instructions about the offering of firstfruits is found in Leviticus 2:12, 14; 23:10, 17; Numbers 28:26.

2   See Hian's chapter on 'Leaders as Examples' (1987:47–58).

3   Elliott (1981) suggests that *oikos* in this passage should be translated as 'house' or 'household' rather than 'spiritual temple', linking the word closely to the 'priesthood'; however, I believe that since the image grows out of the reference to the living stones, and leads immediately into the description of Christ as the cornerstone, it is better taken as a 'building' in which priests serve; thus Peter moves back and forth between two images in these paragraphs, a building and a priesthood.

Table 2

Taxonomy of New Testament terms, roles and images describing followers of Jesus

1. People

    1.1. Emphasis on Relationships

        1.1.1. Relationship by birth
            1.1.1.1. Member of household (*oikiakos*) (*oikeios, oikos*)
                1.1.1.1.1. Sibling
                    1.1.1.1.1.1. Brother (*adelphos*)*(**adelphotes**)
                    1.1.1.1.1.2. Sister (*adelphe*)*
                1.1.1.1.2. Child
                    1.1.1.1.2.1. Child (*hyios*)*
                      1.1.1.1.2.1.1. Son (*hyios*)*
                      *1.1.1.1.2.1.2. Daughter (**thygater**)*
                    1.1.1.1.2.2. Child (*teknion*)*
                    1.1.1.1.2.3. Child (*teknon*)*
                    1.1.1.1.2.4. Child (nepios)*
                    1.1.1.1.2.5. Child (paidion)*
                    *1.1.1.1.2.6. Baby (**brephos**)*
                    *1.1.1.1.2.7. Heir (**kleronomos, synkleronomos**)*
                    *1.1.1.1.2.8. Descendant (seed) (**sperma**)*
                    *1.1.1.1.2.9. Child by adoption (**hyiothesia**)*
                *1.1.1.1.3. Parent (**goneus**)*
                    *1.1.1.1.3.1. Mother (**meter**)*
                      *1.1.1.1.3.1.1. Nursing Mother (**trophos**)*
                    *1.1.1.1.3.2. Father (**pater**)*
              1.1.1.2. Member of a people
                1.1.1.2.1. Images of association
                    *1.1.1.2.1.1. Member of race (**genos**)*
                    *1.1.1.2.1.2. Member of nation (**ethnos**)*
                    *1.1.1.2.1.3. Member of people (**laos**)*
                    *1.1.1.2.1.4. Citizen of heavenly city (**polis,*
                                    sympolites, politeuma)*
                    *1.1.1.2.1.5. Neighbor (**plesion**)*
                1.1.1.2.2. Images of disassociation
                    *1.1.1.2.2.1. Temporary resident (**parepidemos**)*
                    *1.1.1.2.2.2. Stranger (**paroikos**)*

1.1.2. Relationship by appointment
    1.1.2.1. Chosen (*eklektos*)*
    1.1.2.2. Twelve (*dodeka*)*
    *1.1.2.3. Saint (**hagios**)*
    *1.1.2.4. Freedman (**apeleutheros, eleutheros**)*
    *1.1.2.5. Member of assembly/church (**ekklesia**)*
    *1.1.2.6. One who is called (**kletos**)*
    *1.1.2.7. Priest (**hiereus**)*

1.1.3. Relationship by voluntary association
    1.1.3.1. Friend
        1.1.3.1.1. Friend (*philos*)*
        1.1.3.1.2. Friend (*hetairos*)
    1.1.3.2. Wedding participant
        1.1.3.2.1. Friend of bridegroom (*hyios tou nymphonos*)
        1.1.3.2.2. Friend of bride—virgin with lamp
        1.1.3.2.3. Guest at wedding banquet
        *1.1.3.2.4. Virgin engaged (**parthenos**)*
        *1.1.3.2.5. Bride (**nymphe, gyne**)*
    1.1.3.3. Follower
        1.1.3.3.1. Disciple (*mathetes*)*
        *1.1.3.3.2. Imitator (**mimetes**)*
        *1.1.3.3.3. Follower of the way (**hodos**)*
        *1.1.3.3.4. Believer (**pistos**)*
        *1.1.3.3.5. Christian (**Christianos**)*
    *1.1.3.4. Beloved (**agapetos**)*
    *1.1.3.5. Partner (**koinonos, synkoinonos**)*
    *1.1.3.6. Patroness/helper (**prostatis**)*

1.2. Emphasis on Tasks

    1.2.1. Task executed under the authority of another
        1.2.1.1. Servant (*doulos*)* (**syndoulos, doule**)
            1.2.1.1.1. Relationship words
                1.2.1.1.1.1. Hired servant (*misthios*)
                1.2.1.1.1.2. Low status servant
                    1.2.1.1.1.2.1. Manservant (*pais*)
                    1.2.1.1.1.2.2. Maidservant (*paidiske*)
                1.2.1.1.1.3. Member of household (*oiketes*)*
            1.2.1.1.2. Function words
                1.2.1.1.2.1. Personal helper (*therapeia*)
                1.2.1.1.2.2. Assistant for tasks (*hyperetes*)*
                1.2.1.1.2.3. Server for meals (*diakonos*)*
                1.2.1.1.2.4. Manager (*oikonomos*)*
                *1.2.1.1.2.5. One who serves God (**latreuo**)*
                *1.2.1.1.2.6. One who renders public service (**leitourgos**)*
                *1.2.1.1.2.7. Guardian (**paidagogos**)*
        1.2.1.2. Shepherd (*poimen, poimaino*)*
        1.2.1.3. Worker (*ergates*)* (**synergos**)

*1.2.1.3.1. Farmer (**georgos**)*
　　*1.2.1.3.1.1. One who plants (**phyteuon**)*
　　*1.2.1.3.1.2. One who waters (**potizon**)*
*1.2.1.3.2. Yokefellow (**syzygos**)*
1.2.1.4. Apostle (*apostolos*)* (**apostole**)
1.2.1.5. Messenger
　　1.2.1.5.1. Messenger with good news (evangelist)
　　　　　　　　　　　　　　　　　　　　　　*(**euaggelistes**)*
　　*1.2.1.5.2. Herald (**keryx**)*
1.2.1.6. Ambassador (**presbeuo**)
1.2.1.7. Soldier (**stratiotes, systratiotes**)

1.2.2. Task executed independently
　　1.2.2.1. Witness (*martys*)*
　　　　*1.2.2.1.1. Eyewitness (**epoptes**)*
　　1.2.2.2. Fisherman (*alieus*)
　　*1.2.2.3. Athlete (**athleo**)*
　　　　*1.2.2.3.1. Contestant (**agonizomenos**)*
　　　　　　*1.2.2.3.1.1. Wrestler (**pale**)*
　　　　　　*1.2.2.3.1.2. Boxer (**pykteuo**)*
　　　　　　*1.2.2.3.1.3. Runner (**trecho**)*
　　　　　　　　*1.2.2.3.1.3.1. One who finishes the race (**dromos**)*
　　1.2.2.4. Leader/Director
　　　　*1.2.2.4.1. Expert builder (**architekton**)*
　　　　*1.2.2.4.2. Royal ruler (**basileia, basileuo**)*
　　　　*1.2.2.4.3. Overseer (**episkopos**)*
　　　　*1.2.2.4.4. Leader (**hegemonos**)*
　　　　*1.2.2.4.5. Pilot (**kybernesis**)*
　　　　*1.2.2.4.6. Elder (**presbyteros**)*
　　　　*1.2.2.4.7. Leader (**prohistemi**)*
　　1.2.2.5. Teacher (**didaskalos**)
　　　　*1.2.2.5.1. Instructor (**katecheo**)*
　　1.2.2.6. Prophet (**prophetes**)

2. Things

2.1. Emphasis on Relationships

2.1.1. Images of weakness/dependence
　2.1.1.1. Sheep/flock (*probaton, poimnion*)*
　2.1.1.2. Mist (**atmis**)

2.1.2. Images of suffering/rejection
　*2.1.2.1. Scum (**perikatharma**)*
　*2.1.2.2. Refuse (**peripsema**)*

2.1.3. Images of honor/dignity
　*2.1.3.1. Temple (**naos**)*
　*2.1.3.2. Creation (**ktisis**)*

2.1.3.3. Treasure
    2.1.3.3.1. Special possession (**peripoiesis**)
    2.1.3.3.2. Treasured possession (**periousios**)

2.1.4. Images of interconnection
    2.1.4.1. Building (**katoiketerion, oikodome**)
        2.1.4.1.1. Foundation
            2.1.4.1.1.1. (**hedraioma**)
            2.1.4.1.1.2. (**themelios**)
        2.1.4.1.2. Stone (**lithos**)
        2.1.4.1.3. Pillar (**stylos**)
    2.1.4.2. Branches of olive tree (**elaia**)
    2.1.4.3. Members (**mele**) of body (**soma**)
        2.1.4.3.1. Members together (**syssomos**)
    2.1.4.4. Batch of dough (**phyrema**)

2.2. Emphasis on Tasks

2.2.1. Images related to growth
    2.2.1.1. Soil (ge)*
        2.2.1.1.1. Field (**georgion**)
            2.2.1.1.1.1. Productive soil
            2.2.1.1.1.2. Unproductive soil
                2.2.1.1.1.2.1. Pathway
                2.2.1.1.1.2.2. Rocky soil
                2.2.1.1.1.2.3. Thorny soil
    2.2.1.2. Branch of vine (**klema**)
        2.2.1.2.1. Fruitful
        2.2.1.2.2. Unfruitful
    2.2.1.3. Wheat (**sitos**)
        2.2.1.3.1. Seed (**sperma**)
    2.2.1.4. Firstfruits (**aparche**)
    2.2.1.5. Something newly planted (**neophytos**)

2.2.2. Images related to dispersion/influence
    2.2.2.1. Salt (**halas**)
        2.2.2.1.1. Savory
        2.2.2.1.2. Lost savor
    2.2.2.2. Light (**phos**)*
        2.2.2.2.1. Lamp in a house
            2.2.2.2.1.1. On lampstand
            2.2.2.2.1.2. Under a bowl
        2.2.2.2.2. Star (**phoster**)
    2.2.2.3. Aroma
        2.2.2.3.1. Fragrance (**euodia**)
        2.2.2.3.2. Aroma (**osme**)
    2.2.2.4. Letter (**epistole**)
    2.2.2.5. Model/pattern (**typos**)

2.2.3. *Images related to service*
    2.2.3.1. *Vessel (**skeuos**)*
    2.2.3.2. *Spiritual house (**oikos**)*
    2.2.3.3. *Workmanship (**poiema**)*
    2.2.3.4. *Crown (**stephanos**)*
    2.2.3.5. *Seal (**sphragis**)*

13
Reflections on the themes

In chapter four we identified seven themes that were expressed repeatedly in the terms chosen by Jesus to describe his followers. As we explore the ways in which these terms are used by the writers of the early church, and as we examine the new terms that are introduced, we discover that the same themes continue to recur.

Although the New Testament writings show considerable diversity in style, vocabulary, and imagery, a deep underlying unity becomes evident when we look at the basic ideas about discipleship and leadership that are expressed. We find that we are not listening to new and original melodies, but to variations on a theme. We do not uncover totally new patterns of thought and life, but new perspectives and further insights into teaching already given by Jesus to his followers. In this chapter we will look at some of the ways in which the seven themes are developed.

1. Function

The disciple is called to participation in a community as well as to a task.

One cannot read the New Testament letters and the Book of Acts without being impressed by the depth of loving commitment that tied together the early Christian communities. The frequent affectionate references to one another as brother and sister, and the tender parental concern shown by the apostles toward the congregations they established and nurtured, testify to the warmth and strength of the bonds of this new spiritual family. The many appearances of *oikos* (household) and its compounds, descriptions of believers as a chosen people, and the frequent use of images such as the building and the body express the essential unity of the Church.

During the Last Supper, Jesus spoke at length about the love for one another that would be the hallmark of his true followers. In the remainder of the New Testament we see much more about the ways in which that love was expressed. In the Gospels, the competition between the disciples is often more evident than their teamwork; but in the early church we observe numerous *sun-* compounds—fellow-worker, fellow-citizen, fellow-athlete, fellow-soldier, yokefellow,

fellow-elder, fellow-member, fellow-heir, fellow-imitator—all expressing a cooperative and sympathetic spirit of oneness. Other images express the bonds that tie believers together as imitators of one another, followers of the same Way, sheep led by the same shepherds, branches grafted into the same tree, and a body that suffers and rejoices with each of its members. Although the differences between believers are acknowledged, images like the body show that there is unity amidst the diversity of gifts.

The community unites, but it also separates. The heavenly citizenship that brings Jews and Gentiles together simultaneously makes them aliens and strangers to their own society. The call to be saints involves separation from the world. As light they are responsible to expose and rebuke the darkness.

The metaphors of the New Testament letters often highlight the privileges that accompany membership in the community—such as the bride's experience of her husband's loving nurture, the slave set free, the son adopted into the family, the temple as the dwelling of God's Spirit, and the church as God's chosen people and treasured possession. The disciples can rejoice not only for all the new dimensions of relationship to one another, but also for the intimacy of fellowship with the Lord who has called them his friend.

Yet, the emphasis on community does not overshadow the importance of the task committed to followers of Jesus Christ.[1] The metaphors drawn from priesthood and temple, including words for 'serve' like *latreuo* and *leitourgeo*, point to the duties of worship, praise, and thanksgiving, as well as the consecration of the entire life as a type of spiritual sacrifice. The church is called to serve and to build up one another through the functioning of the spiritual gifts in the body, through acts of imitating and modeling, and through the nurture of younger believers as parents with children.

The primary focus of the church's service in the world is presented as the proclamation of the good news of Jesus Christ, expressed through the use of terms like apostle, evangelist, herald, and ambassador. Broader dimensions of service and good works are implied in images like light, stars, and fragrance.

This engagement with the world involves conflict. The images of striving as an athlete in competition, and fighting as a soldier with the forces of darkness, appear frequently.

In addition to the tasks to which every follower of Jesus is called, several images accent the specific and different tasks for which various ones are responsible as stewards of different parts of the household, or as different members of the body. In particular, new terms are introduced that apply specifically to leaders within the fellowship: words such as *episkopos* (overseer), *kybernesis* (administration), *presbyteros* (elder), and *prohistemi* (leader), in addition to the further development of terms like *poimen* (shepherd), *apostolos* (apostle), and *hegemonos* (leader) that were used by Jesus. In the Gospels, the main emphasis is on the responsibility of the disciple as servant to follow; but the remainder of the New Testament reveals more of the dimensions of responsibility and oversight to which various servants are assigned.

So then, both dimensions of community and task remain equally prominent throughout the New Testament.

2. Authority

The disciple is under authority.

The image of the servant remains a central motif in the New Testament letters. The apostles describe themselves as servants of Christ. Even the freedom of the Christian is seen as freedom to serve, not as absolute autonomy. Terms that imply one who is under authority include frequently used words like sheep, soldier, steward, and apostle, as well as terms like ambassador, pilot, herald, and vessel. Christ is the head of the body, and the cornerstone of the building. He is the chief shepherd of the flock.

A new dimension of living under authority that emerges in the early church is the authority exercised within the community by its human leaders. Believers are called to obey their leaders, to respect them, and to submit to them. To describe elders as shepherds and overseers is to imply that the congregation must follow their direction. The call to imitate Christian leaders is to accept the authority of a pattern of life.

To be a disciple is also to live under the authority of the Word of God. The image of the athlete is associated with the need for strict training and discipline.

3. Responsibility

The disciple exercises authority.

The responsibility of the disciple to exercise authority was implied by Jesus in some of his stewardship parables, in his promises to the disciples about judging the twelve tribes of Israel in the coming kingdom, and in his exhortation to Peter after the resurrection to 'feed my sheep.' Yet, as we have seen, the greater emphasis in the Gospels is on the disciples' need to come under the Lord's authority, rather than on their own exercise of authority.

However, after Jesus' ascension to heaven, the role of leadership in the Christian community undergoes considerable development. Prophets and apostles provide overall direction for the church, based on the authoritative proclamation of the Word of God. Various leadership gifts begin to function. Soon elders and deacons are appointed to oversee the affairs of local congregations. Several of the terms used specifically imply the provision of direction and the exercise of authority—especially *apostolos, episkopos, hegemonos, kybernesis, oikonomos, poimen, prohistemi,* and *presbyteros.*

In addition to these specific authority roles, believers in general are appointed to positions of responsibility by the risen Lord. All are instructed to exercise their spiritual gifts as stewards (*oikonomoi*) of the many-faceted grace of God. As a kingdom of priests, all are promised a share in Christ's rule in the coming kingdom. All are invited to represent as ambassadors the King of Kings, proclaiming the message of reconciliation.

4. Derivation

The disciple is one who has responded to the call of Jesus.

The statement of this theme has two aspects. In the first place, it emphasizes that God is the initiator; everything comes from him and starts with him. On the other hand, to be a disciple is to respond willingly to the call, not to be conscripted as an unwilling recruit.

Just as Jesus did, the New Testament writers place great emphasis on the gracious call of God. The very word *ekklesia* (church) pictures an assembly that has gathered in response to a call. Paul describes himself as called to be an apostle, and appointed to be a herald; he says that by God's grace he has been allowed to lay the foundation upon which others are building. The grace, mercy, and love of God are the foundations for our adoption as God's children and his choice of us as a holy nation.

The complete dependence of the church on Christ is expressed in the pictures of Christ as head of the body and cornerstone of the building. The sheep cannot survive apart from the Great Shepherd. Although one plants and another waters, it is God who causes the growth. Every enablement for ministry is a spiritual gift distributed according to God's design. The evangelist, the prophet, and the herald pass on messages given to them by God, not of their own invention. Each believer is a 'new creature', endowed with life that only God can create. Even our very physical existence is like a mist, here only for as long as God's grace allows.

Yet the New Testament images do not express God's initiating role alone. They also indicate the importance of willing human response. The follower of Jesus is a disciple, an imitator, a follower of the Way, a believer.

5. Status

Disciples are on the same level in relationship to God, even though they may have different areas and amounts of responsibility.

Although different levels of responsibility and authority become increasingly evident as the early church develops and becomes more organized, most of the New Testament imagery emphasizes what believers have in common, rather than the ways in which they are different.

On the one hand, there are terms that indicate that no one is higher than anyone else. The ministry of all, including apostles, is called simply *diakonia*, service as a table-waiter. Even the greatest leader is no more than a servant of the Master. All are children of God, and brothers and sisters to one another. Paul describes himself as a common clay pot holding the priceless treasure of the gospel. Both the one who plants and the one who waters the field are merely doing the task assigned to them.

On the other hand, there are numerous terms indicating the high status that all believers now enjoy because of their union with Christ. Privileges that other societies confer on only a few are now the possession of even the humblest Christian. Each one is a royal priest. Each shares in the rule of Christ's kingdom. Each has been adopted as a child of God. Each one's body is a temple of the Holy Spirit. Each is a full citizen in the new Jerusalem. Each is called saint, chosen, beloved, freedman, heir and treasure.

Yet functional differences remain. Wives are still to be subject to their husbands, children are to obey parents, slaves are to serve their masters cheerfully. Members of the congregation are told to obey and to submit to their leaders, and to keep on paying taxes and giving respect to government authorities. But the one with authority is to remember that he or she is not better than the others, and the one under authority is to remember the dignity and freedom of his or her calling. Whatever may be their differences in social standing in the eyes of society, or their various responsibilities in the church, they are first and foremost partners, fellow-workers, fellow-heirs, children of the same Father.

6. Identification

To be a disciple is to identify with Jesus, both in his pattern of life and in his suffering.

To follow Jesus is not simply to accept a body of beliefs but to adopt a pattern of life. To be Jesus' disciple is to become like him. This emphasis on life transformation and training through personal identification is continued through the use of terms like imitator, disciple, model, and follower of the Way.

The distinctive identification of the believer with the life of Jesus Christ is implied in the application of the nickname 'Christian', and in the call to behave like an alien and a temporary resident. The child of God is expected to be holy as is the heavenly Father. The fragrance of the believer's life is supposed to make people aware of Jesus.

Identification with Jesus means not only imitation of his character but also participation in his mission, even to the point of suffering and death. Many of the New Testament images are associated closely with the suffering that the believer will experience for Christ's sake. The apostles lead the way into the arena of death, and are seen by many as the scum and refuse of the earth. The saints in the book of Revelation endure through tribulation. The athlete must run the race with endurance, and must wrestle with the forces of darkness. The witness often becomes the martyr. The Christian as soldier contends with deadly opposition, and can survive only as protected by God's armor. To be an alien is to be excluded and sometimes persecuted for one's differences. To serve is to suffer.

The leader is not exempt in any way from these hardships and sacrifices. No, the leader is to be the model of pouring out one's life as a sacrificial offering.

7. Accountability

The disciple will be evaluated by the Lord, in terms of his character as well as his service.

Just as Jesus contrasted those who were faithful and effective servants with those who were not, so the New Testament writers speak of vessels of honor and dishonor, fields that produces a crop and others that drink the same rain but yield only thistles, those who have matured and those who remain as infants, those who have become teachers and those who still must be taught. The athletic images illustrate again and again that there is a prize to be won, a crown to be awarded, but that not everyone will even finish the race, let alone be honored as a victor.

Fellow-believers may presume to evaluate one another's performance. But several images suggest caution. The believer is a servant who stands or falls to his own master (Romans 14:4). Paul claims that his faithfulness in stewardship is known only to the Lord, who will make the true assessment at the last judgment (1 Corinthians 4:1–5). He defends himself before his critics by saying that the churches he has planted stand as his crown, his seal, his letter of recommendation. The evaluation for which the believer must prepare is the one that will take place at the judgment seat of Christ (2 Corinthians 5:10).

Note

1 Anderson and Jones, citing images like salt and light, hold that the church differs from other community groups in that it is 'called to be rather than to do' (1978:133). Cedar believes that 'serving as a leader in Christ's kingdom relates to people more than to tasks' (1987:90). Van Engen, however, after reviewing the New Testament images of the church, concludes that 'all of them signal a task to be done' (1981:69). R. Anderson provides a balanced summary: '... leadership from a biblical perspective is not so much task oriented as it is community oriented, although in many cases it does involve the performance of a task or the enabling and equipping of others to perform tasks' (1986:69).

14

Conclusions and implications

We began this investigation with the observation that leadership is a process of influence, and that even though Jesus did not use the words 'leader' or 'leadership', he called his disciples into a development process, through which he prepared them for leadership in the Christian community after his ascension.

Yet Jesus' primary focus in teaching the disciples was not to help them to master the skills often associated with leadership—setting goals, formulating strategies, organizing personnel and resources, exercising authority and discipline. He gave almost no direction about how the early Christian community should be organized, how authority should be delegated, how decisions should be made, how visions should be translated into action, or how others should be mobilized or equipped for the task.

Instead, Jesus showed his disciples how to follow, how to obey, how to respond to the authority and call of God. He knew that the effective leader must first learn how to be a faithful follower. Jesus also knew how destructive the attitudes of pride and ambition could be within the community of disciples. Therefore, he taught them attitudes of humility and self-sacrifice, using the image of the servant, and reminded them of their equal standing before God as brothers. Jesus wanted his disciples to think of themselves as 'among' one another, as brothers, and 'under' one another, as servants, more than 'over', as those in authority.

Jesus was also concerned to help the disciples realize that they were being called to significant relationships as well as to important tasks. They were not just workers; they were also friends. They were not only fishers of men, but also guests at a wedding. Celebration and joy and love were to be as much a part of their vocabulary as responsibility and accountability and diligence. They would be evaluated by their love for one another, and their personal commitment to Jesus, as well as by their faithfulness in completing their assigned tasks and investing their divinely-given resources.

Variations on a theme

To impart such lessons as these, Jesus used many images. We have detailed thirty-five, and have referred briefly to some others. But the primary images used by Jesus can be grouped into two categories—those that describe the followers as members of a spiritual family (brother, child), and those that picture them as servants (of the Lord and of one another). The first group focuses on relationships. The second group focuses on the task.

These same two clusters of images remain in the foreground throughout the New Testament writings. Some new terms are added, but the essential emphasis remains the same—the Christian has been incorporated into a loving, interdependent family, and has been commissioned to serve the Lord as part of the mandate to make disciples of all the nations.

What it means to be a follower of Jesus remains basically the same. The seven themes discussed in chapters four and thirteen are revealed in the teaching of the epistles as fully as in Jesus' instructions to his disciples. Implications are spelled out in more detail, and new images are introduced appropriate to new contexts, but we are hearing variations on a theme, not a totally new melody. Even when specific leadership functions are described for the first time in the book of Acts or in the epistles, the underlying concepts echo ideas that Jesus had previously introduced to his followers.

The leader's perspective

How should an understanding of these biblical images and themes influence leadership behavior in the church? I would like to propose some ways in which reflection on these topics can shape the leader's perspective of his/her own role, and the place of other believers as followers and potential leaders. In this way I will seek to demonstrate the rationale for studying all the biblical terms used for followers of Jesus, rather than simply those that are applied exclusively or at least primarily to leaders.

THE LEADER AS FOLLOWER OF JESUS

Again and again in our reflection on the Gospels, we have noted that Jesus focused more of his attention on teaching the disciples how to follow than on giving them instructions on how to lead.[1] The single most important lesson for a leader to learn is that he/she is first a sheep, not a shepherd; first a child, not a father or mother; first an imitator, not a model. Rather than thinking only about those biblical images that set him/her apart, the leader should reflect on the many, many more images that apply to him/her as fully as to any other believer.

The leader is only a mist, mortal and frail; when he/she is gone, God will raise up others; there is no place in the church for the building of dynasties, or the creation of celebrities or personality cults. No matter how grand the leader's title, or large his/her responsibility, he/she is still a steward, not an owner; a partner, not an independent contractor; a fellow-worker, not a boss; a member of the body, not the head; a branch of the tree, not the root; a servant, not a master. The common clay pot must not forget that the treasure is in the pot, not the pot itself.

THE LEADER'S VIEW OF OTHER FOLLOWERS

Just as the leaders ought not to have too high an opinion of themselves, so should they beware of assuming too low an opinion of the other followers of Jesus. They should remember the terms of dignity and honor by which all followers of Jesus are described. The people they lead are royal priests, precious treasures, full citizens. They have spiritual gifts that are just as essential to the welfare of the body as any exercised by the leader. The leader's role is to equip God's people, to empower them, to help them to become as effective as possible in the service of the King. Believers are salt, light, the very aroma of Christ; scattered throughout society in their various vocations, they can become ambassadors and heralds, witnesses and fishers of men.

Many have the ability to become teachers and models for younger believers. Some have gifts of administration and leadership that need to be encouraged. Some are still 'newly planted', not yet ready for the responsibilities of leadership, but if given time to mature, they will become able overseers and shepherds.

Many educators have observed that people tend to become what the leader expects them to be. How important it is, therefore, for the church leader to see the other church members as potentially fruitful branches, productive fields, and victorious athletes; as sturdy building blocks, shining stars, and sweet aromas; as beloved brothers and sisters, chosen people, valued fellow-workers, and precious friends. And how essential it is for the leader to help the people to see themselves in these terms as well! When leaders respect, honor, recognize, and affirm those they lead, they will find others far more willing to follow them; and when leaders realize the true worth and dignity of those they lead, the leaders themselves will be more ready to lay down their lives in service for those who are so precious to God.

THE LEADER'S SPECIAL ROLE

Yet neither leader nor followers can afford to lose sight of the particular function and calling that is given to the leader. We have noted the special leadership words like *episkopos*, which means one who oversees, and *kybernesis*, which means the work of piloting a ship, and *hegemonos*, which indicates one who takes charge. One cannot 'go in front' as *prohistámenos* (leader) unless others are willing to come behind; the shepherd cannot lead the flock to pasture if every sheep wanders off on its own path.[2] There can be no teaching without some who are willing to be instructed, and no mature guidance without others being willing to yield to the wisdom of the *presbyteroi* (elders).

An emphasis on the priesthood of every believer and the importance of every gift can become an excuse for diminished respect for the leadership function. The teaching of the headship of Christ must not become the denial of the legitimacy of any human authority within the church. We are not free to focus only on the images of discipleship which buttress the egalitarian spirit of our age, while rejecting the images that point to the need for authority and submission as essential for both order and forward movement in a loving community.[3]

The search for appropriate images

A question which we must ask continually is whether the images we use, or any of the other symbols we employ, 'stir the imagination and the religious feeling of the modern beholder' (Dillistone 1986:217). Sometimes we need new images to stir us from our slumber. Messer reminds us that:

> New metaphors have the power to create new realities. Old images sometimes lose their capacity to empower or to transform because they have lost their original novelty and vitality due to trivialization, habitual use, or cultural acceptance and assimilation (1989:171).

The search for appropriate terms and images for church leaders today is complicated by the fact that the more exactly suited a certain image is for a particular time and place, the more difficult it may be to understand it in a different context. How do we speak of precious treasure in fragile clay pots to an aluminum and plastic society? How do we capture the power of the shepherd image with urban youngsters who have never been to a pasture, let alone a zoo, to see a flock of sheep? How meaningful is it to speak of a 'kingdom' to those living under a revolutionary socialist government, or to use the image of a cornerstone with those who construct their homes from mud and thatch? Some might question why we should start with the Bible at all for our imagery, when our own society is twenty centuries and thousands of miles removed.

I would suggest that the most important reason to begin with the biblical imagery is to identify the themes that underlie the images. Those who believe in the full inspiration of scripture will acknowledge that the images themselves are part of the inspired text, and therefore deserving of our careful study.[4] Once we have identified the basic ideas conveyed by the biblical terms, we can evaluate the extent to which other terms express similar meanings.

For example, we have seen from our study of the biblical terms that the disciple is one who is under authority. If our own society does not have masters and slaves, there may be other useful images that convey an authority relationship, such as an army recruit with a drill instructor, or a soccer player with a coach, or a factory worker with a supervisor. To take another illustration, in order to express the idea of the disciple, who imitates another, we may explore relationships like the skilled craftsman with the apprentice, or the guru with the follower, or the musician with the young student.

Each image will have its own associations within a given cultural context. Our task is to determine whether the ideas suggested by that image correspond closely enough to the concepts of discipleship and leadership expressed by the biblical metaphors.

We would be wise, however, in our search for culturally appropriate terms, to stay close to the biblical images as well. For one thing, the Bible is so full of pictorial and metaphorical language that we cannot teach it adequately without helping people to develop a clear understanding of the biblical images in context. We should not underestimate people's ability to grasp and to apply a biblical image once they have understood its background.

Nor should we overstate our own distance from the biblical

images. There are many rural societies in the world today that would have little difficulty understanding the agrarian imagery of the Gospels. Modern societies still have athletes, soldiers, children, resident aliens, and ambassadors. People of all places and times understand light, aroma, and the human body; most know the meaning of letters, trees, and the functions of planting, watering, and harvesting crops. Some of the biblical images like seal, crown, adoption, priesthood, apostleship, and freeing of slaves require more cultural and historical explanation for full understanding, but many of the terms are quite accessible to the modern reader.

The biblical images and the themes that underlie them should also suggest boundaries which will help us to determine which images are not appropriate. As we have seen, not every first-century term for leader was taken into the Christian vocabulary. Most of the terms associated with the synagogue[5] and the pagan religions[6] were avoided. So were the strong authority-laden *arch-* compounds, as well as most other words that denoted ruler and ruled.[7] With images like 'shepherd', which had strong positive associations from the Old Testament writings but unsavory connotations among the rabbis (who scorned shepherds as unreliable and dishonest), the biblical writers chose the particular aspects of the image that they wanted to emphasize.[8] Perhaps a similar evaluation could be performed with words that may carry either positive or negative connotations when applied to leaders in a Christian community—like 'manager' in industrialized societies,[9] and 'guru' in a south Asian context.[10]

The development of leaders

A study of the biblical images can help present-day leaders of the church to examine their ideas, their attitudes, and their patterns of behavior. Such a study can also suggest directions for the development of future leaders. How shall we follow in the footsteps of Jesus to nurture leaders for the church of tomorrow?

In the first place, we must develop leaders who have learned how to follow, who see themselves as lifelong students and servants of the Master. Unless one can accept direction cheerfully, one is not ready to give direction to others. Leadership training begins with obeying the order to leave our nets, and cheerfully picking up fragments of food in baskets; it involves patiently lingering to attend to the sick, staying awake for prayer, and humbly washing feet. Leadership training should not be connected with éliteness and special privilege, but with harder work, greater discipline, and more sacrificial service.

Second, leadership training should provide instruction within the context of personal apprenticeship. To be a follower of Jesus is to learn a pattern of life, not simply to give assent to a creed. Such training in attitudes and behavior cannot possibly occur in a classroom setting alone. There must be opportunities for leaders to live, eat, work, travel, serve, and share with emergent leaders. A life that is not observed cannot be imitated.

Third, the development of leaders needs to involve them in commitment to a community as well as training for a task. The emergent leaders must learn to function effectively as members of a team. They must learn to love their fellow-believers, including other leaders, as members of one family. They must come to rejoice and to suffer with the other members of the body, and to respect the contribution of their fellow-workers.

Fourth, the spiritual aspects of leadership must be stressed. More and more tools of management, planning, and organization are available today. But there is a crying need for leaders who will pray fervently, love deeply, and wage spiritual warfare courageously. Leaders need to be schooled in faith, learning total dependence on the Lord as branches of the vine and members drawing life from the head. They must learn that however much they plant or water, God causes the growth, that he is Lord of the harvest. They must be determined to spread the light and aroma of Christ, not to become well-known themselves. Their message must be delivered as faithful ambassadors and heralds, communicating the words given to them by God's Word and Spirit, not depending on their own intellect or eloquence. In short, they must believe that Christ is everything—*everything*—and that apart from him, they can do nothing (John 15:5).

Yet the ministry of leadership today takes place in a world that is increasingly urban, international, complex and technologically sophisticated. The leader is called to be a steward, a wise manager of all of God's resources—which may include accounting procedures, mass media, computer technology, staff and volunteers with specialized training, and greatly increased knowledge about organizational functioning and cross-cultural communication. Leadership training must include orientation to as much of this modern knowledge and technique as is necessary to foster good stewardship of God's resources. Any tool can be useful in the hands of God's steward, as long as the tool remains the servant and does not become the master.[11]

Some final thoughts

Images are powerful. They shape what we see, by highlighting certain features and moving others into the background. They dominate our patterns of analysis and reflection. They suggest explanations of why we relate to one another the way we do, or why certain structures exist. They support particular understandings of the past, interpretations of the present, and scenarios for the future. They promote some values and discourage others. They suggest priorities, and awaken emotions.

The choice to emphasize a given metaphor and to put aside another can set the direction of a community and its leadership. Therefore, we must become aware of the images we use, and how we are using them. In particular, we must examine the metaphors we use in the development of our future leaders. For example, what is the balance between our use of 'task' metaphors and our use of 'relationship' metaphors? To what extent do our images reinforce a sense of accountability to God in our future leaders? Do they think of themselves first as 'brothers/sisters' and as 'servants', or as rulers and bosses? Do they speak of their relationships to others more in terms of 'among' and 'under', or in terms of 'over'? Do they understand that there are legitimate differences in responsibility and authority that can be assigned within the community? Or does their emphasis on equality for all in the fellowship blind them to their own need to be willing to come under the authority of a fellow-servant, or perhaps to exercise authority as a fellow-servant?

Our answers to questions like these today will determine the shape of the church in which we serve tomorrow.

Notes

1 Paul Cedar says, '... one of the true tests of our qualifications to be effective servant leaders is whether we are willing to become true servant followers. First, we follow Jesus Christ as Lord, and then we follow those whom God has designated as our human leaders' (1987:131).

2 Michael Harper says: 'If every society needs leadership, and leadership needs to be in the hands of a team, then every team requires a captain' (1977:212). Likewise,

Morris observes: 'The minister ought to regard himself as no more than a servant to his people, but his people should regard him as a shepherd over the flock. Great harm is done when the minister thinks of himself as supreme over the flock, or when the people regard him as no more than their servant' (1964:77).

3 Cf. comments by Messer (1989): 'Clergy who think of themselves solely as "enablers" or "facilitators" need to rethink the meaning of ordination and the authority of the clergy. The purpose of theological education is to develop a learned clergy and laity who can give leadership to the church and the world in Christ's name' (p. 73). 'By accenting the powerless servant image to the exclusion of the leader metaphor, people eventually discover that their own self-worth suffers and the church struggles for vision and vitality. Many contemporary churches are hurt more by pastoral default than by pastoral domination' (p. 104). The same warnings about the limitations of the 'enabler' ideal are sounded strongly by Wagner (1984:73–106).

4 Not all are willing to agree that the images as well as the underlying themes are inspired. For example, Barbour holds that 'the images themselves are not directly God-given but arise from man's analogical imagination' (1976:18). Similarly, McFague objects to the view that 'the words and images of the Bible are the authoritative and appropriate words and images for God,' holding that such ideas are a symptom of the religious literalism of our time (1982:4). The basic issue is whether or not one believes that 'all Scripture is God-breathed' (2 Timothy 3:16).

5 Meeks (1983:79, 81); Stambaugh and Balch (1986:142).

6 Stambaugh and Balch (1986:138).

7 Küng (1967:495–498); Meeks (1983:134); Schweizer (1969:171–180). However, the word *archegos* (leader, in the sense of pioneer or founder) is applied to Jesus in Acts 3:15; 5:31; Hebrews 2:10; 12:2.

8 Cf. Messer (1989:171–174).

9 Richards and Hoeldtke (1988) strongly reject the manager metaphor for the pastor; Hutcheson (1979) and Dibbert (1989) also raise many concerns. In contrast, Anderson and Jones (1978:44) as well as Campbell and Reierson (1981:92) speak of the pastor as 'chief executive officer', and Jones says that 'the biblical roles of ministry and management are essentially just different dimensions of our calling to be pastors and Christian workers' (1988:28).

10 Fernando (1985) is one who uses this image in a positive sense, even though others have used the 'guru' and his disciples as an example of the sort of blind following of authority that should never be found in the church.

11 An excellent theological and practical analysis of the use of management techniques within the church can be found in Hutcheson (1979).

References cited

Adams, Jay Edward, 1986, *Shepherding God's Flock: A Handbook on Pastoral Ministry, Counseling, and Leadership*, Grand Rapids, Michigan: Ministry Resources Library

Anderson, James D. and Jones, Ezra Earl, 1978, *The Management of Ministry*, New York: Harper and Row

Anderson, Ray Sherman, 1986, *Minding God's Business*, Grand Rapids, Michigan: Eerdmans

Atkins, Robert Alan, Jr., 1987, *The Integrating Function of Adoption Terminology Used by the Apostle Paul: A Grid-Group Analysis*, Ph.D. dissertation, Northwestern University

Banks, Robert J., 1980, *Paul's Idea of Community: The Early House Churches in Their Historical Setting*, Grand Rapids, Michigan: Eerdmans

Barber, Cyril J. and Stevens, Gary H., 1982, *Leadership: The Dynamics of Success*, Greenwood, South Carolina: The Attic Press

Barbour, Ian G., 1976, *Myths, Models, and Paradigms: A Comparative Study in Science and Religion*, New York: Harper and Row (paperback ed.; 1st ed. 1974)

Barnett, James M., 1981, *The Diaconate: A Full and Equal Order*, New York: Seabury Press

Bauer, Walter, 1979, *A Greek-English Lexicon of the New Testament and Other Early Christian Literature*, Translated and adapted by William F. Arndt and F. Wilbur Gingrich. 2nd. edition revised and augmented by F. Wilbur Gingrich and Frederick W. Danker. Chicago: University of Chicago Press

Best, Ernest, 1988, *Paul and His Converts (The Sprunt Lectures, 1985)*, Edinburgh: T. and T. Clark

Bradley, K.R., 1987, *Slaves and Masters in the Roman Empire: A Study in Social Control*, New York: Oxford University Press

Brown, Colin, editor, 1975, *The New International Dictionary of New Testament Theology*, 3 volumes, Grand Rapids, Michigan: Zondervan

Brown, Raymond E., S.S., 1970, *Priest and Bishop: Biblical Reflections*, New York: Paulist Press

Campbell, Thomas C. and Reierson, Gary B., 1981, *The Gift of Administration*, Philadelphia: Westminster Press

Campenhausen, Hans von, 1969, *Ecclesiastical Authority and Spiritual Power in the Church of the First Three Centuries*, translated by J.A. Baker, Stanford, California: Stanford University Press

Cedar, Paul A., 1987, *Strength in Servant Leadership*, Waco, Texas: Word Books

Cobble, James F., Jr., 1988, *The Church and the Powers: A Theology of Church Structure*, Peabody, Massachusetts: Hendrickson Publishers

Dale, Robert D., 1984, *Ministers as Leaders*, Nashville, Tennessee: Broadman Press

Dale, Robert D., 1986, *Pastoral Leadership: A Handbook of Resources for Effective Congregational Leadership*, Nashville: Abingdon Press

DeBoer, Willis Peter, 1962, *The Imitation of Paul: An Exegetical Study*, Kampen: J.H. Kok

Dibbert, Michael T., 1989, *Spiritual Leadership, Responsible Management: A Guide for Leaders of the Church*, Grand Rapids, Michigan: Zondervan

Dillistone, F.W., 1986, *The Power of Symbols in Religion and Culture*, New York: Crossroad

Dulles, Avery, 1987, *Models of the Church*, Expanded edition. New York: Image Books, Doubleday. (1st ed. 1978)

Dunn, James D.G., 1975, *Jesus and the Spirit: A Study of the Religious and Charismatic Experience of Jesus and the First Christians Reflected in the New Testament*, Philadelphia: Westminster Press

Elliott, John Hall, 1981, *A Home for the Homeless: A Sociological Exegesis of 1 Peter, Its Situation and Strategy*, Philadelphia: Fortress Press

Engstrom, Theodore Wilhelm, 1983, *Your Gift of Administration: How To Discover and Use It*, Nashville, Tennessee: T. Nelson

Fernando, Ajith, 1985, *Leadership Lifestyle*, Wheaton, Illinois: Tyndale House Publishers

Fleming, Kenneth C., 1989, *He Humbled Himself: Recovering the Lost Art of Serving*, Westchester, Illinois: Crossway Books

Gangel, Kenneth O., 1974, *Competent To Lead*, Chicago: Moody Press

George, Carl F. and Logan, Robert E., 1987, *Leading and Managing Your Church*, Old Tappan, New Jersey: Fleming H. Revell

Getz, Gene A., 1984, *Serving One Another*, Wheaton, Illinois: Victor Books

Gibbs, Eddie, 1987, *Followed or Pushed?* Bromley: MARC Europe

Green, Edward Michael Banks, 1964, *Called To Serve: Ministers and Ministry in the Church*, London: Hodder and Stoughton

Greenslade, Philip, 1984, *Leadership, Greatness, and Servanthood*, Minneapolis, Minnesota: Bethany House Publishers

Hanson, Anthony Tyrell, 1962, *The Church of the Servant*, London: SCM Press

Harper, Michael, 1977, *Let My People Grow: Ministry and Leadership in the Church*, Plainfield, New Jersey: Logos International

Harvey, Anthony Ernest, 1975, *Priest or President?* London: S.P.C.K.

Hian, Chua Wee, 1987, *The Making of a Leader: A Guidebook for Present and Future Leaders*, Downers Grove, Illinois: Inter-Varsity Press

Hill, David, 1979, *New Testament Prophecy*, Atlanta: John Knox Press

Holmberg, Bengt, 1980, *Paul and Power: The Structure of Authority in the Primitive Church as Reflected in the Pauline Epistles*, Philadelphia: Fortress Press

Hutcheson, Richard G., Jr., 1979, *Wheel within the Wheel: Confronting the Management Crisis of the Pluralistic Church*, Atlanta: John Knox Press

Jones, Bruce W., 1988, *Ministerial Leadership in a Managerial World*, Wheaton, Illinois: Tyndale House Publishers

Kee, Howard Clark, 1980, *Christian Origins in Sociological Perspective: Methods and Resources*, Philadelphia: Westminster Press

Kraemer, Hendrik, 1958, *A Theology of the Laity*, Philadelphia: Westminster Press

Kruse, Colin G., 1985, *New Testament Models for Ministry, Jesus and Paul*, Nashville, Tennessee: T. Nelson

Küng, Hans, 1967, *The Church*, London: Burns and Oates

Lakoff, George and Johnson, Mark, 1980, *Metaphors We Live By*, Chicago: University of Chicago Press

Lampe, Geoffrey William Hugo, 1949, *Some Aspects of the New Testament Ministry: Being the Albrecht Stumpff Memorial Lecture Delivered at the Queen's College, Birmingham, on 3 May, 1948*, London: S.P.C.K.

Le Peau, Andrew T., 1983, *Paths of Leadership: Guiding Others Toward Growth in Christ through Serving, Following, Teaching, Modeling, Envisioning*, Downers Grove, Illinois: InterVarsity Press

Lightfoot, Joseph Barker, Bishop of Durham, 1901, *The Christian Ministry*, London: Macmillan

Lim, David Sun, 1987, *The Servant Nature of the Church in the Pauline Corpus*, Ph.D. dissertation, Fuller Theological Seminary

Lindgren, Alvin J. and Shawchuck, Norman, 1977, *Management for Your Church*, Nashville, Tennesee: Abingdon

Luecke, David S. and Southard, Samuel, 1986, *Pastoral Administration: Integrating Ministry and Management in the Church*, Waco, Texas: Word Books

McCord, James I. and Parker, T.H.L., editors, 1966, *Service in Christ: Essays Presented to Karl Barth on His 80th Birthday*, Grand Rapids, Michigan: Eerdmans

McFague, Sallie, 1982, *Metaphorical Theology: Models of God in Religious Language*, Philadelphia: Fortress Press

McKenna, David L., 1989, *Power To Follow, Grace To Lead: Strategy for the Future of Christian Leadership*, Dallas: Word Publishing

Malherbe, Abraham J., 1983, *Social Aspects of Early Christianity*, 2nd edition. Philadelphia: Fortress Press (1st edition 1977)

Malina, Bruce J., 1981, *The New Testament World: Insights from Cultural Anthropology*, Atlanta, Georgia: John Knox Press

Meeks, Wayne A., 1983, *The First Urban Christians: The Social World of the Apostle Paul*, New Haven, Connecticut: Yale University Press

Messer, Donald E., 1989, *Contemporary Images of Christian Ministry*, Nashville, Tennessee: Abingdon Press

Minear, Paul S., 1960, *Images of the Church in the New Testament*, Philadelphia: Westminster

Moltmann, Jürgen, 1977, *The Church in the Power of the Spirit: A Contribution to Messianic Ecclesiology*, translated by Margaret Kohl. New York: Harper and Row

Morris, Leon, 1964, *Ministers of God*, London: Inter-Varsity Press

Oden, Thomas C., 1983, *Pastoral Theology*, San Francisco: Harper and Row

Oxenrider, Jack La Von, 1982, *Sharing Leadership in the Brethren Church: A Leadership Design for an Elder (Pastor) within the Tradition and Polity of the Brethren Church*, D.Min. dissertation, Ashland Theological Seminary

Price, Nelson L., 1989, *Servants, not Celebrities*, Nashville, Tennessee: Broadman Press

Purkiser, W.T., 1969, *The New Testament Image of the Ministry*, Kansas City, Missouri: Beacon Hill Press of Kansas

Richards, Lawrence O. and Hoeldtke, Clyde, 1988, *Church Leadership: Following the Example of Jesus*, Grand Rapids, Michigan: Zondervan. (Revised edition of *A Theology of Church Leadership*, Zondervan, 1980)

Sampley, J. Paul, 1980, *Pauline Partnership in Christ: Christian Community and Commitment*, Philadelphia: Fortress

Sawyer, David, 1986, *Work of the Church: Getting the Job Done in Boards and Committees*, Valley Forge, Pennsylvania: Judson Press

Schillebeeckx, Edward Cornelius Florentius Alfons, 1981, *Ministry: Leadership in the Community of Jesus Christ*, translated by John Bowden, New York: Crossroad

————— 1986, *The Church with a Human Face: A New and Expanded Theology of Ministry*, translated by John Bowden, New York: Crossroad

Schmithals, Walter, 1969, *The Office of Apostle in the Early Church*, Translated by John E. Steely. Nashville, Tennessee: Abingdon Press

Schweizer, Eduard, 1961, *Church Order in the New Testament*, translated by Frank Clark, London: SCM Press

Shawchuck, Norman, 1984, *What it Means To Be a Church Leader: A Biblical Point of View*, Indianapolis: Spiritual Growth Resources

Stabbert, Bruce, 1982, *The Team Concept: Paul's Church Leadership Patterns or Ours?* Tacoma, Washington: Hegg Brothers Printing

Stambaugh, John E. and Balch, David L., 1986, *The New Testament in Its Social Environment*, Philadelphia: Westminster Press

Stevens, R. Paul, 1987, *Liberating the Leadership: Equipping the Saints for Full Partnership*, D.Min. dissertation, Fuller Theological seminary

Stott, John, 1961, *The Preacher's Portrait*, London: Tyndale Press

Swindoll, Charles R., 1986, *Improving Your Serve: The Art of Unselfish Living*, New York: Bantam Books. (1st published Waco, Texas: Word, 1981)

Tidball, Derek, 1984, *The Social Context of the New Testament: A Sociological Analysis*, Grand Rapids, Michigan: Zondervan

————— 1986, *Skilful Shepherds: An Introduction to Pastoral Theology*, Leicester: Inter-Varsity Press

Tillapaugh, Frank R., 1985, *Unleashing the Church: Getting People out of the Fortress and into the Ministry*, Ventura, California: Regal Books

Van Engen, Charles Edward, 1981, *The Growth of the True Church: An Analysis of the Ecclesiology of Church Growth Theory*, Amsterdam: Rodopi

Van Proyen, Dirk Theodore, 1985, *Elder Leadership Enrichment and Development*, D.Min. dissertation, Dallas Theological Seminary

Wagner, C. Peter, 1984, *Leading Your Church to Growth*, Ventura, California: Regal Books

White, John, 1986, *Excellence in Leadership: Reaching Goals with Prayer, Courage, and Determination*, Downers Grove, Illinois: Inter-Varsity Press

Whitehead, James D. and Whitehead, Evelyn Eaton, 1986, *The Emerging Laity: Returning Leadership to the Community of Faith*, New York: Doubleday

Wilson, Robert R., 1984, *Sociological Approaches to the Old Testament*, Philadelphia: Fortress Press

Wimber, John, 1987, *Kingdom Ministry*, Ann Arbor, Michigan: Servant Publications

Youssef, Michael, 1986, *The Leadership Style of Jesus*, Wheaton, Illinois: Victor Books

Zimmerli, Walther and Jeremias, J., 1965, *The Servant of God*, Revised edition. Naperville, Illinois: A. R. Allenson

Index of images

24636637R00117

Made in the USA
Middletown, DE
01 October 2015